Tripping the World Fantastic

Glenn Dixon

TRIPPING THE WORLD FANTASTIC

*A Journey Through
the Music of Our Planet*

DUNDURN
TORONTO

Editor: Allister Thompson
Design: Courtney Horner
Printer: Webcom

Library and Archives Canada Cataloguing in Publication

Dixon, Glenn, 1957-
    Tripping the world fantastic : a journey through the music of our planet / by Glenn Dixon.

Includes bibliographical references and index.
Issued also in electronic formats.
ISBN 978-1-4597-0654-5

    1. Music--Social aspects. 2. Music--Psychological aspects.
3. Dixon, Glenn, 1957- --Travel. 4. Voyages around the world.
I. Title.

ML3916.D59 2013   306.4'842   C2012-907676-7

1   2   3   4   5   17   16   15   14   13

We acknowledge the support of the **Canada Council for the Arts** and the **Ontario Arts Council** for our publishing program. We also acknowledge the financial support of the **Government of Canada** through the **Canada Book Fund** and **Livres Canada Books**, and the **Government of Ontario** through the **Ontario Book Publishing Tax Credit** and the **Ontario Media Development Corporation**.

Care has been taken to trace the ownership of copyright material used in this book. The author and the publisher welcome any information enabling them to rectify any references or credits in subsequent editions.

J. Kirk Howard, President

Printed and bound in Canada.

Visit us at
Dundurn.com
Definingcanada.ca
@dundurnpress
Facebook.com/dundurnpress

Dundurn	Gazelle Book Services Limited	Dundurn
3 Church Street, Suite 500	White Cross Mills	2250 Military Road
Toronto, Ontario, Canada	High Town, Lancaster, England	Tonawanda, NY
M5E 1M2	LA1 4XS	U.S.A. 14150

Contents

ACKNOWLEDGEMENTS

NO ONE BOOK CAN COVER THE MUSIC OF THE ENTIRE WORLD. IN FACT, a book of this size would barely be enough to cover the music of a single village in places like Ireland or Cuba or India. Still, I travelled through more than sixty-five countries to arrive at the pages you hold in your hands. I know it's not enough. I know that people will ask me why I didn't include a chapter on Argentinian tango or the Inuit throat singing of the High Arctic. Believe me, I wanted to. I wanted to include it all, but in the end I decided to limit myself to a single overriding question. Why do we play music at all? Why is it that, in every crook and corner of this planet, there is singing and dancing and playing?

I think, at last, I'm ready to give you some answers and I certainly could not have done it alone. There was a tremendous amount of research to read, most of it very recent and very exciting, and to those scientists and thinkers, I surely tip my hat. I also want to thank my fellow travellers for their camaraderie and curiosity and for pushing me to go ever further. For all the guides and local residents I met, I thank you for your insights and knowledge and patience in explaining things. And for the musicians themselves, all over the world, I want to thank you for your extraordinary gifts. This book, most of all, is dedicated to you.

LISTENING TO THE MUSIC

THIS BOOK HAS AUDIO AND VIDEO LINKS ON AN ACCOMPANYING WEBSITE. Throughout the text, you will see the symbol: ◀ξ LISTEN. Go to *www.tripping-the-world.com* and follow the links or go directly to the chapter samples below by adding the backslash and name to the end of the web address.

0.1 /flute.html
1.1 /kingtut.html
1.2 /bedouin.html
2.1 /sinai.html
2.2 /hurrian.html
3.1 /dervish.html
3.2 /calltoprayer.html
4.1 /santouri.html
5.1 /notredame.html
6.1 /flamenco.html
6.2 /flamencodance.html
7.1 /africandrums.html

7.2 /ivoryhorn.html

8.1 /rumba.html

8.2 /trova.html

8.3 /streetmusic.html

9.1 /redemption.html

9.2 /steeldrum.html

9.3 /cropover.html

10.1 /ballgame.html

10.2 /mayanmusic.html

11.1 /whalesong.html

11.2 /chant.html

11.3 /fiji.html

12.1 /gamelan.html

12.2 /kecak.html

13.1 /ganges.html

13.2 /tabla.html

13.3 /sitar.html

13.4 /snakecharmer.html

14.1 /moscowcathedral.html

14.2 /faberge.html

14.3 /accordion.html

14.4 /krakowtrumpet.html

14.5 /gypsy.html

14.6 /lute.html

15.1 /mozart.html

15.2 /magicflute.html

15.3 /moonlightsonata.html

16.1 /irishjig.html

16.2 /celticharp.html

16.3 /edinburghpub.html

16.4 /bagpipes.html

16.5 /barra.html

16.6 /scottishlament.html

INTRODUCTION

PROFESSOR NICHOLAS CONARD CROUCHED IN THE DARK CAVE, DUSTING at the remains of an ancient cooking fire. He'd found a scatter of flint shards — the remains of a tool-making culture — and as he worked his way down through the layers something light and smooth revealed itself.

It was a bone fragment and it had the marks of tooling on it. Conard's heart began to race as he brushed away the dirt. He'd seen this before — carefully drilled holes, a finger length apart — so that even before he had it fully exposed he knew he'd found another paleolithic flute.

At the University of Tübingen, not far away, the flute was dated to 42000 years B.C.E., making it the oldest musical instrument ever found. It came from a time when the first migrations of homo sapiens had begun shoving in from Asia, entering the new continent just before the climate took a major change for the colder. They came up the Danube corridor, north of the Alps, and then down into Germany, pushing the ill-fated Neanderthals ahead of them.

Both the Neanderthals and our own ancestors inhabited the cave systems that riddle the hills from Southern Germany to the south of France. Some of the caves are all but empty. Others are heaped with

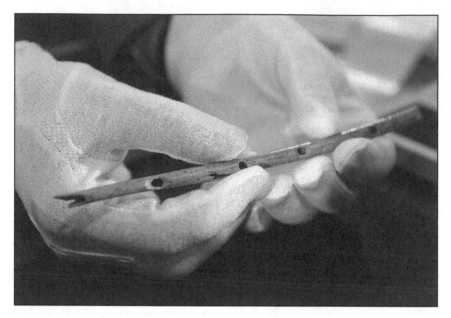

The oldest musical instrument ever found. *(Courtesy of Daniel Maurer/AP Images)*

ancient artifacts. One complex of caves yielded the stone carving now known as the Venus of Willendorf — a squat figure, clearly female, and painstakingly fashioned. In Lascaux, the famous cave galleries were awash with finely rendered bison and dancing antelope. And yet others, just over in the next valley, were virtually empty.

Why would some caves be empty while others were filled with treasures? It was a mystery until microphones were brought in to record the acoustic properties of the cave systems. It turned out that the empty caves were quite flat, aurally, while the ones rich in finds boomed with reverb and echo. They were, quite simply, caves filled with sonic magic.

So we can well imagine this old bone flute, trilling out its notes in the vast cathedral echoes of the Geißenklösterle cave system. This flute is so fragmental that it's almost impossible to know what it would have sounded like. However, Conard, just two years previously, had found a more complete flute dating from 35000 B.C.E. — and this one was close to playable. The flute plays a simple pentatonic scale. You can get a completely functional version of "Mary Had a Little Lamb" out of it. In fact, an exact replica of that bone flute has now been fashioned and I've heard it for myself. I've heard its plaintive tones and even worked out that it plays in the key of D.

◀€ LISTEN 0.1

Music, it seems, has been around for a very long time. Things like simple scales and rhythms appear to be hardwired into our brains. Why this should be is not really understood. Music doesn't seem to have the evolutionary advantages of, say, opposable thumbs or being able to walk upright. And yet every culture on Earth, every culture that's ever existed, has had music. It has been at the centre of our rituals. It has accompanied our stories. It has cheered us up when we are sad and set our toes tapping when we are happy. We bang and pluck and blow, it seems, on almost anything that can make a sound.

I've spent the last few years travelling the globe listening to the music of the world. I've heard extraordinary musical performances almost everywhere I've been. I've felt tingles down my spine and had goose bumps rise up on my arms at the beauty of it all. But why? Why does music — this organized sound, as one composer called it — hold us so completely enraptured?

Well, we do have some ideas now. There's been an explosion of research into music cognition in just the last few years. We're now able to look directly into the neural networks of the brain. We understand the basic physiology of auditory perception and we have some pretty solid theories about evolutionary psychology.

We are just now starting to understand what drove our paleolithic ancestors to fashion bone flutes. We are beginning to understand the tremendous power of music and why humans the world over play and dance and sing.

And the answers just might surprise you.

PART ONE
Music and Evolutionary Psychology

1

EGYPT
THE TRUMPETS OF KING TUT

CROSSING THE STREETS IN CAIRO IS LIKE WALKING INTO A CAVALRY charge. Lanes and lines mean nothing to Egyptian drivers. Dented Mercedes and trucks filled with tomatoes careened past me almost out of control. Sometimes there were five vehicles abreast, sometimes two, whatever it would take to push and swerve ahead of the next driver. Stop signs were ignored and sidewalks were only provisionally for pedestrians so that venturing out on foot was as foolhardy as a winter advance on Russia.

We had just crossed a bridge over the Nile. I thought it was going to be a wide, lazy river, reed-rimmed, with square-sailed felucca boats gliding across the water like Time itself. Instead, I got honking and angry car engines. I bounded after my guide, Yassar, who seemed to take no notice of the chaos. He wore a suit, even in the crippling heat. Yassar was an expert in Egyptian hieroglyphics and he had a great bushy moustache that he stroked when he lectured.

He only stopped and turned to speak when we came up into Tahrir Square. This square, of course, was at the centre of the mass protests that brought down Hosni Mubarak. Yassar pointed out strategic positions and a place where a tank or something had crunched up the curb. He hurried through it all, barely touching his moustache. This wasn't his thing. The history of anything more recent than two or three thousand years ago just didn't seem to interest him and he strode off, after only the briefest of explanations, to a large building, distinctly colonial and more than a little run down, that sat at the edge of the square. This was the Egyptian Museum.

They've been talking about building a new museum for decades but it never seems to happen. The old crumbling building is packed to the rafters with Egyptian treasures — many of them just sort of haphazardly piled around the place. The funny thing is, even the third-rate stuff here would be a centrepiece of almost any other museum in the world.

Inside, the air was stifling and I wilted and stumbled from exhibit to exhibit, trailing after Yassar, trying to keep up with his explanations. Yellow and peeling labels — some a hundred years old — told us that this piece was a carving of an ancient funerary boat and that that one was a plaque commemorating the union of the upper and lower kingdoms in the reign of some pharaoh or other.

Upstairs, we went into the rooms containing the treasures of King Tut, and Yassar strode directly to a glass case containing two fragile trumpets. "Please examine these," he said in impeccable English. "The one on top is silver, is it not?" It was. Only the tip of the horn was clearly silver, and the rest was inlaid with what was either bronze or maybe gold. "It is broken," Yassar began. He took a step back. "A radio reporter tried to play it in 1939, for the BBC." He stroked his moustache. "It broke into three pieces after they tried to play it. But the other one ..."

I leaned into the glass case again. There was a second trumpet there. Not quite as pretty as the first.

"This one is copper. And this one was stolen."

"Stolen?"

"In the troubles, out there on Tahrir Square. There was looting." Yassar paused, clearly pained. "They broke into the museum and stole many things. They stole this trumpet."

"It was returned, then?"

"Yes." Yassar fixed me with a stare. "The thief, all the world would find him. He knew it, and the trumpet was eventually found in a shopping bag on the Cairo Metro."

The trumpets of King Tut in Cairo. (Courtesy of Raquel Rodriquez/Northern Kentucky University)

"On the subway?"

"All the world would find him. This thief."

Yassar moved on to the next case but I lingered at the trumpets. Both of them, as he said, had been played in a 1939 BBC broadcast. We don't know exactly what the music of ancient Egypt sounded like — they left no hieroglyphics of actual musical notation — but we do know what these two trumpets sounded like. For the first time in three thousand years, they were played and we have that recording.

◀╪ LISTEN 1.1

Elsewhere in the museum and up the Valley of Kings, there are plenty of wall murals showing people playing rattles and trumpets. There's a complete harp and various lutes in the Louvre in Paris. The ancient pharaohs would have been completely surrounded by music in the royal processions and religious ceremonies, and even the common people lived in a very musical world. The work crews hauling up the blocks for the pyramids, for example, likely would have had some sort of beat to keep them pulling and pushing in sync.

Music, in some form or another, exists in every culture on Earth — through every time period of history. We play music. It's a universal of human existence.

Yassar plodded on and came at last to what turned out to be my favourite room: the room with the royal mummies. It cost extra money, so Yassar didn't follow me in, but he'd told me before what to expect. The mummies are not what you see in Hollywood movies. They may have been wrapped up at one point, swathed in miles and miles of long, thin bandages, but they're not any more. They're desiccated-looking human beings — all their fingernails intact with strands of hair still cobwebbing off their scalps. They stare up at you through glass cases like butterflies pinned to a board.

In the main mummy room there are nine mummies, all pharaohs except one. Beside a mummy that's now known to be Queen Hatshepsut lies a much smaller figure which at first I took to be a child. It's not. It's a mummified baboon. It had been the favourite pet of this queen and so there it was amongst the pharoahs. Three thousand years from its jungle home.

I was especially drawn to one of the mummies near the door. This, the sign read, was Ramses II. You've probably heard of him. He's the pharaoh who appears in the Old Testament, the one who Moses stood up to, invoking the words "Let my People Go," and whether or not it actually happened like that, here was Ramses II, perhaps the most powerful man on the planet at the time, staring up at me from his glass case. I have the most profound memory of hovering over the glass case, my nose maybe six inches from his, thinking here's me literally face to face with a man who would have been the Napoleon of his time, or something like the pope and the king and maybe Bill Gates all rolled into one.

He was a little dried up and shrivelled but it was a distinctly human face I was looking at, a face still a little contorted by pain. He'd been crippled by arthritis but he lived well into his nineties — almost unheard of in that time period. His hook nose and sharp chin, if you can look beyond his sort of brownish colour, wasn't far off any elderly person you might see on the street. Some cantankerous old goat swearing at traffic.

Downstairs again, Yassar showed us the urns that contained the mummy's internal organs. There were usually four containers — canopic jars, they're called — one for their lungs, one for the stomach, one for the liver, and one for the intestines. They left the heart and the kidneys inside the body and most surprisingly for all the advances of the ancient Egyptians, they removed the brain and simply — like so much snot — tossed it away. It was pulled out in pieces through the nose and thrown away as useless and unimportant gunk.

The ancient Egyptians thought our minds, our consciousness, resided in the heart — which, actually, is why they left that in the body. Even today we have the vestiges of this sort of thinking, imagining love and other emotions to be seated in that most unlikely organ.

They're not, of course. The entire architecture of our being is in our brains although we've yet to fully understand how a lot of it works. We're still at a loss to explain consciousness. No one has found a soul in the hippocampus, or a dream in the corpus callosum. We've yet to find our favourite songs, or even the memory of the lyrics anywhere in the grey matter of our cortex. But it's there all right. It's there. All of it embedded in the grey goo that the ancient Egyptians simply threw out with the garbage.

This is the first thing you have to understand about music and why it's so important to us. Music exists entirely in the brain. It's not really there in our ears at all. What I mean by this is that the eardrum and the cochlea behind it are entirely mechanical — simply a collection bowl for auditory information. Our ears really do nothing to process music. The complexities of melodies and rhythms are completely constructed in our brains. Dogs, I have been told, don't really "get" music, though they hear exactly the same auditory landscape that we do. To dogs, even a Beethoven symphony is just a mush of clanking and droning sounds. Oh yeah, they may bark and croon at certain frequencies, but the music really doesn't come together in any of the ways that we perceive it.

The sense of hearing in all higher order organisms is there for a very specific reason. It helps us survive. This much is true in dogs as well as humans, and it's worth looking at in depth.

Most of the sounds in nature are a sort of white noise. The wind in the trees, the patter of rain, and even the repetitive crash of the surf. It was the sudden changes in sound that made our ancestors' ears perk up. Like schools of fish darting away from the subtle vacillations predators might make, animal and human brains were alerted to danger through sound.

This is the reasoning behind police sirens (or ambulances and fire trucks for that matter). It's not that they're louder than everything else. Sirens are deliberately designed to be unnatural. They waver back and forth, screeching up and down frequencies in a way that specifically triggers the perception that something unusual is happening.

In fact, all our sensory systems are, at root, "difference engines," alert to changes in temperature and movement and odours in the air. In hearing, we have been hard-wired to pay attention to things like sudden loud noises or unusual timbres or even the speed at which a sound is coming towards us. Sound direction and speed is encoded in something called the Doppler Effect. We can hear this effect in things like a race car going by on a track or a train receding into the distance. As a sound source moves towards us, its pitch rises (as does its volume) and as it moves away from us, the pitch descends. It's a natural phenomenon we have learned to use. One that probably lies at the roots of melody.

Changes in the sound environment were often warnings of danger but they were also subtle aural clues about where we could find water or food. One theory in evolutionary psychology, for example, holds that humans all around the world are pleasantly relaxed by the sound of gurgling water. And it's true, we love the splash of fountains and the gurgle of gentle brooks. It only stands to reason that our primeval ancestors would have been drawn to aural landscapes where running water was clearly in abundance. It is necessary for our survival and, to this day then, it is a sound that soothes us and reassures us, a sound that tells us we are in a place where we can flourish.

All this, of course, is elementary sound perception and something that was clearly in place long before we developed music. And, certainly, it doesn't tell us very much about why music has such a supreme power over us.

I trundled out to the western outskirts of Cairo one day in a bus. Along one road, I was looking out the window at apartment buildings and the Egyptian equivalent of a strip mall when there behind the buildings I saw the tip of something strange. I looked again. *That's not...* I thought. *That's not the pyramids, is it?*

But yes it was. The curious sight of the Pyramids of Giza, sticking out above the buildings on the outskirts of Cairo, stays with me. The city ends quite suddenly and there's a sort of sand shelf, high enough I guess that the floods of the Nile couldn't quite make it up, and up on the plateau there are the three great pyramids. There are hundreds of smaller structures too, many still buried in the sifting sand and, of course, off to the left, the enigmatic Sphinx.

I've seen all this a million times in pictures and people had told me their own stories of being a little underwhelmed, so I had actually prepared myself to be disappointed. It's true that hawkers all around the pyramids gather to descend on the tourists, selling everything from bottles of water to dubious camel rides. They're quite insistent and tend to make a big dent in the magic of the place. The tourist police are no help either, dressed in smart white uniforms with black armbands that read "Department of Antiquities." Some of them have machine guns, but you know, they're just as bad as the touts, offering to stand in a picture for baksheesh or giving you unwanted directions and then again asking for money.

Despite all this, and what other people had told me, I stood in awe of the pyramids. Yeah, I'd heard the statistics, how many thousands of slaves, how many years it took, the two million granite blocks — each one the size of a minivan — but staring up at Cheops' pyramid, actually standing there in its midst, was unbelievable. Try this on for size: Cheops' is the highest of the three and it's about the height of a forty-four-storey building.

That made it the tallest man-made structure in the world for almost 4,000 years. It was the thin spire of the Lincoln Cathedral in England that finally outdid it for sheer height. I did a quick mental calculation and figured this pyramid would still be the fourth highest building among all the skyscrapers of my native and very modern city of Calgary.

I craned my neck up and some sort of hawk was riding the thermals up near the top. I watched it swoop and cry. This pyramid was built for the Pharoah Khufu (which is Cheops in Greek). It was finished in about 2560 B.C.E. at a time when the entire population of the Earth was just thirty million people. Funny, because that's about the population of greater Cairo now, a sweeping sprawl of a city running up both sides of the Nile for miles and miles and miles.

Unlike the Valley of the Kings, where most of the mummies come from, they're having a hell of a time finding the royal remains in these pyramids. There are nine "false shafts" in Cheops' pyramid — rigged up with falling granite blocks to hamper grave robbers. One chamber does have an unfinished sarcophagus, but the mummy of Cheops has never been found. Some hold that the remains here were looted long ago, others that there may still be things hidden inside the great pyramid and that apparently even modern ultrasound technology simply can't pierce through the masses of granite here.

A bit like the brain perhaps. Even when we have unravelled all the neural circuits, even when we have developed the tools to see what every square millimetre of the brain is doing, it still won't quite explain the wonder that is human consciousness, the sense of self, and the soul-rattling emotions we feel when we are profoundly moved by music.

Out past the pyramids, there are Bedouin tribesmen who will take you out into the raw burning desert on camels. I arranged to go with them and spend a night in the desert at one of their camps.

Bedouin players at the desert camp.

The camel they gave me seemed too small. My legs dangled out over his sides so that they were almost touching the sand. And weren't they supposed to be nasty creatures, these camels, snapping and spitting? Mine was as gentle as a deer and I thought that maybe this was a toddler camel, trotting behind his tall and strangely elegant mother with a Bedouin herder sitting proudly tall on her, leading the foolish white tourist deep into the desert.

A hot blue sky rocked above me. Far in the distance, pinnacles and strange formations of orange-red rock stood out above the sand. For thousands of years these Bedouin had been nomads in this deep, unforgiving desert. The shadows were lengthening though the air was still a furnace. I bounced and clopped on my little camel amongst a scene that was completely biblical.

Some of the Bedouin men walked, easily trotting alongside the camel brigade. They wore long flowing white robes and walked proudly like characters from *Ben Hur*. It was forty-two degrees Celsius, though it didn't feel a spot over thirty-eight.

At the foot of one of the red rock escarpments we finally came to our camp. Square tents, broadly striped in black, flapped in the breeze. This was no oasis, though. I hadn't seen a tree or plant of any sort for hours.

We'd arrived in the long, slow twilight of the desert and, dusty and tired, I was led to a cooking area surrounded by wattle walls. Carpets had been set on the sand and I nestled my tender backside down into a scattering of embroidered cushions.

And that's when the musicians appeared.

They too wore the long flowing robes of the Bedouin and they sat on two short stools, just across from me. One held a small drum, like a short, fat bongo. This was a *târ*, the backbone of all Bedouin music. With the flat of his hand, he thumped out a few tentative beats. The man beside him had a stringed instrument, a fat-bodied sort of lute called an *oud*.

They signalled to each other, as all musicians do, and then the drummer began to whap out a fantastic rhythm. Only the ends of his fingers rapped across the rim of the drum, although the palm of his right hand would sneak in every few beats, to thump out a deeper note from the middle of the drum skin.

No less a mind than Charles Darwin puzzled mightily over the problem of music. He too had noted that every culture has music and, therefore, he felt that there must be an evolutionary basis for it. His theory of natural selection wouldn't really work if he couldn't account for things like this. But he was surely stumped. "Neither the enjoyment nor the capacity of producing musical notes," he wrote, "are faculties of the least use to man. They must be ranked among the mysterious habits with which he is endowed."

Darwin had already written his great book *On the Origin of Species*. He already figured out how certain traits — anything really that would improve our chances of survival — were likely to be handed down to succeeding generations. Give it a few thousand years and that trait — something we now know is usually carried directly in our genes — would spread through an entire population.

But what about music? There's nothing about it that would give us an advantage, nothing that would help to ensure our survival. It was really quite a mystery.

Darwin began to look at birds for his answer. He mentions them a lot in his writings and he is plainly aware that their "songs" might be something close to the music that we humans also produce.

So, why does the caged bird sing? What about that canary in a coalmine? Well, birds sing for one reason only. They're trying to get laid.

It was this thought that brought about Darwin's second great breakthrough. It took him a further twelve years and another book to amend his theory of natural selection to account for things like music. Natural selection, it turns out, is only one of the processes at work in evolution. The other, and equally important process, is sexual selection. "The chief and, in some cases, exclusive purpose," Darwin wrote about songbirds, "appears to be either to call or charm the opposite sex."

An obvious example of Darwinian sexual selection is peacocks. Peacocks don't really sing. Hell, they don't really even fly. But male peacocks are doing something very important with their shimmering, flashing plumage (and it's redundant to even say male peacocks. The females are properly called peahens and they don't have these big tails). Peacocks can flap around awkwardly for a hundred metres or so, sometimes managing, through sheer force of will, to hoist themselves up into the safety of the lower branches of a tree. But really, the whole act of flying for them is a sad and embarrassing spectacle.

It's a paradox. Surely, their survival is greatly hampered by this gaudy tail of neon green. Pretty easy pickings for any predator around. But the principals of sexual selection hold that "charming a mate" is just as important as escaping from danger, just as important as any of the principals behind "survival of the fittest." It is not enough to survive. Evolutionary logic tells us quite plainly that, even at the cost of personal sacrifice, the game is not about you. The game is about passing your genes along.

So music, in Darwin's view, is a peacock's tail. It is the ornate façade of human behaviour at its finest. The skills of a musician (like these Bedouin players) engendered over tens of thousands of hours of practise, will, presumably, be a flaunting of the laws of natural selection. Instead, such skills suggest that one has so much spare time (in other words, wealth and prestige) that they are literally able to dither away their free time on spurious pursuits. And this, presumably, makes any sane female sit up and take notice.

If you doubt this, think of Mick Jagger strutting his way across the stage. By any objective measure, he is not a particularly handsome man. But by the gift of his peacock tail of musicianship, he has literally become (or in his younger years anyway) a sex god.

Back in the desert and much, much later in the night, the oud player signalled to the other, who put aside his drum. It was time for a solo and, after a beautiful run of notes on his lute-like instrument, he launched into a song I'll never forget.

 **LISTEN 1.2**

He closed his eyes and crooned out a long, sad tumble of melody. "*Habibi*," one of the camel drivers called out, perhaps chiding him for his sorrowfulness. *Habibi* in English means simply "love," and I got one of the Bedouin men to translate the rest for me.

"He is saying," the man said, "that he is the girl's servant. That whatever she asks for, he will do." The man listened a bit more. "He is saying that when he touches her lips he becomes, how do you say — drunk."

"Drunk?

"No, not drunk. He looks like he's drunk but he's…"

"Ah, you mean drunk with love."

"Yes, yes. Everyone will think he has been drinking, but this is not true. He is drunk only…"

"With love."

"Yes, saheeb, it is too true."

The singer crooned with such passion that at the end everyone — and this included the local Bedouin herders — broke into applause. Clearly music, of all sorts, tugs at our heartstrings. Music connects with the things that run deepest in all of us. And for all of us, this is love.

2

PETRA
AUDITORY CHEESECAKE

THE BUS ROLLED EAST TOWARDS THE SINAI PENINSULA AND AN HOUR after we left Cairo a curious sight appeared. An oil tanker as big as five football fields floated across the sands in front of the bus. I shook my head to try to make the mirage disappear, but there it was, a ship drifting across the dunes. What I was really seeing was the Suez Canal. From the road, the canal was just below the level of the horizon, so the tanker looked just like it was moving across the burning sands.

As we neared the canal itself, when we could see the water, a machine gun placement appeared on a hillside. The soldiers waved at us merrily and we dropped down through a tunnel and out onto the other side, out onto the Sinai, a strange triangular-shaped bit of land that straddles Africa and the Middle East.

This was much different than the Sahara. There were cinnamon-coloured boulders, as big as cars, jumbling down from the hills. The view from my bumping bus window looked like footage from the Martian land rover — just a stark bare red-rock field as far as the eye could see.

This was the land of Exodus, a land of biblical wandering for forty years in the sun-baked emptiness. Somewhere near the middle of it all we came to Saint Catherine's monastery. Saint Catherine's is the oldest working monastery in the world and it's built right at the foot of Mount Sinai. *The* Mount Sinai. This is where Moses is said to have received the Ten Commandments and, fighting back my visions of Charlton Heston, tablets held aloft, robes fluttering in the breeze, I eyed the mountain and thought that it didn't look too hard. I'd come to climb the thing, you see, to watch the sun rise over the desert and to see if I'd have any revelations of my own.

I stayed at a little pension in the village nearby the monastery and arranged to go up the mountain for the sunrise. And so, at 2:30 in the morning came a thumping at my thick wooden door. At first, it just assimilated itself into my dreams, then I became conscious of the real world and stumbled up to open the door. "Sirrah," chimed a small Egyptian man. "It is time."

"Mmmfff," I answered eloquently.

"You will need your torch."

"Mmmmfff, torssh."

I assembled myself and indeed I had brought along my Petzl headlight, strapping it to my forehead. It was only five minutes of trudging to the start of the trail and it really was pitch black. There was no moon that night and the stars sparkled above us. Once or twice I saw falling stars. At the beginning of the trail, camel drivers came out of the shadows at me, insisting I should ride to the top. I could see the dim outline of camel humps and occasionally my beam of light straddled across their saddles and heavily carpeted backs.

I chose to walk and so up I went. It wasn't really that steep. A few hours later and near the top, I came to the 750 steps that would take me up to the small Byzantine church at the summit. The steps, perhaps a thousand years old, were crooked and rough, and even the last camel station was now far below us. I say "us" because there was a line of pilgrims, some holding candles, looking like some kind of medieval procession, stumbling up the trail behind me. The sky was dimming, a thin pink line appearing over the mountain ridges to the east.

Up top were a hundred people or so, some of them nestled under blankets in any little niche they could find so that I'm sure they'd climbed up the evening before and spent the night on the mountaintop. I found a rock perch, a couple metres back from a thousand-foot drop, and sat down to await the sunrise. Slowly, slowly the sky began to lighten, a red rim appeared on the horizon, and then the first small spark of the sun.

A lone voice started to sing. I had no idea this was going to happen. It was one of those sublime moments you get sometimes travelling, something completely unexpected. A group of maybe twenty pilgrims — I'm not sure if they'd been waiting there or if they had come up behind me — were being led by a sort of concert master. He was singing the first lines and a lone violin wrenched at the melody behind him. Then, in a call and response, the rest of the voices came in. Twenty voices, baritones and tenors mostly, in rich three-part harmony. They sang just as the sun came peeking over the distant horizon and the music rang out with such solemn invocation that I felt chills race all up and down my spine.

◀€   LISTEN 2.1

I'm not a particularly religious person, but I'll be the first to admit that I was overwhelmed. It was so beautiful. Their voices seemed to echo down over the mountains and ring out across the sky. What other phenomenon can move us as deeply as this? What is it about music that sends us into such cataclysms of emotion?

The singers on top of Mount Sinai were not Christian. I was in Muslim Egypt, though they certainly weren't that either. In fact, when I listened closely I realized that they were Jewish. In their singing, the word "Israel" kept coming up and, dimwitted though I can be sometimes, that was pretty clear.

The words were from the Sh'ma Yisrael. It's the central text of the morning Jewish prayer service, and here we were watching the first glint of the dawn appear over the desert of Moses. There are also subtle allusions to the Ten Commandments in the Sh'ma Yisrael, so that here the song resonated deeply on a whole lot of levels. In fact, the Sh'ma Yisrael is so central and important to the Jewish faith that for the most ardent believers, the words are meant to be said on your deathbed, as your last halting whispers on this Earth.

So, pretty powerful stuff.

I was feeling chills down the back of my neck and goosebumps were rising on my forearms. Endorphins, to be clinical about it, were gushing through my heathen neural circuits, triggering my opiate receptors, the pleasure centres of the brain.

A woman to the left of me began to cry. I could see the tears rolling down her cheeks. Now, everyone knows that tears are salt water. But you probably didn't know that tears are chemically different according to the emotion you are feeling.

Tears of sadness are actually different from tears of happiness or the tears you might get when a speck of dust blows into your eye. Tears of sorrow contain prolactin.

Prolactin is a kind of tranquillizing hormone. It calms us and presumably sees us through the worst of the situation when something horrible happens. It serves to calm us down when we're overwhelmed by emotion.

Our tightly wired brains are a veritable chemistry set, gushing neurohormones like a hose that the neighbourhood dog has gnawed apart. And nothing triggers these gushes of chemicals more readily than music.

But we've got a problem here. I'm acutely aware that there's a big disjunct between profound religious experiences up on mountaintops and all this talk of brain structures and neurochemicals. It just doesn't square up. So, what's really at the heart of it all?

Well, let's go back a step.

At the foot of the Taurus Mountains, near the coast of what is now northern Syria, lie the ruins of the Hurrian city of Ugarit. Ugarit was a sort of outlier city that flourished in the dying days of the Babylonian Empire in the second millennium B.C.E.

In the ruins, the archaeologists found literally thousands of clay tablets. And somewhere among all those thousands was a piece inscribed with music. Lord knows how they figured this out, but it could only have been through absolutely painstaking attention to detail. Somehow, they worked out the fact that this particular tablet was not just another court record of taxes. No, this was something unprecedented. It was not actually writing at all. It was music.

Dated at about 1400 B.C.E., this little ceramic clump contains the oldest piece of music notation known to us. The writing is based on

Sumerian cuneiform so it looks nothing like our modern staff notation. There are words there too to be sung and there's even a bit along the bottom with some murky instructions on how to read it.

There's a lot of debate on how to best transcribe the tablet into modern musical notation, but if we can figure it out, we can hear, pretty accurately, what music sounded like three and a half thousand years ago, and that's a pretty amazing prospect.

Some early attempts at figuring it out produced a deadly dull melody — a sort of droning monotone — and the thought was that that couldn't be right. Why would these ancient people have taken the time to write down something so pedantic? Later ideas about how to decode it came up with something much more complex. And now, we're pretty close to hearing exactly what it would have sounded like.

◀᠍᠍᠍᠍᠍᠍ LISTEN 2.2

The lyrics on the tablet are also worth a look. It's written in a relatively obscure Semitic dialect. Much of it is beyond our ability to translate, but in the scraps that we can make out, something leaps out quite clearly. It's a love song.

"Once I have endeared her to me," goes one line, "she will love me in her heart." That's pretty plain and I can almost imagine some raven-haired Mesopotamian beauty from three and half thousand years ago. I can imagine our suitor writing down this music to impress her, to win her over.

"Love," Darwin had written, "is still the commonest theme of our songs."

Well, I wish I could leave it at that but there's more to the story. The whole thing is a great big red herring because while the Hurrian tablet is a love song, it's not a love song to a woman. Not exactly.

A closer translation of the Hurrian lyrics makes it clear that it's a song to be sung to a god, a female god (probably a moon goddess) and no raven-haired mortal at all. The song commemorates the leaving of ritual offerings to this unnamed female god. The man (or it may be a barren female) singing the song has committed some sort of sin. They are asking the moon goddess to bless them with good crops and, even more importantly, to bless them with children.

So, there's that element of fertility still and the passing on of genes, but this is definitely not about Darwinian sexual selection. This is something more than that. The song here is, like the pilgrims' song on Mount Sinai, entirely religious. It deals with a sense of something greater than ourselves. Something much greater than our little grey brains can understand.

So the fact, I'm afraid, is that Darwin was dead wrong. At least about music. Music is not some peacock's feather that we have arranged to get us a mate. We might use it for that, quite right, but we use it for a pretty extensive list of other things too. We use it at birthdays and weddings and funerals and sporting matches. We use it to worship, to celebrate, to mourn, and sometimes just for the sheer joy of it, with no occasion at all.

It's for our gods and ourselves, and everything in between.

I took a ferry up the Red Sea to the port at Aqaba. On board, I met a fiery Irish girl named Claire. She had been leading tours up and down Jordan and Egypt for years and she knew her way around. She spoke with a tinge of Irish lilt in her voice, an accent that surely has something of music in it.

On board the ferry, you could get falafels and things and, surprisingly, beer. Claire was quite interested in that. Up at the window, though, the Arabic man behind the desk tried to stilt her on the price. He even said something along those lines to his friend behind him. Little did he know that Claire spoke Arabic relatively fluently. She launched into the man in such a tirade of sizzling angry Arabic that he actually took a step backwards from the sheer force of it. He bowed his head low and offered a thousand apologies, and she let him go with only a few more white hot Arabic bullets.

Language is funny that way. Even if you don't know the words, you can make out the intent from the sound of it. There's a word for this. It's called prosody, and it's exactly where language and music touch. Think about it. Even the word "melody" itself has a simple descending line of three notes. That's the prosody of words — their musical sounds.

The best poets and writers know all about prosody and they use it well. The best lyricists too are those who have mastered the art of knowing just what sorts of syllables and vowel sounds will best fit certain lines in a melody. Language and music are completely intertwined in that way. It's no coincidence at all that the pilgrims up on Mount Sinai were singing words of deep religious significance and it's no wonder that the oldest music we have, the Hurrian tablet, is a sort of prayer, a plaintive request put to music.

Claire came back from her little skirmish with a couple of cold beers. The day was toaster hot and I had no problem drilling it back and going up to our now humble Arab for a second round.

Claire asked me about my travels and I asked about hers. "We're lucky today," she said. "The ferry left when it was supposed to. There are times when you can wait in the port for hours. Sometimes it doesn't go at all."

"It must help to know Arabic."

"Of course it helps. Otherwise they'd not listen to a woman at all."

Outside, we were moving slowly up the Red Sea. It's actually a fissure that's a continuation of the Great Rift Valley — the very womb of humanity. Mecca was just a little south of us, off to the starboard. Up ahead of us was Jerusalem and all the holy sites of the world's great monotheistic religions. Places of power and beauty, emotional ground zeroes, where our deepest sense of identity came into being.

We spoke about language and about Ireland. We talked of pyramids and of the grand façades of Petra — something both of us were now off to see. Through the afternoon, the beer softened our views of the world, and we melted into a comfortable hum of conversation. I started telling her all about Darwin and his theories on music.

He's not the last word on music and evolution though. Far from it. Along about the end of the 1980s, evolutionary psychology started to come into vogue. Important breakthroughs were happening in language, especially in how language was configured in the brain. Noam Chomsky was claiming that grammar is hardwired into us, that we are preprogrammed to learn languages. And one of Chomsky's disciples, Stephen Pinker out at M.I.T., wrote a book titled *How the Mind Works*. It was filled with some pretty amazing insights into the ways we've evolved.

When Pinker came to music, he focused on the neurochemicals washing through our brains. Physically speaking, he wrote, much of this starts in our limbic systems. The limbic system is a set of structures just above the brain stem, which includes the hippocampus. Now, I'm no brain surgeon but I do know this: the hippocampus is the seat of the four F's — feeding, fighting, fleeing, and, um, well... mating. It regulates everything from increased heart rates to sweaty palms — all the things we need to deal with the situations we get into.

Pinker figured that music is an "exaptation." This means that it is not a proper evolutionary adaptation. We don't need music to survive nor does it enhance our sexual proclivity. Instead, our brains seem to have found that it's a short cut that produces gushes of pleasure — or gushes of soothing hormones in times of sorrow.

Music, Pinker brazenly claimed, is auditory cheesecake. Those were his exact words. Now cheesecake, for those of you who have never seen a dessert menu, is a heavy confectionary of fats and sugars. A hundred thousand years ago, this is exactly what our paleolithic bodies needed to survive. Nowadays, we've learned how to bake them up simply and easily, but those essential ingredients still trigger all the same pleasure centres hardwired into our gullible brains.

Music is much the same. It's an exaptation or a borrowing from other processes and this is, in fact, not at all rare in the animal kingdom. There are all kinds of amazing exaptations out there. We now know, for example, that feathers on birds are an exaptation that goes back to the age of dinosaurs. Feathers first evolved for simple insulation and temperature regulation. It was only a by-product — the hollow cores — that also happened to make them very good for flight.

Pinker, I told Claire, was simply claiming that we'd developed music as a short cut to pleasure. It was an exaptation. And probably an exaptation from language.

"I don't believe that," Claire said. "Music and language are not the same thing at all."

"No. One is an exaptation of the other."

"That's complete rubbish."

"It's not my theory, Claire."

"How do you know that language is not an exaptation of music? Maybe music came first. How about that?"

"Actually, that's a real possibility."

"I like that theory better. I'm going to call that one mine."

"Okay, Claire. That one can be yours."

We eventually sidled into the docks at Aqaba. The whitewashed city of Aqaba sits in an odd little triangle that presses it — with Israel on one side and Saudi Arabia on the other — into a stretch of beach that is only a few dozen kilometres long. You can literally see the buildings of Eilat in Israel just to the west, maybe ten kilometres away, though you have to look over a fence that has like a gazillion volts of electricity running through it.

Claire and I clambered up the docks and out into the country of Jordan. Aqaba is its second biggest city, quite pretty really, a little oasis on the tip of the great Arabian desert.

"I know a place that serves a decent pint of beer," said Claire, eyeing up the waterfront.

"Right then," I said, heaving up my backpack. "Let's go."

With a mouth tasting like your parents' shag carpet, I got on the bus the next day for the long trip to Petra. Claire crawled in beside me. The bus chugged through the haunts of Lawrence of Arabia. Out in the raw desert she pointed out some railroad tracks. They were narrower than usual. "Those are the old Turkish tracks," she said. "The lines that Lawrence blew up. Have you seen the film, then?"

"Not for a while."

"Well, it's a brilliant scene. He was a bit of a wingnut but he united the desert tribes against the Turks."

These lands, I guess, have always been a crossroads. This empire and that empire. This war and that. And hidden among the valleys of central Jordan is one of the most interesting civilizations of all.

The Rose-Red City of Petra is one of those lost cities, so deep into the weave of canyons and caves that no European saw it until 1812. In fact, it was a real short cut for the camel caravans running between the Persian Gulf and the ancient Mediterranean ports at Gaza. The route through the red rock cliffs cut weeks off the longer desert route, so the Nabateans built Petra here and became fabulously wealthy by controlling the water sources then selling that lifeblood of the desert to the desperately dry caravans.

We turned off the highway and down towards the site. My head was walloping and I hadn't had enough sleep. I could've used a little water myself. Near the entrance, the Bedouins have set up carts and horses to take you down the pathways and into the ruins. Claire and I chose to walk instead. A long dirt road led down to a cleft in a cliff and there, right at the beginning, were a couple of rock-carved tombs. The colour of the rock really was a vivid orangey-red and my hangover began to forget itself.

You enter the city down a long *siq*, a narrow canyon, sometimes no wider than an arm's length with walls that tower three hundred metres straight up. Lined in rusty reds and browns and calcium whites, they were like huge walls of Neapolitan ice cream.

I walked down the long siq in awe. It's as if the two walls of the Grand Canyon had been pushed together leaving only a trail three or four metres wide. Claire had been here before and she was getting a kick out of my astonishment. I kept craning my neck up at the ice cream cliffs until she nudged me to point out a niche in the rock. In it was a heavily eroded statue of one of the Nabatean gods. In places underfoot were the remains of a cobblestone road and at the side of the cliffs were runnels, dry now but once meant to catch the water from the flash floods and direct it down into reservoirs and pools.

The siq suddenly opened up into a natural amphitheatre, and I'm sure a thousand tourist cameras have captured this exact moment, coming around the bend and seeing the shining building carved out of the rock face there. The monumental façade is called *Al-Khazneh*, which translates as "The Treasury."

And it is astounding. It's as if the Parthenon of Athens had been fully restored and airlifted whole, dropped down here into the middle of the Arabian Desert. Huge carved columns rise up four or five storeys tall, holding up a pediment as big as a courthouse and above that more fluted columns and statues.

Claire laughed at me. "Do you see up there on the top?" She was pointing up at a huge stone urn above the pediment. "For a while they believed that the urn contained the treasure. Do you see how it's riddled with bullet holes?"

It was true. The rest of the façade was pristine but the urn was crumbling away and pretty beat up.

The treasury at Petra.

"Your man shot the thing up trying to get it to spill its contents. Like a bloody piñata. There was nothing inside the urn. There's not even nothing — it's all solid rock."

The idea of this thing as a treasury really is an illusion. Inside the building is one big stark and empty room with a couple of niches off to the side. Claire looked around at the big empty space. "Look at this," she said, "there's nothing. It's architectural cheesecake."

She was a quick study, Claire was. I laughed. I think I actually snorted. She'd hit the nail on the head.

"It's like a spandrel," I said.

"A what?"

"Pinker actually used the word 'spandrel.' It comes from architecture."

Claire looked at me strangely. "I have no idea what you're on about."

"Well look, let's say you're building an archway for a door. You put in the door but you still have this semi-circular space left over above it. You have to fill it in with something, a nice fresco or some stained glass or something. That's a spandrel."

"So what are you saying?"

"Not me. Pinker. Pinker was saying that music is a spandrel."

"Of what? Are you on about language again?"

"Well, yes, it could be that music is a spandrel of language."

"Ah, there you go again."

"It's not my theory, Claire."

"Well," she said, sagely, "at least that makes more sense than cheesecake."

Music and language have both evolved from an attention to our auditory worlds. That much is certain. Both are tied — evolutionarily — to our most primal sounds. Cries of distress, laughter, sighs of contentment, the moaning of pain or the roaring of anger — those immediate communicators — are at the beginnings of both.

Dr. David Huron, a professor in Music Cognition at Ohio State, went on to explain that we've had a million years of learning to read the voices of others. It was to our advantage to be able to read another's moods — sometimes quite in contrast to the actual meaning of the words they were speaking. Recent work even hints that we look to prosody in speech as a sort of lie detector test. We can say any words we want, true or false, but our intonations may give away our sincerity. A tightness in the throat, a slight heightening in pitch, tells us much more about the emotional state — and honesty — of a speaker than the words themselves. And we have become very, very good at reading these cues.

But does that make music a spandrel of language? Well, not exactly. It might be some sort of half-twin of language — something that's come from the same evolutionary trunk of the tree — but despite what Pinker said, it's probably not its spandrel. No more than language is a spandrel of music. Music works on an emotional level that language just can't attain. It's something intimately entangled with our deepest memories. It's something that makes us move and dance and speak to our gods. There just has to be more to it. There has to be.

Past the so-called Treasury, the siq empties out into a wider canyon. The Bedouin have set up camp there, some of them living in the caves dotting the hills. I could see their cooking fires rising from the rocks. They have a little market in the space that's opened up — a few spices laid out on a table and cups of coffee strong enough to melt stone. You can sit there for a while and watch the camels wobble by on their knobbly knees.

A man there was playing a flute. It was exotic, like a snake charmer whirling up through a minor scale. It echoed through the canyon. In fact, I had heard it when I was in the big stone room behind the façade of the Treasury, wondering where it was coming from. It made me think of the paleolithic flute in the caves of Germany. It was timeless and haunting.

Claire and I went on after that, down into the valleys. There are more than a thousand archeological sites mapped out here. Some of them are tiny but a few are almost as grand as the Treasury. Up against one great cliff face, there's a façade called the Palace. Inside it too there's nothing more than a big empty space. Down further there are the ruins of a colonnaded street from Roman times and up over a little hill a Byzantine church, the last hurrah before Petra disappeared into the shadows. And towards the end of the complex, up a grueling set of narrow steps, not unlike the steps up to Mount Sinai, there's a façade called Al-Dier, "the Monastery" in English. It's the single largest building at Petra. Just the entrance, the doorway alone, is eight metres high. It towers up well above that in columns and pedestals and porticoes.

And inside?

Nothing. It's just as empty as all the others.

All this was a mystery until relatively recently. In 2003, the tomb of a Nabatean king was found under the Treasury. It dates to 26 B.C.E. There was nothing in the empty recesses behind the grand façades, but there was sure as hell something under them. They're not spandrels at all. They're tombs. Each and every one of them.

They are the final resting place for the souls of kings.

3

TURKEY
THE WHIRLING DERVISHES

MARCO POLO SLEPT HERE. I CAN IMAGINE HIM, CURLED UP IN A FETAL position, an innocent teenager cowed by the cavernous building and the strange languages washing all around him. I was four or five days out from Istanbul at the very beginnings of the Silk Road and I'd just come into this ancient caravanserai. A fountain in the courtyard dripped and plopped water in the shimmering heat. A thousand years ago, the camels would have drunk from it and inside the men would have slept, knives tucked into their belts, their goods safely piled up beside them.

Along this Silk Road came textiles and spices and hidden treasures. Marco Polo's uncle carried a small flask of holy oil from Jerusalem, destined for the distant courts of Kublai Khan. In the packs of the long caravans came all manner of merchandise, as well as ideas. Along these roads, the traders brought medical advancements and mathematics and sometimes the melodies of distant and unfamiliar music.

I had come across the Strait of Bosphorus out onto the land bridge of Asia Minor to this crumbling stone building in the desert. I'd been dragged along by a Turkish woman named Bahar. "You will see something special here," she said. In the haunts of Marco Polo, she was taking me to hear and see and experience the legendary Whirling Dervishes.

The caravanserai we came into was silent. These way-stops were placed every seventy kilometres or so, which apparently is about the distance a camel can cover in a day. But the caravans are long gone, replaced now by dented Soviet-era trucks making the runs out to the distant ports on the Black Sea, or trundling up through the mountain passes and into Iraq. And so this caravanserai has long been abandoned and deserted.

We entered through a massive wooden door, two storeys tall and banded by iron strips like the slats of a barrel. The doors creaked opened and we were led into a cavernous hall with a great arched ceiling.

The room was dark. Candles flickered up on the stone pillars. Bahar sat me down on a wooden bench along the wall. A stillness fell over the place and a lone male voice began to sing in the shadows.

If it weren't for Bahar I would have thought it was the Muslim call to prayer.

The inflections were the same, the strange tumble of quarter tones, the same shape-shifting melody, wandering up and down the scale.

The Whirling Dervishes, Sufis, are a sort of outlier sect of Islam. They are mystics, with an almost Buddhist-like preoccupation with meditation and altered states of consciousness. This singing is called *Naat,* and it starts with invocations of praise for Muhammad in the ancient Persian tongue of a legendary poet named Rumi.

We sat very still and listened and waited for something to happen. At some indefinable point, the singing simply trailed off and was immediately taken up by a flute. Still no one moved. No one had come out to introduce the ceremony. In fact, the place was mostly empty, just a handful of curious travellers and the haunting call of this flute from somewhere in the darkness. It echoed off the stones and I thought that, yes, again, like the paleolithic caves, here was a place of power and magic.

From the shadows the Whirling Dervishes entered. They came in single file, five of them, wrapped in long, sweeping black cloaks.

 **LISTEN 3.1**

The flute song curled up around the pillars, mournful and breathy. The Dervishes stepped slowly into the candlelight in single file until all at once they halted. They stood still a moment and then, in perfect synchronization, they swung the dark cloaks off their shoulders, whirling them like matadors. The cloaks dropped with a flourish, floating to the floor to reveal that the Dervishes were all in crisp, shimmering white gowns.

"That's their souls," whispered Bahar, leaning over and clutching my forearm.

"Their whats?"

"They have cast off their earthly egos." It sounded like she was reading from a pamphlet. Obviously, she'd given this speech before. "They have cleansed themselves of their worldly selves. Now they are ready to join with God."

"Wow," I said. "What's that on their heads?" Each man wore a high conical hat with some sort of felt covering.

"Tombstones."

"I beg your pardon?"

"Tombstones. The hats represent tombstones. They represent the death of their egos." She looked at me as if every fool already knew this.

"Very Freudian," I said.

"Shhh. They're about to…"

"About to whirl?"

"Exactly."

The Dervishes moved out into the centre of the room like ghosts, arranging themselves so that one stood in the middle with the others standing at each of the four corners. And as they came into their positions, they began to swirl around, slowly, methodically, just one foot stepping over the other to turn them around and around.

Every culture on Earth has music. Every culture on Earth also has dance. They are inseparable, like two sides of a coin. It's only in our modern Western society that we have severed the two. We've created professional classes in both dance and music, and the vast majority of the rest of us have become just passive listeners and watchers.

But why were music and movement ever entwined? One theory has it that music arose to synchronize work. Imagine hauling the ten -ton blocks of granite to build the pyramids for example. It would have been handy to have everyone pulling on the same beat. Or, say, rowing Roman galleys. Or prison work gangs in Mississippi. It's all movement synchronized to a beat and, although there's something to that idea, most anthropologists now believe that this is probably not widespread enough to account for ubiquity of either music or dance.

If you think about it, music has a much more primeval link with movement. The human ear is not only the organ of hearing, it's also the organ of balance. The inner ear contains the complex vestibular organ which orients our bodies to gravity. Up, down, left, right, back, front, we calibrate ourselves to the outside world through our ears. The vestibular organ also registers acceleration and angles of turn — and these Whirling Dervishes were deliberately messing with that. They were spinning to throw their perceptions out of whack. To lose themselves, so to speak, in order to get closer to God.

Why balance should be connected with sound is a sort of conundrum until you realize that one of the functions of our auditory system — again, evolutionarily speaking — is to be able to tell where a sound is coming from and therefore where exactly the danger is. Human ears can pinpoint a sound to within three degrees of its real source. That's pretty good. In fact, by having two ears, we almost involuntarily turn our entire heads toward the source of a sound, balancing the signal in each ear to locate its position, and it's only then that our eyes take over.

It used to be that our entire ears would move, like a cat's or a dog's. Every one of us still has these muscles — remnants of a prehistoric past — which can move our pinnae, the fleshy bits of the ear. We've just forgotten how to use them. There's a great line in the book *Music and the Mind* by Anthony Storr in which he talks about moving our ears. "We use this now," he says, "only for party tricks — to amuse children and confound creationists."

Each of the Whirling Dervishes' arms were now crossed over their chests as if they were hugging themselves, their hands holding loosely to the opposite shoulder.

"Do you see," announced Bahar, "how they are arranged?" They were still whirling slowly, the five of them, spaced like the five on a roll of dice.

The Whirling Dervishes.

"Yeah...?"

"The one in the middle represents the sun."

"Okay."

"The others are the planets. The whirling is the entire universe. They are representing through their dance the entire creation of God."

"Four planets?"

"That's what the wise men of the time would have known. Only four of the planets were clearly visible to the..."

"The naked eye?"

"The naked eye, yes." Bahar turned back to the performance.

I looked into the eyes of these Dervishes. Well, actually their eyes were closed, but I studied their expressions, looking, I suppose, for any hint that they might be faking it, that they might just be hamming it up for the tourists. To say they were in ecstasy may be a bit of a stretch, but certainly they really were going into some sort of trance. As they spun — a little faster, though never very quickly (everything was quite meditative) — their skirts swept up with the centrifugal force, like umbrellas opening. The flute song still danced around the ancient stones and it was like time was suspended. After a few minutes, each man unfolded his right hand from his left shoulder — all still perfectly synchronized with each other — and their right arms rose slowly above their heads, their hands outstretched, cupping their palms as if they were catching raindrops. At the same time, their left hands dropped from the other shoulder and moved slowly to point downwards at the floor.

I leaned over to Bahar, a questioning look on my face.

"Now they are channelling."

"Channelling what?"

"Heaven," she said.

Like lightning rods, they were directing the light and peace of God down to our woebegone Earth. Nice.

I never did see the musician playing that flute. It was lonely sounding and incredibly beautiful and it alluded to a line by Rumi. "Listen to the reed flute," he wrote, "and the tale it tells. How it sings of separation ..." The notes were long and sad and the Sufi directly interpret this flute song as the sorrow of being separated from Allah.

All their movement and all their ceremony was meant to address this loneliness, to free themselves from our earthly desires and troubles. To touch, if only for a moment, the divine.

For about fifteen minutes the Whirling Dervishes spun, slowly, counterclockwise. The flute song echoed around the stones but at some moment in the movement, some catch maybe in the melody, the Dervishes brought their arms back across their chests and, still perfectly synchronized, they slowed and finally stopped. They bowed, their high tombstone hats sweeping down towards the ancient stone floor and then, one by one, they floated out of the room in ghostly single file, just as they had come in. The flute trailed off and we were left in the echoing darkness, wide-eyed and silent.

Someone had given our driver an Indy 500 baseball cap and he'd surely taken it to heart, for now he raced down the road, stirring up the dust of the central plains of Turkey. I sat in the back seat, gripping onto anything I could, tossing from door to door with each wild, careening turn. Bahar sat up front with the driver and, on a relatively safe straightaway, she turned back to me, smiling awkwardly. "He is crazy," she apologized. "He is a crazy man."

Out past the window, the whole place was crazy. Just south of the caravanserai of Marco Polo is a region known as Cappadocia. Bizarre volcanic cones rose up out of the ground. More than a thousand years ago, early Christian churches had been carved into the cones and it was this that brought most of the tourists to this bizarre valley.

I'd come, though, to see an underground city — something that existed nowhere else on Earth. Bahar mentioned that she could get me there and I jumped at the chance. So it was that we tumbled into an old car that appeared one morning, off to see Derinkuyu, one of the most remarkable places on Earth.

We sped south for forty-five kilometres before our driver burst through his imaginary checkered flag and hit the brakes in a tumbling cloud of dust. A nondescript wooden shack sat by itself out in the middle of an empty field. There didn't seem to be anything there. The driver, however, was already out of the car, testing the flashlight we'd given him and signalling for us to follow him. Inside the shack, a set of stairs wound down into a narrow passageway. It was like plunging down the rabbit hole in *Alice in Wonderland*. A warren of passages and tunnels and dark echoing canals led off into the darkness.

We wound down into a long, descending passageway and the darkness became total. I had to follow the sound of footsteps and whispers ahead of me.

The underground city of Derinkuyu was lost to the outside world for hundreds of years, until it was rediscovered by a chicken about forty years ago. The chicken, apparently, was being chased about the field by a farmer intent on making it his meal when it suddenly disappeared into a mysterious hole in the ground. A further exploration of the "hole" revealed an entire hidden underground city, level after level of rooms and passageways burrowing down deep into the soft volcanic rock.

There are eleven levels plunging down eighty-five metres below the surface. At its height, the city held about three thousand people, mostly early Christians who had gone into hiding from the spread of Islam through this region in the seventh century.

Cappadocia, it should be said, lies at the centre of what used to be called Asia Minor. It's the crossroads between Europe and Asia, and the locals here have always been stuck in a sort of no man's land between the great powers of the ancient world. Everyone from Alexander the Great to Genghis Khan swept over these fields and the inhabitants wisely realized that the only enduring safety lay in going underground.

The shallowest levels of the city date back a good three millennia. These levels were later turned into underground stockades so the people could bring their livestock down into safety as well. There are rock troughs and loops carved into the rock to tie up the animals. Down deeper are the living areas — a real warren of niches and spaces where the people would have waited out the passing of armies overhead. There's even a schoolroom, complete with desks and a lectern carved out of solid rock.

We kept going down and down and at one point the driver (now our guide) got ahead of us and we had to stop in the complete and utter darkness. We had to yell at him then, our voices ricocheting off the rock, until we could hear the clip clop of his boots coming back to us.

It's a curious fact that we perceive sounds as if they are inside our heads. We internalize them to a much greater degree than things we see. Things we see are outside of us. Things we hear are somehow more inside of us. Music, of course, seems to be right inside our heads so much so that we even talk about getting a song stuck in our heads and trying to get it out. It's deeply lodged in there.

You have to remember that our distant ancestors would have spent half their time in total darkness. At night, besides the moon and stars and perhaps a few very fragile cooking fires, it was a very scary world out there and our sense of hearing was all we could depend upon. It really was quite crucial that we evolve a way to orient ourselves to the things around us.

This includes the movement of things — towards us and away from us. I talked before about this Doppler effect of sound. It would have been apparent to the people hiding down here in Derinkuyu as the Mongol hordes rumbled past overhead. The oncoming roar of hooves would rise in pitch as the army approached. Directly above them, I suppose the passing army would have literally rattled the tufa roofs, dislodging chunks here and there. The candles would have sputtered and the underground people would have huddled there quietly, just listening. The army would pass over, never knowing that they had just ridden over an entire hidden city, and the sound of it all would slowly drop in pitch and fade away into the distance.

This is the evolutionary foundation of pitch perception, one of the most basic building blocks of music. Pitch is simply the frequency of the sound waves striking our eardrums and, like our sense of balance, it's a brilliant piece of engineering.

A healthy young human ear can detect pitches between 30 and 20,000 hertz (or cycles per second). In our inner ears we have about 3,500 hair cells. Each one of these has anywhere up to a hundred projections on it, fine little filaments called cilia. And so (very basically, mind you — I don't wish to pretend I'm any sort of ear specialist) one of these cilia gets jangled and, there you go, you hear an E flat.

Essentially, that's it. A vibration of approximately 311 hertz hits our ear drum, jangles a particular cilia filament, which is then converted into an electrical impulse. This impulse travels up through the auditory nerve batting around the brain stem like a ping pong ball, up through the thalamus to finally be registered in the auditory cortex itself. And there, in what is probably the most easily understandable mechanism in the entire brain, there is a tonotopical mapping of neurons. That just means that there's a broad band of neurons that are lined up very much like a piano keyboard, lower notes at one end, higher pitches at the other. I've even heard neuroscientists say that with a precise enough measurement, they can literally see what neurons are firing there and say that that's an A flat or that's an F sharp.

Unfortunately, that's about the only thing that's self-evident in the auditory cortex. For one thing, there is not one auditory cortex but two — one in each hemisphere, each about the size of a spindly French fry. Both register pitch but after that they do different things. The right auditory cortex, for example, registers things like the quality of a sound. Is the sound source bouncing off a hard stone surface or is it muddied by something softer? Are we in a small confined space or a great cathedral? Sorting out all this auditory information — and it's very complex — is just another example of how the brain locates itself within the world.

At the bottom of Derinkuyu, we came to an underground church. It was unadorned. It was simply too dark to paint any of the sorts of religious icons you would find in the churches above ground. This rock church is in the simple shape of a cross and there is one set of stairs that goes even deeper. We inched down it to a small room below, a confined, spooky space almost one hundred metres below the surface of the Earth. This was the crypt. They kept bodies there until all was safe again, then they were carried back up to the surface where they would have been properly buried. We stood there a moment in the deafening silence with thousands of tons of rock above us. It was dark and claustrophobic and no place for a living human to linger for long.

The spires and minarets of Istanbul rise up like fairy tales. Down by the gleaming waters of the Golden Horn sits the palace of the sultans with its four courtyards and massive gates. In the treasury there are gilded swords encrusted with jewels and an ebony throne inlaid with ivory. In what used to be the privy chamber — the private rooms of the Sultan — lay the most holy relics of Islam. Astonishingly, there's a letter signed by the Prophet Muhammad himself as well as his cloak and several other treasures. An imam sits there rocking in a chair, intoning suras from the Koran, hour after hour, his prosody wafting through the echoing spaces like music.

Between the first and second courtyards, behind a high wall, are the four hundred rooms of the harem. It's not exactly what you think. Sure enough, hundreds of girls were kept under the watchful eye of the sultan's mother. They were slave girls from all across the Ottoman Empire and, most desirably, the Caucasus, thought to be home to the most beautiful women in the world. These dark-eyed beauties would be trained in dance and music and all the secrets of love. Some would rise to become concubines of the sultan and some would eventually become one of his many wives.

The sultan's children were also kept here, protected from the world in their golden cage. One of the male children would rise to become the next sultan and then another harem girl would become head of the harem — mother of the new sultan — and easily one of the most powerful women on Earth.

I stood on a balcony there, locked behind a massive wall, with a view out over the Bosphorus Strait and Asia on the other side. Behind me and just out of sight was the Blue Mosque, surely one of the most gorgeous buildings on Earth. It was about one in the afternoon and the call to prayer was just starting up.

The call usually begins with a crackle of electricity. The mosques in Istanbul broadcast over speakers now, and a sort of warm up, a "testing, testing, is this thing on," cry in warbling tentative quarter tones rose up across the medieval walls.

"Allah Akbar," the call rings out — though these four syllables are warbled through for a good thirty seconds or so — sometimes even for several minutes, dropping and ascending through dozens of notes. The call to prayer is called *adhān.* The Arabic root comes from the verb "to permit," though it's also related to the word *udun* or ear. It comes five times a day in Muslim countries. In the cities, you can hear the minaret speakers popping on across the neighbourhoods, slightly out of sync with one another, sometimes seemingly competing to be the loudest, or project the furthest. And each singer's call is different — particular to himself — something to be perfected and developed over years and even decades.

◀€   LISTEN 3.2

The singers, which in Arabic are called *muezzin,* are masters of pitch. The words are exactly the same across thousands of mosques but the actual melodies are individually improvised. Each muezzin has his own particular call and to our Western ears, it's all exceedingly exotic.

It's the quarter tones. They sound out of tune to our sensitive Western ears but I can assure you that these pitches are absolutely precise. They waver and hover around our more staid old scales like heat waves on Istanbul cobblestones.

More than a hundred and fifty years ago, Alexander John Ellis, a reportedly tone deaf mathematician, divided the range between semitones into one hundred equal steps which he, logically enough, called "cents."

Ellis, by the way, was the basis for the character of Henry Higgins in *My Fair Lady*, the professor who insisted on training Eliza Doolittle with "the-rain-in-Spain-falls-mainly-on-the-plain." And while I'm throwing out these little facts, it's also worth saying that decibels (the measure of volume) were named after Alexander Graham Bell.

At any rate, our brains can detect change in pitch at about 4.3 cents for the middle range notes on a piano. That's the difference at which a good piano tuner will start to hear a note as being ever so slightly sharp or flat. These muezzin quarter notes are a good 50 cents apart, so we are readily aware of them. But they are not the 100 cent difference in a semi tone that we are used to — the step between a white key and the next black key on a piano keyboard — and therefore, culturally, we're not quite sure how to fit them into our musical schemes.

There's actually a fair bit of a debate over this in musicology circles. If music is some sort of evolutionary adaptation, then why is the music of the world so different? People of all races and cultures have opposable thumbs (barring some sort of industrial accident), and our hearts are pretty much in the same place. All the bits and pieces of our brains are wired in similar ways yet musical habits are radically diverse.

Or are they?

The so-called quarter notes — the micro tunings of Middle Eastern music — may not be as unusual as you think. These quarter tones are never the notes that a phrase will end or begin on (or even linger on for long). And this is important. The notes that the Call to Prayer do rest on, where a phrase begins or ends, are exactly the same notes — the octave or the fifth, say — that will be the most prominent in any music from the West.

Most of the world's music today appears to be based on seven main pitches (the white keys on a piano) and five secondary pitches (the black keys). This twelve-tone chromatic scale has a biological basis that I'll talk about in the next chapter, but it does not include the quarter tone notes of the muezzin. So, where do they fit in?

Well, and again this is controversial, these quarter tone pitches flash by quickly, usually on the way to another more conventional note so that the quarter tones could be considered simply *glissandos* — something Western music does quite often. Glissandos, as the word might imply, just means that the notes slide from one to the other. They're not a lock step movement up to the next pitch. It's just that Middle Eastern music allows the singer to rest on some of the middle points of the slide a little longer than we're used to.

Good musicians all over the world wrench out loads of emotional capital by hitting a note at first slightly, slightly flat and then pulling it up into the accepted pitch. Guitar players bend strings like elastic bands, sliding off a flatted third up to the major resolution. Think of B.B. King bending out notes, his face all scrunched up, on his fabled Lucille, a guitar he's owned since 1949.

It's just a bit of frosting on the cake, a squeezing out of the emotional juice. And it's one of the things that makes music really tick. We play all the time around, on top, or under the precise numerical value of a pitch, and that's what makes music emotive. It's what makes music human. This is a fantastically important point.

And that's where the different musics of the world divide up. It might be fair to say that there is a basic architecture to all music and that it has a very solid basis in the physics of sound. It's encoded into electrical impulses and it triggers specific neurons in the brain. It's only in the flourishes, the ornamentation, that we create discrete cultural differences.

Now, this is a contentious issue among musicologists (to say the least) but the research is saying pretty strongly now that the world's music has far more in common than it does in difference. One sure universal is the octave, and it's pretty clear that perfect fourths and fifths are almost everywhere too. And, as we shall see, there's increasing evidence to suggest that we are hard-wired for certain scales and chords and melody lines. There is a physiological basis to it, just as the evolutionary psychologists have said. We just need to pick it apart a bit more, to unravel the complexities, and finally come to some kind of real understanding about music.

Our brains all do contain the same auditory structures and, if we can get beyond what we've become used to hearing, we can hear beauty in all the music of the world. The fundamentals run deep. They are quintessentially human.

4

ATHENS
THE SCALES OF PYTHAGORAS

HIGH ABOVE THE STREETS OF ATHENS A GREAT FORTRESS OF ROCK rises up. This is the Acropolis, and perched along its top are the temples and walls and marble columns that mark the very beginning of Western civilization. Socrates would have walked among the shadows of these buildings, dragging along his pupil Plato. And later Aristotle shuffled along, thinking about the both of them and how he could probably do better.

Nowadays, the tourists file up the steep stairs to the top, slipping and sliding on the highly polished marble. Most of them head straight for the Parthenon, the largest of the remaining buildings, and, even in its advanced stage of dissolution, what's left of it makes it among the most iconic structures in the world.

I stood looking up at the fluted columns and broken pediments and the German cranes that are now trying, Humpty Dumpty-like, to put it all back together again. They never will, of course, because the whole point of the Parthenon was that it enclosed a massive silver, ivory, and gold statue of Athena herself, and that's long gone, damaged so badly by successive fires until what eventually remained was carried off by the

The santouri player underneath the Acropolis.

barbarians. The silver spoon in your cupboard may contain a speck of her fingernail. The gold in your watch might have a smidgen of her just and tranquil nose.

A sheen of greatness still lingers in the ruins, though. There's a fantastic optical illusion, for example. The thick columns bulge up three stories into the hot blue sky and perspective should have made them seem to bend in towards each other at the tops. But the Greek architects understood this phenomenon and flared the columns with absolute mathematical precision so that they would always appear straight as an arrow all the way up — even though they are not. Such was the genius of the ancient Greeks.

For a few hours I wandered around the stones like any other tourist, then, tired of the crowds and the heat, I retreated down the steps and away from the bus parks and souvenir stands at the bottom. There's a shaded little pathway that swings around to the north, and very quickly I left the rush behind and strolled along a walkway lined with stone walls and ancient little houses with their doorsills and windowsills painted in brilliant blue. A tinkling of notes appeared and against a wall a man played a zither-like instrument spread out in front of him like a coffee table.

He wore a traditional white *foustanella* (a sort of dress) with a short, embroidered vest and big white pom-poms on the toes of his shoes. He was certainly dressed for the tourists, but I was the only one around now. He stopped playing when he saw me and we talked for a while. The instrument, he said, spreading his hands over it, is a *santouri*. Dozens of strings wound around the tuning bars but they were strung together into twelve main rows like railroad lines of chromatic possibility. It's a very old instrument, a sort of trapezoid shape of walnut and pine, that's been played in Greece for thousands of years.

I asked him to play something for me and he solemnly bent his head and raised the little mallets he carried in each hand. Then he just let them fall, easily, tapping down onto the strings, bringing out a sparkle of notes. The chiming of the strings was something like a harpsichord — but struck, not plucked. It is the great, great grandfather of our modern piano and he played shimmering arpeggios that hovered between minor and major scales. It was as if he were experimenting with the scales themselves, changing only a single note here and there so the scales moved and changed like wisps of clouds.

 LISTEN 4.1

Two and a half thousand years ago, even before the Parthenon was complete, mathematicians like Pythagoras were working out the principles of music. Just below the Acropolis is the ancient agora, mostly rubble now. This was once the marketplace of Athens. The story goes that Pythagoras was walking down these streets, probably thinking of triangles, when he became aware of the hammering of anvils from a blacksmith's shop. The funny thing was that the anvils were bonging away in perfect harmony with one another. One would clang and then another beside it would chink out a perfect fifth while another behind that one would fill in the minor third. Curious, Pythagoras went down into the shop and almost immediately he could see what was causing this. It was the size of the anvils.

I suppose Pythagoras interrupted a rather annoyed blacksmith shop foremen to weigh the anvils precisely, and this is what he found: it's all about ratios. Music is all about ratios.

You would think that the notes in scales are just linear mathematical progressions of frequencies (Do being 100 Hz, say, then Re being 200 and so on). Well, they're not. It's much more complicated than that. What Pythagoras found out is that a twelve-pound anvil and a six-pound anvil would ring in a perfect octave to each other. That's because the ratio is 2 to 1 (or 2:1 in mathematical notation).

But if you take that same twelve-pound anvil and hit an eight-pound anvil beside it, the eight-pounder will give off a perfect fifth. Again, it's the ratio. This time it's 3:2. Now, that's very strange. Why should our ears — or our brains, more correctly — hear ratios? And it certainly doesn't end there. Every single note in a scale — any scale — sits in a specific ratio to the tonic, or central octave note of the scale.

But of course you had to be Pythagoras to figure all this out. He took the ideas back to his workroom and began to measure the strings on instruments, and sure enough, there were exactly the same ratios. Complicated but undeniable. A perfect fourth is 8:6, a minor third is 6:5 and a single whole note interval is 9:8.

This, by the way, is what humans hear and dogs don't. Our brains comprehend the complex relationships between notes, and that is what scales or, for that matter, what melodies are. Dogs hear the pitches all right and sometimes even howl at them, but their dog brains can't pick out the relationships between them. They couldn't comprehend the interval of a minor third if you balanced it on their nose.

For human beings, basic pitch is processed in both hemispheres of our brain. But the relationship between the notes, the building of scales and melodies and chords seems to be primarily a function of our right auditory cortex. The left auditory cortex processes the length of notes and the repetition of sounds, so you start to get the beginnings of rhythm there. At least a part of the research here comes from stroke and accident victims. A stroke affecting the left auditory cortex can leave a person without much of a sense of rhythm. A stroke affecting the right side can leave us all but tone deaf.

Some really fantastic things are going on in our little auditory cortices. There are neural circuits leading up to our auditory cortices that actually select sounds for our attention. This is how we manage to follow the thread of a conversation in a loud cocktail party. This is how we're able to focus in on certain sounds and mask out the others. An interesting side effect of this is that we don't hear our own voices. We don't need to, of course, because we already know what we're saying. All this leads to the curious phenomenon of the telephone answering machine. When we hear our own voice on some such recording, we're often surprised. "Is that really what I sound like?" we ask, amazed. Our brains have literally kept us from the sound of our own voices.

There are certain musical ratios too, which we can't really hear, or more properly, that our brains can't process. There's an interval for which our brains are no more advanced than a Rottweiler's or a Chihuahua's. This is the Tristan Chord. It's an augmented fourth (if you start with a C then it will be that and the F# above it). For many thousands of years and all over the world, putting these two notes together was shunned. In the middle ages, it was called the *Diabolus in Musica* (the Devil's music) and it does, to this day, strike us as discordant — as brash and distinctly unpleasant. Oh, it's been used a few times by some very brave composers. Wagner used it in the opening to *Tristan und Isolde* in 1865 (thus the name of the chord) and Stravinsky toyed with it in his *Rite of Spring* (which, famously, caused the audience to riot at the premiere in Paris in 1913). You'll hear it in the occasional Miles Davis or Charlie Parker solo, but on the whole, you won't hear an augmented fourth in any of the music of the world.

And why? Because the ratio is the square root of two over one and, as any math student can tell you, the square root of two is an irrational number. It's stark raving mad. The decimal places have been calculated up to ten million places and still there's no end. It's a number that doesn't exist in any stable way in the real world. You can play this Tristan interval on a piano, and the two notes will fight and clash and jar with each other.

It is literally the sound of a square root, an irrational square root, and so, just as a dog might struggle to make out a melody, our human brains can't quite unravel this devil's interval. We hear it as not making sense, and to me that's fascinating. It's as if the mathematical truth of the universe is hardwired into us.

Is music, then, simply a matter of our brains experiencing the mathematics of sound waves? Well, it's a beautiful idea and there's at least a little something to it. But on the whole, no. It's still what we do with all these ratios and intervals, how we manipulate them, that makes music human.

The notes shimmered off the old stones and when the santouri player was finished, he passed his hand over the strings, quieting them, though the resonances still hummed in the pinewood. Someone else was standing behind us now, and he started clapping loudly.

"Brilliant," said the man, though I noticed he did not throw any coins into the musician's upturned case. I turned around to see a hardcore backpacker. I knew the type. Clothes a little ragged. Long stringy hair and proud of the fact that they've been travelling for eight months solid — or a year — or more, well out of money, but just following their hearts across this great big world, a kind of modern-day hobo.

I tossed a few Euros in the musician's case, nodding to him, and turned to go.

"Where you from, man?" the backpacker asked.

"Canada," I said, maybe a little more brusquely than I needed to.

"You coming around to the theatre?"

"The theatre?"

"The Theatre of Dionysus — it's one of the oldest theatres in the world. It's just around the corner."

He looked harmless enough. Beneath a massive nose, he had a warm smile and there was intelligence in his eyes.

"Where is it?"

"Just down around the corner there. That's where this path goes."

"Okay."

"I'm Rod," he said, holding out a big meaty hand.

"Well, pleased to meet you, Rod."

I followed him down the path and sure enough we came in very short order to the remains of a theatre slanting up the slopes of the Acropolis. In its day it once held 15,000 people, but there wasn't a whole lot to see anymore. Cracked slabs of marble form the benches and down in the centre is a flat area that would have been the stage. Rod and I took a seat there and he looked down over the ruins a little philosophically, imagining as I was the performances that used to take place here. He tugged at something in his coat and pulled out an oilskin of wine. "For Dionysus," he said.

"The god of wine."

"And drama."

"And fertility."

"Quite a guy," said Rod. "Did you know that theatre began with festivals to Dionysus. Lots of singing and dancing. Gradually they formed into proper performances."

"Are you in the theatre business, Rod?"

"Pathos," he said.

"What?"

"Pathos. It's the opposite of Logos."

"Logic. And mathematics."

"That's right. Dionysus was all about Pathos. He was all about music and emotion … and drinking."

"Party on."

"Yup." Rod took another swig from the wine flask. "Pathos is the human condition. It's all about sadness and anger, and love, and laughter, all of it. It's the thing that makes us human."

"So, you're an actor?"

"Not exactly. I'm a busker. I'm heading out to Ios tonight. Gonna make some money there."

"I'm heading for Naxos. Good beaches," I said.

"It's the same ferry."

"Great," I said. "So, you're a busker. Are you a musician?"

"No," said Rod. "Not exactly."

We spent the rest of the day wandering around the ruins and then took the train down to Piraeus, the dirty and slightly rundown port of Athens. Now, I've got to say that the Greek islands are pretty much my favourite place on Earth. The ferries run out from Piraeus and they usually leave in the evening so that you wake up in the morning in heaven.

Just out from the harbour, in the pink setting sun, a dolphin jumped in the wake of the ship. All around me, young travellers settled across the decks, climbing into sleeping bags, piling T-shirts under their heads for pillows. I stayed up by the rail, watching the sky purple and the stars come out over the wine-dark sea.

Rod set up a place somewhere and then came over to join me. We stood awhile, looking out over the rails. The constellations came out, many of their names coming down to us from the ancient Greek mariners. I was still thinking of the santouri player up by the Acropolis and said so.

"Yeah, he was good," Rod allowed. "Though I couldn't quite make out the song. Just sort of runs of scales."

"You know Pythagoras, right?"

"Triangle guy?"

"Yes. Well he also wrote that the planets and stars must make a sound as they travel through space. He called it 'the Harmony of the Spheres.'"

Rod closed his eyes. "Yeah, I've heard of that." He closed his eyes. "On really quiet nights I shut my eyes and try to hear it."

"You do?"

"No, I don't. I'm not dim. It's a vacuum out there in space. There's no sound at all."

I nodded.

"Nice idea, though," he admitted. "Quite poetic." Rod turned from the rails. "Gotta go get some sleep," he said. "Big night in Ios tomorrow."

"You playing in the square?"

"Yeah, something like that."

"So," I said, "Are you a juggler … sword swallower?"

"No, no," he said. "Not exactly."

The Greeks, then, were the first ones to sort out musical scales. There really are exact mathematical reasons why we've divided up the octave into twelve notes.

I should first say again that the octave is the one unequivocal universal in all the world's music. It is, of course, simply the doubling of a frequency, a ratio of 2:1, and it's so perfect that if you play two notes exactly an octave apart, they will still really only sound like one note — just richer and fatter.

Interestingly enough, an adult male voice and an adult female voice are pretty much exactly an octave apart. It's pretty easy to sing with someone from the opposite gender for this reason. We will naturally slide into melodies an octave apart — very useful for singing such ditties as "Happy Birthday." In fact, the octave is such a fundamental interval that there have even been experiments with other animals. It is thought that all mammals, even our lowly dog, can actually comprehend an octave. How these studies were done — and why — is a bit of a mystery to me. But there you go. Even dogs can hear this much.

But how we divide up the octave, well that's a whole other story. There is actually a very solid mathematical reason for dividing it into twelve. Now bear with me here because it does get confusing. If you start with an octave and divide the two frequencies exactly in half, you get the perfect fifth. That's simple enough. But then if you take that same perfect fifth, go up a full octave from there (say the perfect fifth of a C scale — G and go up to the high G above that) then divide those frequencies in half again, you get second of the original scale (in other words you get D — the second note in the C major scale). So, if you just keep going up dividing the octaves in a perfectly mathematical way (D up to a higher D now, which, divided, gives you A) you will eventually go through twelve steps before you come back to the original note. This gives you the 12 notes of the chromatic scale — the seven white keys and five black keys on a piano keyboard.

This is a mathematical reality and it forms the basis of all music. And this is what the Greeks worked out two and a half thousand years ago.

And where these clever Greeks went with this was that they tried out all the combinations of diatonic scales (just the seven dominant notes) and made a table of what these scales would sound like if you started on a different note but kept the intervals the same all the way up. The most basic one to us is called the modern Ionian scale. It's your basic do, re, mi, fa, so, la, ti, do. This is the major scale that is the basis of most of the music of the so-called Western world.

But there are many other possibilities and the Greeks worked them all out with sometimes crazy names like the Mixolydian scale or the Hypolydian or Hypophrygian scales. I'm not going to worry about all the details here, but what's most important is that they noted that each scale had a particular feel, a particular mood to it.

Aristotle believed that the Mixolydian scale was mournful and solemn but that the Phrygian was too emotional, putting men "into a frenzy of excitement." Plato, writing in *The Republic*, wanted to banish most of the scales, thinking that they would lead to laziness and a lack of purpose. He thought they should only keep the Phrygian and Dorian scales because one was good for use in battle and the other was good for reassurance in times of misfortune. All the rest were good for nothing but pathos, just useless emotions.

I don't know about that but I do know that, through all the years, in the West at least, we've gradually winnowed the scales down to two we use most often. There is the modern Ionian, which, as I've already said, is our basic major scale. The other is the modern Aeolian scale, which is our minor scale.

However, just in the last seventy or eighty years another scale has actually been resurrected. This is the Dorian scale, which we now call a blues scale. It's the same one that Plato thought brought our moods up in times of misfortune. The flatted third and the minor seventh do tug at the heartstrings, giving it a sort of sad swagger, and it appears today not only in blues music but also in jazz and certainly in rock and roll.

As we'll see, this Dorian scale came to back to the modern Western world in a most roundabout way, sailing over the seas in the holds of the slave ships from Africa. There's no doubt about it. These scales, once worked out by the ancient Greeks, were largely forgotten in Europe but were alive and well in sub-Saharan Africa. Later, they formed the backbone of spirituals on the old cotton and sugar cane plantations and in time became the basis of much of our popular music today.

A funny thing happened to me on the Greek island of Naxos. Well, maybe not so funny. I fell in with a group of people and we traipsed up to the old town to find a terrace to have a drink. I should say that Old Naxos town is an absolute maze of little lanes and dead ends and stairways that go nowhere. It was built this way deliberately because, a few hundred years ago, there used to be a lot of pirates in these parts. So, the idea was to fool the pirates, maybe even trap them, by making the town into a veritable labyrinth that only the locals would understand. It was a real Tristan chord of urban planning.

Anyway, we dipped into a few bars here and there and by the end of the night I was a bit pickled. It was after midnight and we were sitting in some little square, completely lost, and someone in the group had a guitar. Now I can whap out a tune with the best of them, especially when I've got a few drinks in me. So, when the guitar got passed around to me, I stood up and laid into my best impression of Keith Richards. I think I actually was playing "Sympathy for the Devil." I sang it out at the top of my lungs, much to the laughter of my new friends and the evident anger of a man who lived in a little apartment just above the town square.

Somewhere near the end of my inebriated performance, a balcony door opened above us and a local Greek man very sensibly told us to shut the hell up. All in Greek, of course. Someone, and it wasn't me, yelled back at him. I was still playing the guitar and I don't think I even noticed all this happening. But the Greek man came stomping down into the square with a knife. I was the one making all the noise, so he made a bee-line for me, and as I remember it — it's all a little bit foggy — he pushed in towards me, brandishing a knife the size of his forearm.

I smiled politely, handed the guitar back to whomever it had come from, and exited the square in a boundless display of courage, no doubt roundly impressing my new friends by the speed of my running. I ran for all I was worth, my heart thumping like a drum solo.

Emotion in music, of course, is tied to these prehistoric fight-or-flight instincts. An accelerated rhythm has an obvious correlation to our heartbeat. When our heartbeats are racing — as mine was down the narrow Greek lanes — we are aroused. Well, in my case, terrified. And it's exactly the same sort of beat or rhythm we would expect to hear in the soundtrack of a movie when things are getting a bit hairy. Mathematically, it's a tempo that matches the speed of our heart, say, 150 beats per minute in this case, maybe more.

Slower tempos, by contrast, are soothing and calming. They lend themselves well to sadness. Or to reflection and reverence. And those tempos would be exactly the timing of a heart at rest. It's still all based on mathematics.

Emotions, though — Rod's Pathos — are a little more complex but, seen in the light of evolutionary psychology, they make perfect sense. Our basic instinctual emotions, anger and fear, for example, are pretty straightforward reactions to danger in the environment but even the more subtle feelings — jealousy, embarrassment, disgust, suspicion, sympathy — all these have their roots in our evolutionary past as well. Jealousy, obviously, is a part of Darwin's sexual selection, urging us to act if we are in danger of losing our sexual partner. Embarrassment might serve to ensure that we don't make the same foolhardy mistake twice. Disgust, suspicion, sympathy, can all be decoded as evolutionary responses. They propel us to do things, to avoid things that may be dangerous, to help others in our social circle and so on.

Obviously, music encodes some of these feelings better than others. Think about it. We can have lyrics about humiliation or disgust, but the music itself doesn't directly generate those feelings. We don't have music that makes us feel suspicious, for example. We don't have pop tunes that make us feel embarrassment. Occasionally, music can instill feelings like trepidation or terror. Movie soundtracks do this well. The famous shower scene from Hitchcock's *Psycho* is usually held up as a pretty good example, though the truth is that that scene is more sound effect than real music.

No, music is best at generating something pretty specific. Music works with feelings than run along the spectrum of sadness and joy. Chords and scales and meter alone seem to be very good at making us feel real sorrow or, alternatively, lifting our souls to real happiness. And it's worth noting that this is probably the widest spectrum in human emotions. It encompasses everything from tranquillity to ecstasy, and from grief to glory.

Now, something important to understand about these particular emotions is that they are more than simple reactions to events in our world. In fact, we now think these emotions are largely about expectations. We think something will happen and if it does, especially if it exceeds our expectations, then we are happy, joyful even. But if something doesn't turn out quite as we planned it, like a relationship gone wrong, then we feel sadness or even despair.

This is called "dissonance theory" and it actually fits in nicely with what we know about music. Music is largely about anticipation, as the prominent music researcher and evolutionary psychologist David Huron insisted in his book *Sweet Anticipation*. It is based on mathematical sequences, and when something doesn't quite match our anticipation of what the next note or the next beat in the sequence should be, it sets up a complex reaction in the brain, one that reverberates emotionally.

Good composers know this. They set up expectations and then gradually fulfill them. After a long suspended chord, we expect to hear a resolution and experience measurable relief when it does come. We are surprised, pleasantly, when a song modulates up to another key signature and we are electrified when a piece of music suddenly breaks into double time.

Good musicians will play with these expectations as well, squeezing out a note at first slightly flat and then bending up into the proper pitch. A good drummer will lay a little behind the beat or really push at it to create a sense of groove. This has a powerful emotional impact, because it defies the brain's expectations. It plays ever so slightly with the mathematical precision of meter, and this is what really calls out to us as human beings.

We are most likely to get chills down the back of our necks when a singer suddenly hits an unexpected high note, leaping above the others, holding it for all she's worth. That's what brings tears to our eyes or sends us clambering to our feet in a standing ovation. And that's what music is all about.

I got on the ferry at dawn. We swung out of the harbour out past a rocky promontory. There's a great marble door sitting there on the end of it. It's called the Portara. There's nothing else there, just the marble frame of a giant door. The temple that used to be attached to it is long gone. In fact, it was never properly finished. Even two thousand years ago, there were money problems and political crises, and not even the gods remained unscathed.

We pulled out into the blue Mediterranean, never really too far from the sight of another couple of islands. This whole archipelago is called the Cyclades. It's a broad circle of islands, nestling in sun-spar-kled waters, though each island is really quite different. From Naxos, it only takes about three hours to cross over to the furthest southern reaches of the group and pull into the sunken cauldron that is the island of Santorini. There's nothing else quite like Santorini in the whole wide world. Towering cliffs push straight up out of the sea — the remnants of a massive volcanic explosion — and at the top, draped across the volcanic cliff tops, is the whitewashed town of Thera.

From the docks at the bottom, a bus will take you up a terrifying switchback of roads, up the cliffs to the town at the top. I found a place to stay up there then set out wandering. Just back from the plunging cliff, a little town square butted up against a Greek Orthodox church. I was walking across the plaza when I heard someone call my name. I turned around. A few pigeons fluttered above the cobblestones. Over by the church, a group of children had surrounded a lone figure. He was making them balloons, squeaking and twisting them into bubbly swords and Dachshund dogs. His face was powdered white and he wore a big round bright red nose over his own. Even his hippy hair was tucked underneath a grand mop of woollen orange hair.

"Rod," I said. "Is that you?"

"Who's Rod?" he said, winking at one of the children. "I am only a simple clown." Rod performed a deep and dignified deep bow in my direction. The children squealed. "I am the purveyor of laughter. I am the connoisseur of tears."

"Pathos," I said.

"You got it, man."

5

PARIS
THE INVENTION OF HARMONY

"BUT OF COURSE," THE GUIDE BEGAN, "THE DEVIL AND THE ARCHANGEL Michael made a bet."

Is this a joke? I thought. *It sounds like a joke.*

"Their wager was for all the souls of Brittany and Normandy."

I looked out over the steely-grey Atlantic. Just up the coast from here were the beaches of Normandy. To the west was Brittany. Somewhere straight out in front of me, lost in the fog and distance, was the English Channel. I was standing on a cobblestone terrace outside the cloisters on the island of Mont Saint Michel, surely one of the most fantastic places on this Earth. It looks like a set from *Lord of the Rings*. Behind me, towering above everything, were the ramparts and flying buttresses of a massive cathedral rising from the very top of the tiny island like a crown.

"There, do you see the other island?" the guide continued, pointing off into the mists.

I looked out over the rock wall, out across the grey water. A bare shard of granite sat out there in the cold waters between England and France. "The Devil, he says, 'let us have a competition. Let us see who can build the most beautiful palace.' He says, 'I will take that island and you will take this one.'" The guide paused and looked at us all. His voice grew sombre. "'Twenty-four hours you will have. Twenty-four hours to win the souls of all the people.'"

"Now," the guide said, "who do you think won our little game?"

Well, clearly, the archangel had built Mont Saint Michel. It's named after him and there's a golden statue of him at the top of the highest spire.

"The archangel?" I ventured.

"No." The guide pursed his lips in the way that only the French can do. "The Devil won."

"Then, how...?"

"This place — Mont Saint Michel — she is directly on the border of Normandy and Brittany." He allowed himself a chuckle. "The Normans say that the souls of the Bretons went to the Devil. The Bretons say the souls of the Normans went to the Devil."

"Of course," I said. "But how..."

"It is not for us to know where the souls go." He shrugged.

"But..."

"Ahh, the story. The Devil's palace was out there — on the second island."

"I, uh … I don't quite get it. There's nothing there."

"The Devil's palace was even more beautiful than Mont Saint Michel. But the Devil, of course, he is a liar. He, how do you say..."

"He cheated?"

"Yes, he cheated. He made his palace only out of ice. With his fires, he carved out the ice."

"It is a bit cold out."

"It was more beautiful than even this." He pointed up at the spires of the cathedral. "But in the morning, before the twenty-four hours is finished, the sun comes up and she is gone."

"So, the archangel won?"

"No, the Devil won."

"But, Mont Saint Michel is still here. The Devil..."

"We are right on the border of Brittany and Normandy." The guide looked at me as if to shut me up. "The Normans say the Devil took all the souls of the Britons. The Britons say..."

"That the Devil took the Norman souls."

"Yes, so you see, it was..."

Mont Saint Michel.

"A tie?"

"*Mon dieu.* Okay, yes. It was a tie."

We ducked down out of the oncoming rain, in through a narrow set of stairs and into the cloisters of the abbey. A plaque there told me that the archangel Michael appeared to a certain Bishop Aubert on October 16 of the year 709, commanding him to build an abbey here. That sounded a bit more reasonable than the ice palace story. This place is surely very old, and the first buildings here do date back to the Dark Ages. In fact, there were probably monks living in the caves at the very beginnings of Christianity. The rocky promontory would have been a safe haven then. Every day the tide sweeps in and leaves the place an island for twelve hours and, even when the sea is out, Mont Saint Michel is surrounded by a quagmire of mud. Much of it is quicksand, so that the pilgrims who came here would have to seriously pray before stepping out onto the mudflats. And even today, occasionally, someone will get a little too adventurous and go out too far onto the mudflats — and they are never seen again.

Over the centuries, a medieval village grew up around the base of the rock. A cobblestone road spirals up around the island, and at the top, precariously perched on a series of crypts and buttresses, above everything, is what the French call simply "Le Merveille": the Abbey of the Saint Michael.

The guide led us through a weave of winding little staircases and passageways, up through chapels and ancient kitchens with blackened fireplaces as big as walk-in closets. In one room was a huge wooden pulley used by the monks to ferry up supplies during times of siege. During the Hundred Years War, after, well, a hundred years of assaults, no army was able to get past the quicksand and the medieval fortifications. During the French Revolution, the place was used as prison, and more than a few of its inhabitants met their untimely ends at the blade of a guillotine.

The cathedral itself is largely unchanged in a thousand years. It's a vast, echoing, cavernous stone room. And unlike some of the other great cathedrals of Europe I've visited, this one was all but empty of people. It felt like I could have been walking into medieval France, especially when up near the front, a priest or monk, I'm not sure which, began to tug on a long rope. The rope dangled down in front of him, and he was really hauling on it. It almost lifted him off his feet when the rope pulled back up. I traced the long line with my eyes, way up, three or four storeys above us, where it disappeared into a hole in the roof. And from somewhere above that, the cathedral bells began to gong.

You could hear them for miles and miles, stirring up the lost souls of Brittany and Normandy. Now, bells — especially bells of this size — are a special sort of instrument. They have some very unique properties. They're made out of bronze, first of all. They clang and ring and throw their reverberations huge, huge distances. They also contain more harmonics than almost anything else human beings have invented.

Harmonics are the sympathetic vibrations that ricochet above and below the main note. A small hand bell can be tuned to a specific pitch, though even the smallest ones are rich in harmonics. These cathedral bells at Mont Saint Michel were the size of Volkswagen cars and they produced hundreds if not thousands of separate harmonics ringing and humming above the prime.

It is these ghostly harmonics that actually make instruments sound different from one another. A B flat on a trumpet obviously sounds different than a B flat on a clarinet. It's the same note, but it's the harmonics set up by the metal as opposed to the wood, not to mention the shape of the instruments and even the particular nuances of the breath travelling through them, that tell our brains they are different.

But there's nothing quite like bells for harmonic complexity. You'll find them all over the world. There are gongs in some countries and the pot-like gamelan in Indonesia. Cymbals are nothing more than flatter versions of the same thing. I know that in recording studios it is often the sizzle of the cymbals that is the most difficult sound to completely and accurately capture. And most of these sorts of instruments are made of bronze or at least coated in bronze. Guitar strings, for that matter, are twined in bronze. There's just something about it that resonates in a way that other metals cannot.

Much of sound is a matter of physics. I think we've covered that already. The materials and the manner in which they're put together, even the spaces in which they are struck or played or blown through, all set up a wildly complex set of frequencies. It's all math, really. And somehow our brains have become really, really good at decoding it all and even appropriating it to our own uses.

A funny little footnote is that the monks of Mont Saint Michel, even a thousand years ago, were very clever fellows when it came to acquiring this valuable bronze. By ancient rights — soon after the Norman invasion of England in 1066 — they came to control certain lands in Cornwall and Devon over in England. And, later, they even forged documents (sly devils) to retain control over these lands. And why? Well, we can't be one hundred percent certain, but in all likelihood it was because of the tin mines over there. Tin is the secret ingredient in making bronze. Bronze is nine parts copper to one part tin. The copper was easy to come by but the tin … not so much. So, it's possible that for several centuries, these Benedictine monks in Mont Saint Michel completely controlled the tin trade to the continent and had a monopoly on the forging of cathedral bells across most of Europe. Tell that to the Devil.

Medieval Paris surely stank. The inhabitants simply dumped their waste out into the streets. I was staying in the winding cobblestone lanes of the Latin Quarter just across the Seine from Notre Dame Cathedral. It's called the Latin Quarter because this was where the students lived — learning Latin, apparently — at what is one of the world's oldest universities, the Sorbonne.

Every day that I stayed there, I walked over the bridge to stand in awe of Notre Dame. It's one of my favourite cathedrals, partly because of the stained glass windows but mostly because of the gargoyles. Along the sides and especially up on the bell towers are hundreds of fantastic nightmarish creatures that strike me as a singularly illogical form of adornment for a church.

Just to the left of the main entrance, you enter a tiny winding staircase that takes you up the south bell tower. At the top, there's a great view over old Paris off to the Louvre on one side and to the right, where the Seine disappears into the distance, the far-off, almost delicate lines of the Eiffel Tower. The tiny stairwells and wood braces up here were haunts of the hunchback, Quasimodo. I can picture him ringing the bells, and up near the top I heard one of the great bells as it bonged out four o'clock. It damn near knocked me off my feet.

I stumbled back out and onto a thin stone walkway that ran around the outside of the south tower and came face-to-face with some of the finest of the gargoyles. These ghoulish apparitions are carved out of the very stones that make up the walls of the church. One of them had its head in its hands looking woebegone at its fate, sitting up there on its haunches over the long centuries. Another was chewing off a rabbit's head. I don't know what it all meant, but there were dozens of them. Maybe they were supposed to ward off evil spirits or something. I don't know. They looked like evil spirits themselves.

A gargoyle on Notre Dame Cathedral in Paris.

In practical terms, what they really are, are drain spouts. The old medieval mortar between the stones is fragile. A few decades of rain will corrode the mortar into sand. So these spouts were designed to carry the water out away from the walls, splashing happily down onto the heads of the peasants far below. *Gargoyle* comes from the French word *gargouille*, which originally meant throat (and from which we get the English word "*gargle*").

It's worth saying at this point that, beyond bells, there is almost no instrument with as much harmonic richness as the human voice. Technically, it's a reed instrument, with air passing over our vocal cords much like air passes over the reed of a clarinet or oboe. The vowel sounds in any language are particularly fat with harmonics and it's that which makes each and every human voice unique. And it was here, under the gargoyles in the cathedral of Notre Dame that a huge breakthrough was made in vocal music, in fact a sort of quantum leap in the whole history of music.

The music of the church before about the twelfth century was almost entirely Gregorian chant. It was named after Pope Gregory the First, who lived between the years 540 and 604. He never wrote a single note of

Gregorian chant himself but he is credited with ordering the cataloguing of much of the early church music, and for that he is now considered the patron saint of music.

At any rate, the chanting named for him was the music you would have heard in places like Mont Saint Michel and all the ancient churches of Europe in the early middle ages. It was also called plainchant. It's monophonic — a simple kind of droning melody called the *vox principalas*. Over top of that they did have the rudimentary melodies created with the fourth or the fifth. These were called *vox organalis* and they moved in a strict lockstep progression with the *vox principalas*.

All that changed in Notre Dame Cathedral in the twelfth century. A small group of scholars and monks and musicians put together — and as far as we know, quite independently of anyone else — the first principals of polyphony, whereby two or more singers would sing completely separate lines of music that would somehow, almost magically, weave together. And this was the beginning of almost everything we know in the Western world about music. This was the invention of harmony.

I just happened to be in Paris one August night when (and they only do this once or twice a year) there was to be a concert in the nave of Notre Dame Cathedral. And the concert would be that very music — the first polyphonic music — from these early masters of the School of Notre Dame. We even have a few of the composers' names. A man named Léonin lived in the 1100s. His breakthrough was to slow down the Gregorian chant and then add a melodic line above it with two or three notes to every one below. It was meant to just be another form of ornamentation, but it sounded damn good. This Léonin also probably invented a musical notation system and began to codify the rhythmic schemes, writing the phrases into bars that have since become the staple of our modern written music. The other name is Pérotin, who may have been a student of Léonin and may have been connected somehow to the new university across the river at Sorbonne. Certainly he was called Magister, or master, and we have at least a few pieces of written music, early polyphony, that can be directly attributed to him by name. Both of them worked right here, in the cathedral, literally inventing the music that would become the music of the Western world.

On the night of the concert, I got a seat in the very front row. They'd set up six chairs just in front of the altar and six music stands. It was a long summer twilight, and the evening light was dripping down through the Rose Window above us, speckling the ancient pillars with little triangles of blue and green and red.

Six musicians appeared. The first thing they performed came from a manuscript found in the Medici libraries in Florence. But it was from the School of Notre Dame, written somewhere in the 1200s, and it was a sort of round. What surprised me were the instruments. Along with the singers there were a harp and a violin and a guy playing a big flat handheld drum. I'd seen these sorts of drums before. They're called "bodhrán" in Ireland and they are distinctly Celtic. I guess that stands to reason. A thousand years ago, the people here would have been largely Celtic. Now the Celts have been pushed up into the far edges of Scotland and Ireland, though they still live out by Mont Saint Michel too, on the peninsula of Brittany in France.

At any rate, they played a few things that were actually something more like popular songs than church music. Chansons, they were called, like early versions of the songs the minstrels and troubadours sang. It drew up visions of chivalry and knights and all the things that went along with this medieval world. This was the sort of music that would have been played outside the cathedral, in the squares and taverns, and I suspect a little bit frowned upon by the bishop and his priests. It was a sort of warm-up, I guess, because then three of the singers stood and the cathedral hushed.

Their voices lifted, and there it was, three-part harmony for possibly the first time in history. It was a hallelujah for the Virgin Mary. The words were in Latin and it was as if a thousand years of history had just come to life again. I looked over at one of the side apses. There's a statue there of Joan of Arc, who was burned at the stake in Rouen, just to the east of here. Her ashes were cast into the Seine and would have floated right past this cathedral. Now she's one of the patron saints of France. I kept looking over at her face and I could almost imagine a smile on that stone visage, hearing again this ancient music ringing up to the heavens.

Harmony is like the third dimension of music. Rhythm and pitch are the first two. It's a nice little analogy — though not completely accurate. I read one scholarly article that claimed it was no coincidence that this third dimension of harmony appeared at about the same time that painters were first working out the principals of perspective. That seems like a bit of a stretch to me, connecting vision in this way with music, but there you go. Maybe there's something to it.

A better interpretation might be that it was a time in which they really were starting to figure out the world in a mechanistic sort of way. The astronomers were figuring out the rotation and elliptical paths of the planets. Architects were perfecting domes again and, in all, a brave new renaissance of thinking was on its way.

Music was a bit ahead of the game here in Notre Dame Cathedral. I don't think they understood the math behind it all but they sure got the sound, and it literally began to change the way we performed and listened to music.

In essence, it was a move beyond the simple harmonic possibilities of the perfect fourth and the perfect fifth. The School of Notre Dame introduced, probably for the first time in Western music, independent vocal lines that fit together like a jigsaw puzzle. And what came out of this was the rise of "the third."

All of a sudden, you have the third appearing as a feature of music. It's a major hallmark of Western music in general, and the magic of it comes in that ever so slight change between a major third and a minor third.

This is one of the big mysteries left in music cognition studies. What is it about a minor third that makes it sound sad? And why should a major third sound sprightly and happy? It's really only an infinitesimal difference in frequency. So why this massive sea change in the emotional perception of it?

Interestingly enough, although the third is a staple of Western music, the perception of its inherent qualities don't seem to be limited to Western ears. In cross-cultural studies, the melancholy of minor chords is easily recognized, as is the optimism of major chords. Infants as young as four months old also seem to innately perceive the moods that are somehow embedded into these chords, though we don't completely understand why.

Our best guess goes back to brain studies and simple evolutionary psychology. We have studies showing that fingers scraping on a chalkboard — that sound we all love to hate — is actually unpleasant across any culture (though how they got a chalkboard into the jungles of New Guinea eludes me). Likewise, we know that there are other sounds, like gurgling water, that are pleasant across all cultures. There is something deeply hardwired into us about all this. Like scales, there seem to be basic principles at work here, natural properties of acoustic waves and our brain's ability to perceive them.

In terms of pure pitch, particular neurons are triggered to fire with specific auditory frequencies coming in from the ear. We know that already. What's more interesting is that when two notes in harmony are played, the two sets of neurons attending these notes fire but not at exactly the same time — just very, very closely together, within microseconds of each other. It turns out that when two notes are in perfect harmony, the fine timing of these neurons is almost simultaneous. But when two notes jar (like an out of tune piano) the brain neurons take a little more time to process them. There's a lag of milliseconds while the brain tries to figure out what's just happened. We will hear those notes, then the chord that's produced, as discordant. It seems to be a matter of the timing of the neurons.

This is true of the Tristan Chord we talked about before. It's also true when we hear our drunken uncle singing slightly out of tune and it's true of nails on a chalkboard. Our brain just can't sync the sounds up very well, and we almost physically feel the discordancy.

In the natural harmonics of the world, the major third is a structurally solid ratio. It's 5:4, only a little less prominent than a perfect fourth or perfect fifth. On the other hand, the minor third, with that ever so slight drop in pitch, gives you a slightly more complex ratio. It's not that bad. It's still a 6:5 ratio, but that slight difference and the brain's difficulty in parsing it, well, that tends to make us hear it as just a little more anxiety-ridden, a little less pleasing, and, though it's not quite understood, a little more sombre and sad.

Really, we don't have a good handle on this phenomenon but, so far, that's about as close as we've come. It's about the brain's processing of frequencies and the relative complexities involved. Our brains parse out incredible amounts of information from the raw data coming in through our ears. We've apparently set up some sort of exaptation that taps deeply into our movements and emotions and memories. We are starting to understand how all this is done but the question of "why" remains. And that's the most important question of all.

When the concert in Notre Dame was over, the singers bowed and I went up briefly to talk with one of the men. His name was Sylvain Dieudonné and I'd already learned that he was the director of this ensemble. Sylvain had played the violin on a few of the pieces but it was he who had put this whole concert together. He'd spent a lifetime digging around in dusty libraries, pulling out these old manuscripts, like a kind of archeologist of music. I saw the script for the hallelujah they had played. The music was not like our modern notation, but it was sort of recognizable, like a precursor of our staffs and bars and notes. And I could make out the words underneath the music, printed carefully there on the page, staring out across the years.

Sylvain showed me two of his violins, one from the thirteenth century and one from the fourteenth. They were boxy little affairs but clearly ancestors of our modern violin. These ones were actually modern copies, painstakingly reconstructed from old drawings and written accounts. In a couple of the pieces he'd played them and I remember them sounding often like the drone, like that low note on the bagpipe that plays underneath the rest of the melody, certainly not like the frenzied pyro-techniques you can get in modern classical music.

There was an ancient harp there, too, small, almost hand-held. And, of course, the drums and even a couple of flutes, almost like recorders or penny whistles. I'd thought the concert was going to be all about vocal music. And it was, for the most part. I'd never stopped to think that there would have been other instruments involved.

Right beside the Eiffel Tower there's a museum that most people forget about in the cornucopia of museums in Paris. Most people only have time to whip through the Louvre or make a pass through the fantastic Museé d'Orsay. You see the Mona Lisa and a few Van Goghs, and you're off to the next city. I didn't even know about the Museé Du Quai Branly until I started researching music. This little museum is something to see, though. It houses a massive collection of cultural artifacts, much of it acquired in the years when France was a colonial superpower. Certainly, some of the great figures in anthropology were French. Claude Levi Strauss comes to mind and his name does pop up all over this particular museum. Right near the entrance, though, they have a sort of rotunda that's a full three floors high. It's stacked to the rafters with musical instruments from around the world, shelf after shelf of flutes and drums and harps from Africa and Asia and the Americas.

In the fine old tradition of ethnomusicology, there is a sort of genus mapping of these musical instruments. "Aerophones" include all woodwind and brass instruments, anything basically that is blown through to get a sound. "Chordophones" are the stringed instruments like the harps and lutes and zithers — even if they only have a single string. These, like a biological phylum, are subdivided into bowed instruments and plucked instruments. Third comes the "Idiophones," instruments that vibrate like rattles and cowbells, gongs and cymbals, and church bells. These idiophones make up the largest group in world music, perhaps because they are the most basic. And they are also related to the last group, the "Membranophones." Membranophones (who came up with these names?) are instruments which vibrate, like the others, but which have a particular membrane that vibrates. Essentially this is the skin of all drums.

There's a rebel upstart group of ethnomusicologists who have been keen on introducing a fifth category — electrophones — to include synthesizers and digital sound processors. I get the impression that the staid older crowd doesn't like this very much. An electric guitar is still a guitar, they'd say. And an electric keyboard is still a chordophone; it's just that the vibrations produced are digital.

I don't know. I have to say that walking through these endless shelves of instruments just made me think of butterflies pinned in collection boxes.

All the rooms were in a sort of twilight darkness, sunlight I suppose being the enemy of the fragile woods and strings. But it left me feeling a bit empty. A bit sad even.

This endless cataloguing of music and musical instruments seemed to me to be beside the point. It perhaps told us a lot about the "what" of music around the world — but once again it seemed to be missing the "why." And isn't that what it's all about?

Maybe there's a bit of a clue in the next major change in music. After the school at Notre Dame, three or four hundred years went by and polyphony became widespread. Composers played with the new harmonies and chords, and new instruments evolved. Along about the seventeenth century, by the time a young Johann Sebastian Bach was practising his chops, a major mathematical problem was becoming very apparent.

Composers had begun to switch between different key signatures — within the same piece. This was the Baroque era, a time in which ornamentation was pushed to its limits with fugues and toccatas and great complex façades of music and architecture.

But there was a problem. The Pythagorean system of scales and ratios had worked well for a thousand years. But that was because the compositions stayed in just one key signature. Now, the composers were toying with diminished chords and major sevenths and, most of all, flipping back and forth between different key signatures, all within the same piece.

Now, if you work out all the Pythagorian ratios starting in, say, a C major scale, then mathematically, the note G, the perfect fifth in that scale, will, of course, be a certain frequency. A certain exact hertz. But, and this is a big but, if you start off in another scale, say an E major scale (in which the G note would be the minor third), the note G there is actually a slightly different number. It doesn't actually work out to the same hertz. It's close, but not exact. So, when these baroque composers started transposing between keys, things went out of tune pretty quickly.

Today, on a modern piano keyboard, a G note is a G note, no matter what the key. So what happened?

Well, there was a lot of confusion about this little math problem for a long time. In the end, the instrument makers came up with the idea of "tempered" tuning. What they did was just sort of average the notes together. It's no longer mathematically exact, but it sounds right to our ears. Johann Sebastian Bach actually proved this with his Well-Tempered Clavier, a series of preludes and fugues in every possible key signature. On his new-fangled harpsichord with its new-fangled "tempered" tuning, it all worked. As one rogue put it, "Every note is now perfectly out of tune." Just by a bit.

So it turns out our brains are not just reacting to precise mathematical principles. We are not the product of some deterministic, blind watchmaker universe. The physics took us a long way but when it comes to music we seem to have bent things to our own will. We made it our own, and I find this strangely comforting.

This is something more than an "exaptation," something more than our basic auditory machinery evolving into other uses. We seem to have taken at least some conscious control over these processes. We are bending our own physiology and the very physics of sound to our own uses.

But why? What is it about the "organized sound" that moves us so deeply? Singing to our gods. Wringing out our souls in cascades of carefully crafted melodies and harmonies. Every culture on Earth seems to do it, so there must be a reason.

Well, we're almost ready for an answer, though we still need to look at what is probably the most basic property of all. We still need to look at rhythm.

6

SEVILLE
FLAMENCO AND THE RHYTHM OF OUR HEARTS

THEY CALL SEVILLE THE FRYING PAN OF EUROPE. IT'S HOT, ALL RIGHT, but charming. Courtyard gardens peek out behind wrought iron gates. Narrow cobblestone streets weave past ancient churches. It's easy to lose yourself for an afternoon in the labyrinth of tiny lanes, but all of them eventually funnel down into a massive stone plaza. The cathedral is there and the high walls of the Alcázar Palace. For a couple of hundred years, this was probably the most powerful square kilometre in the entire world. And, certainly, it was the richest.

This was the court of Queen Isabella of Castile and King Ferdinand of Aragon. Their marriage had merged two kingdoms, but it wasn't the family money that made Seville rich. The city had become powerful beyond belief because of a sea captain with a wild, almost unimaginable idea.

Christopher Columbus and his hair-brained scheme had already been turned down by the king of Portugal and just about every other monarch in Europe. The world was round, he claimed, and although this was by no means news, the idea of sailing around it, going west to get to the east, was a radical idea to these monarchs. Give me a flotilla of ships, Columbus said, and I will sail to India by heading straight out into the Atlantic.

"And fall off the edge of the world?" the king of Spain may have muttered.

"No, wait. Let him speak," said Queen Isabella, though in fact it was not the idea that caught her attention. There was something about this rough mariner's dark eyes. There is a story making the rounds now that she took quite a shine to Columbus. She did that sort of thing, apparently. We have no formal proof of an affair, but there are boatloads of corroborating evidence. A few weeks after he first came to them, Queen Isabella, like the other monarchs, actually turned down Columbus's request. At first, this might not seem like confirmation of an affair — quite the reverse — but the fact is that she turned him down not on the advice of her scientists or her accountants, but on the strong words of her confessor. So it seems there was something guilty riding on her conscience.

Then it was King Ferdinand who actually called Columbus back. Columbus was already leaving the city, dejected, riding on the back of a donkey. The king, you see, was shrewd and if there had indeed been an affair then he wanted Columbus completely and utterly gone forever. So he quite wisely agreed to the plan. What could be better? By agreeing to Columbus's request, Ferdinand was sending him off into the endless sea in three rickety boats. King Ferdinand also offered to raise a crew for him. The king kindly emptied the jails of Seville and put all the men on Columbus's ships. A pretty astute move. There'd be no more trouble, he thought, from this amorous sea captain.

Queen Isabella actually did die of an infection "down there," as the guide told us in the palace. And King Ferdinand, who'd apparently been a sex machine in his youth, had a rather unfortunate death himself. He died of indigestion and when the court physicians performed an autopsy, it was found that his guts were all blocked up with bull's testicles. Bull's testicles were, apparently, the Renaissance version of Viagra, but the king had eaten so many of them that the balls literally killed him.

Such are the rhythms of the human heart.

At any rate, Christopher Columbus set off and sailed the ocean blue and pretty much changed the course of human history. Unfortunately, he didn't seem to fully realize what he'd done. He pig-headedly believed to his dying day that he had found India when, really, it was the Caribbean and the coasts of Mexico. But, India or no India, he'd discovered a place with enough gold to make the new united Spanish kingdoms the richest and most powerful empire on Earth. And the sweet frying pan that is Seville became its capital.

Seville is an ancient city. There were Romans here and even before them the Phoenicians. It was pretty much the end of the world. Just past the gates of Hercules, the narrow straits between Morocco and Gibraltar, the blue Mediterranean empties out into the cold grey Atlantic. Nothing lay beyond that, just a great emptiness of sea monsters and unfinished maps.

So, the lands around Seville became a sort of bottleneck of peoples over the centuries. Most famously, the Moors came up from Africa and ruled here for five hundred years. They named this land Andalucía, coming from the Arabic word for "paradise," and truth be known, the Alcázar palace and many of the finest buildings are a paradise of Moorish design. Theirs was a kingdom of tolerance and one of the first truly multicultural civilizations on Earth. Jews and Gypsies lived in peace with Moors and Christians. The architecture of the palace reflects all this and so does a rather famous little form of music.

Seville, besides frying pans and sea captains, is probably most famous for the music we call flamenco. All over the world, the United Nations declares certain places to be World Heritage sites. But it is only in Seville that they have declared a form of music something of the same. The official UNESCO designation declares flamenco a "Masterpiece of the Oral and Intangible Heritage of Humanity."

So, obviously, I had planned on going to see one of the big flamenco shows while I was here. I'd looked a few up online but when I got here, the good people at the Garden Backpacker Hostel told me to come along with them to a little place they knew about. The tourist shows down by the cathedral were like big Las Vegas reviews, they said. They're worth seeing, but this one would be at a local tapas bar. Tiny. Intimate. The real thing.

I stumbled off behind an Italian guy who worked there, down through the weave of cobblestone streets, and we ended up at the Tablao Huelva just off the Plaza del Salvador. The place was small, a living-room-sized square in the back of the bar. They'd set it up so it looked like a room in someone's house. A painting hung on the wall and candles flickered on a fireplace hearth. They had some chairs set up around the back and side walls, maybe enough room for a dozen people to sit, and at the front, three wooden chairs (like kitchen chairs) for the musicians.

When the musicians came in they were relatively young, all in their late twenties or early thirties. The one on the right had a guitar. Off in the corner, two older men came in too. They sat there through the performance, just like the two old guys up in the balcony in *The Muppet Show*. These two old men were locals, as were the musicians, but they weren't here to heckle, exactly. I got the impression that they were connoisseurs of the art form, making the rounds, checking out the new talent, and here they were seated in a dark corner watching the new young bucks with doubtful eyes and expressionless faces.

It was the guitar player who began. He swept out a few chords then his fingers licked up the fretboard in a lightning-fast run of notes. *Okay*, I thought, *this guy can play.*

Beside him, in the middle, sat the singer. In flamenco this is called the *canto* but the singing itself is called *quejillo*. Now that's a terrific word. It literally means "to complain," and I'll admit I didn't quite get it until I heard this guy sing. What quejillo really means is a sort of crying out against one's fate. It's a raging, boiling, impassioned plea to whatever gods may be. And I'd never heard anything quite like it. The canto began gently, a mournful note or two above the guitar, but after a few bars, the singer drew his clutched fists into his chest and really began to blow apart the room. He sang as if the rapture had taken him, his face contorted in feeling, his eyes closed, tearing out his soul right in front of us.

It was a stunning, commanding performance, and just as he hit his stride, the third young man, the one sitting on the far left, began the staccato hand claps that are called *palmas*. He smacked out a vigorous and rock-steady beat and the singer, raising his own hands, joined in, clapping sharply in syncopation with the first. The guitar player turned to them, listened for a moment, and then leapt all over the rhythm, and the entire room exploded.

 **LISTEN 6.1**

One of the older men, one of the Muppets, stemmed his glass of wine and leaned into the other to comment. They both seemed to approve, nodding sagely, and one of them started bobbing his head ever so slightly with the rhythm. The young ones seemed to be winning them over.

In the great cathedral of Seville, the altarpiece contains enough gold to sink a ship. It climbs three storeys high, and when I first saw it, I thought it must be polished brass. No, I was told, that's solid gold. I tipped my head up towards the far-off ceiling and all the way up there was gold, tons and tons of gold. It had been wrought into thirty-six different scenes from the Old Testament and the lives of saints — and each scene was the size of a bay window. Begun ten years before Columbus and not completed until halfway through the next century, the altar was finished with the pillaged gold of the New World. In an alcove to the right is the tomb of Christopher Columbus. His coffin is an ornate marble affair but it's hoisted up on the shoulders of four marble kings, bearing him in honour across the centuries.

High above the cathedral is the bell tower called the Giralda. It's actually the only part of the building remaining from the central mosque that had stood here in Moorish times. The Giralda was a minaret tower and it's still so high and massive that when I walked up it, there weren't stairs inside, but ramps. This was so that, in the old days, the muezzin could ride his horse up — inside the tower — to sing out the call to prayer, five times a day.

In 1492, the very same year that Ferdinand sent Columbus off in the ships loaded with convicts, the last of the Moors were chased out of Andalucía, back across the straits and into North Africa. The Jews, meanwhile, were slaughtered and the darkness that was the Spanish Inquisition closed down over the land.

The gypsies were spared, probably because they were at least nominally Christians. And it was these gypsies who first performed the flamenco music. The rhythms are those of the Roma peoples. Likely it arose here in the poor barrios across the river, in the Triana district. In the early days, there were not even guitars, just the palmas and singers, clapping out the rhythms and intoning their protests to an unlistening god.

The tomb of Christopher Columbus in Seville.

We don't even know where the word *flamenco* comes from. It may be a gypsy word or it may be Moorish, a bending perhaps of the Arabic words for "escaped peasant." Some claim it comes from the Spanish word for fire, and I quite like that one. Whatever it means, it's clear that this is not the music of the cathedral. This is not the music of emperors or kings or sea captains. This is the music of the people.

The musicians in the Tablao Huelva had taken a break after playing for about an hour. When they came back in from their cigarettes out in the laneway, the palmas, a young man with movie star good looks, remained standing. He was dressed all in black, with a leather vest, looking for all the world like a gunslinger in the Wild West. His long black hair already glistened with sweat, but he jutted out his chin proudly and rose up as if he were daring the world to comment. Then the guitarist lit off into another lightning run and the gunslinger's feet cracked against the floorboards.

To say he danced does not do it justice. He strutted. The hard soles of his shoes ricocheted across the wooden floorboards. He flung an arm above his head and turned, whirling, while his feet accelerated with the rhythm.

His dark hair whipped around, spraying droplets. Then he stopped, just for a millisecond, striking a pose like a matador before he was off again, the soles of his shoes detonating across the floor. He was magnificent, and the two old men bent into each other again, whispering and nodding.

Rhythm is one of the basic properties of music, of course. You can strip away all the rest and we are still willing to call it music. Rhythm seems to be foundational, something without which music just wouldn't exist. More than one scholar has speculated that this has to do with our heartbeats. After all, the sound of our mother's heartbeat in the womb is our first real perception of the outside world. Our own heart thumps steadily away throughout our entire life, and when it stops, so do we, so you would think that it might account for our deep sense of rhythm. In fact, it's really only a part of the answer.

What we think of as rhythm is actually three separate facets of sound over time. The first (and simplest) is tempo. It's just the speed at which a piece of music is played. And, yes, this idea of tempo may well be related to our heartbeats. It's quite obvious that when we are aroused our hearts and our breathing speed up. So it is with music. The faster the tempo, the more stimulating the music, and the slower the tempo, the more relaxing it seems to us. Simple.

And like our heartbeats, there is a range of speed. Beats that are more than 1.2 seconds apart are so slow that we don't really parse them into recognizable rhythms. That works out to about 50 beats a minute, which is just a little slower than a heart at rest. Likewise, beats separated by less than 200 milliseconds are just too fast to be recognized as music. It's more like machine gun fire. That's about 300 beats a minute, and I can assure you that your heart would literally explode at that terrifying rate.

There is a preferred tempo range for music right around the world. It works out to somewhere between 85 to 120 beats a minute, and a quick check on the metronome will show you that most of the music we play or listen to does fall within these extremes.

Back in the flamenco bar, the musicians were pushing at these limits. It was an intangible masterpiece. This really was music on fire.

Rhythm is more than tempo, of course. That's only the speed of the piece. What we usually think of as rhythm comes from the other two aspects of sound over time: its meter and the patterns within that meter.

Meter is synonymous with bars in written music. Most commonly this is 4/4 time. Time has no natural unit like the octave, but this pattern of fours comes close. And again, like breathing or heartbeats, more than a few researchers have hinted that there's a physiological basis for it. Most likely, it has to do with human locomotion — with walking. Right leg, left leg, right leg, left leg. It's not exactly about moving our legs and striding off along down the street, though. It's a little more complex than that. It has to do, we think now, with how the brain sets up and sequences things like walking. It's about how the brain keeps patterns going and makes things like walking automatic to us. As someone once said, walking is basically organized falling. One miscue in the brain and our musculature and bones, like a house of cards, would simply tumble to the ground.

So a steady 4/4 beat, even a 3/4 beat, probably links deeply into the brain's structuring of movement. I'm not sure about 3/4 time (waltz time) but I wonder if it has to do with us moving either sideways or backwards. That's more of a three-step motion and still quite natural and automatic for us. It's the automaticity that is key here. When we first learn a new series of motor movements, say riding a bike for the first time, the process is overseen by a part of the brain called the basal ganglia. Now, I'm no brain surgeon, but I've been told that when we master this sequence — when it becomes automatic to us — it gets shunted off to another part of the brain to free the brain space up for other things. That's the brain being efficient. And it seems to be just this process that has been appropriated by rhythm.

We know a fair amount about all this from reverse engineering locomotion problems in patients with diseases like Parkinson's. There are different manifestations of the disease, but most often there is a corollary loss of coordination and balance. Walking becomes problematic, but it's not that the Parkinson's sufferers' leg muscles have atrophied. It's not about muscles or bone degeneration. It's about the neurotransmitters that regulate habitual sequential movements.

In a series of quite famous studies, Parkinson's patients who had trouble walking could regain some of their natural gait by listening to music, especially music they liked. The researchers tried different things, even a mechanical click track at a very specific tempo. That did nothing at all. It had to be real music and it had to be music the patients had an emotional connection to.

So, our sense of rhythm is deeply associated with the neural networks involved in automatic motor control. All the repetitive movements we typically make during any given day, from walking to typing to chewing, all seem to have been subsumed into our sense of rhythm. It goes deep. A newborn can be rocked to sleep, which, when you think about it, is pretty counterintuitive. There's just something about that steady, consistent movement that has a profound effect on us. It's something that goes to the very heart of our appreciation of music. Something I was certainly witnessing here in the little flamenco bar.

Halfway through what I guess you could call the second set, a woman appeared. She swept into the room in a long peasant dress. Her long black hair was tied back into a loose bun and she strode to the front where the others awaited her. This was what I had mentally associated with flamenco music. She was the very image of the art form. She wore a white lace shawl draped over her shoulders, its fringes ready for the sweeping turns and pivots. She was heavily mascara-ed and there were red and white roses in the band that tied back her long black hair.

She also had that same proud countenance, the almost matadorial stance, as the man. They did not dance together. They never do. Flamenco is not about romance or love. There is a tragic bravery to it. A raging against the heavens, and when she began to dance, her eyes squeezed shut, almost as if she were in pain.

The guitarist once more began, and with the two others now clapping, the woman began to step. It takes years, decades, to master flamenco dance. And even if you get the steps and master the fantastic rhythms she was fracturing the air with, you will not have understood flamenco until you've got the attitude and the passion that goes along with it.

◀€ LISTEN 6.2

Truth be known, the dance was a later addition to flamenco. What had begun in the poorer barrios gained status in the nineteenth century. Certain performers attracted followings. Their electric energy could not help but inspire movement and a whole new element appeared in style and posture. And though the dancer's arms rise up dramatically and their heads are held high, the dance is still all about the rhythms that their hard-soled shoes produce in syncopation with the palmas.

The guitarist was ripping through chords. The singer was now principal palmist and he was smacking along in a beautiful counterpoint to the dancer's gunshot footings. It was like she was tap dancing in a marble palace, her head held high like an Olympian goddess. One of the old men in the corner broke into a wide smile, rising an inch or so off his wooden chair. In flamenco, they call this indefinable element, this spark of human passion, *duende*. It is the mysterious and almost untameably powerful force created by a great performance. It is a force that takes over the audience, enrapturing them, leaving them spellbound and profoundly moved. Some call it "the gift." And these performers certainly had it. This was pure magic.

The third aspect of rhythm works within the meter. In fact, it is this third aspect that most people would likely call the "rhythm." It's the patterns. It's the backbeat on the two and the four in rock and roll. It's the upswing of the guitar in reggae. It's the rat-ta-tat-tat and the knock on the door that goes "Shave and a haircut … two bits."

In the brain, we know that neurons in the left auditory cortex fire when a sound repeats at a particular rate. This is the basis of rhythm perception (in contrast to the pitch predominance of the right cortex). We know that tempo and meter are connected to our brain's ability to sequence movement. But it's in the rhythmic patterns within the meter where we get the real Morse code of groove. It's in the accents and inflections here that the human brain plays with time like a four-year-old on a swingset.

We usually perceive rhythmic patterns in blasts that last less than five seconds. That's about the limit of our auditory short-term memory. Then we repeat them, over and over, and set up what can be a highly infectious beat.

You put chords and a melody over top of that and you have music. It all coalesces in the brain in the secondary auditory cortices — larger areas that surround the spindly central auditory cortices. Animals don't have much for secondary cortices, and that's why they don't get it and we do. This is where we put it all together. This is where all the auditory information unites into our holistic sense of a song. But that's not all of it. Not by a long shot.

We have many other neural networks spinning out from there, connecting music to our motor cortices and our basal ganglia. We have networks linking music with our memory systems and the limbic system of our emotions. In all, there are at least thirty different networks in the brain that are necessary for music to exist. In fact, the perception of music is thought to take up more real estate in the brain than any other single human pursuit.

And, of course, there's still the human component to it. Music is not just about neurons firing. That's a reductionist fallacy. It's simply impossible to account for the power of music by focusing solely on neurochemicals and brain structures. It's not some sort of auditory cheesecake. This is the stuff of the human soul. Music moves us to tears. It shapes our very lives.

I've always liked the analogy of clocks and clouds when it comes to these sorts of things. It's an idea that comes from the famed philosopher of science, Karl Popper. Western science, Popper claimed, tends to think in terms of clocks. Western scientists believe that things are best understood by taking them apart, by looking at all the little cogs and gears and levers that make them run.

The problem is that many things just don't work like this. The weather, our economy, social interactions, and even consciousness itself are nothing like clocks. These complex systems are more like clouds: diaphanous and ever shifting. They are, generally speaking, things in which the whole is much more than the sum of the parts.

Music certainly falls into this category. There is no doubt now that evolution has appropriated various parts of the brain in the construction of music. But music is more than this. We have to look at it through a wider lens.

It's as if all these physical systems of the brain are being put to work for another purpose — some sort of higher purpose. It has to do with communication, certainly, but not at the level of language. It's something deeper. Something more fundamental. Something, maybe, as basic as wanting to know that our fellow human beings are out there. We hear each other in the music we produce; we hear the deepest parts of ourselves.

And to really understand this, we'll need to set off once again. This time, we'll start in Africa, where the very earliest humans once walked the Earth. There is where we'll find the elusive "why" of music.

PART TWO

Music and the Social Animal

PART TWO

7

AFRICA
DRUMS IN THE NIGHT

A FLASHLIGHT BEAM BOUNCED TOWARD ME THROUGH THE AFRICAN night. A rusty gate squealed opened and the night watchman appeared, standing aside to let me into the compound. He had a baseball bat tied to his belt. It clunked against his gum boots and he was grim as he led me over to my accommodations.

"Is there trouble?" I said, pointing at the bat.

"Do not go onto the beach after dark," he said in a deep, low voice. I looked around. It was definitely dark. "Do not go up into the village either."

A thin veil of cold rain was coming down, which surprised me. This was supposed to be sub-Saharan Africa, and it was the middle of summer. Off in the distance I could hear the sound of the surf pounding up onto the shore. It sounded stormy and foreboding.

"This is Big Milly's, right?" I asked as he fumbled through a great metal ring of keys. He hardly looked at me. When he found the right key he pushed opened the door to my room for the week. It was basically a cot on a cement floor and a thatch roof.

"Close the door tight," he said. "There are mosquitoes."

"But where is everybody?" The place was dead. There wasn't a soul around but for the watchman, who'd already turned to walk off.

"Friday," he said. "They will come for the cultural show." He clumped off into the darkness, his flashlight beam dancing in front of him.

"That's why I'm here too," I said, but now I was just talking to the rain. So, this was the famous Big Milly's Backyard. I'd heard about it for months. It was on a long stretch of sand called Kokrobite Beach, just to the west of the capital of Ghana, Accra. It's where everyone comes. Just not tonight.

Up the road from here had been a place called the Academy of African Music and Arts. It had been run for about a decade by a master Ga drummer named Mustapha Tettey Addy. It was closed down now, though I'd heard that here at Big Milly's you were still likely to hear some of the finest African drumming in the world.

In the morning, I woke up to a grey sky. Down by the beach, the fishermen were coming in with their catch. The men stood in the back of the heavy, long boats, as sure-footed as surfers, steering the boats in to shore through six-foot breakers. The women walked elegantly down the beach to meet the incoming boats. They wore brightly coloured dresses like saris and carried big metal cooking pots and plates of pineapples and peanuts balanced on their heads. There was a rough market of sorts set up on planks just outside Big Milly's compound. Fires sprang up here and there and people huddled around them, cooking up pots of fish and rice and beans.

Every morning I would watch this scene unfold. Sometimes the beach was almost lost in mist. I saw the fishermen haul their heavy boats up onto the sand, a dozen or more men hauling on a thick rope while others manoeuvred logs in front of the prows of the boats, rolling them up onto the beach like pyramid blocks.

Throughout the week, the compound began to fill up. People were coming in from all across the country. A few backpackers arrived on the shared taxis — *tro tros* — dropping them off just outside the gate. Dean, a bellicose Afrikaner, had driven his Land Rover in from his farm off in the east of Ghana. He'd left Johannesburg, he told me, after his mother was murdered there in 1994. Tanguy was from Belgium and was slightly uneasy about his role as the overseer on a multinational "fair trade" banana plantation. Annabelle had been volunteering at an orphanage up by Cape Coast. She'd gone back home for a year but had now come back again to see her "kids."

Everyone was talking about the drumming. Amongst a grove of palm trees, a large concrete slab sat empty, though by Friday morning there were drums stacked up there, piled like oil barrels flung up onto shore after a maritime disaster. As the sun began to set on that day, a couple more pickup trucks rolled into the compound. They pulled up near the makeshift stage and several dozen people piled out of them. The women flashed with colour, wearing batiks of red and purple and emerald greens. The men wore whites and yellows and grinned great toothy white smiles. It looked like half the village had shown up, and I was thinking that they couldn't possibly all be drummers.

A small crowd of onlookers had gathered around the stage. We sat in a semi-circle, leaving a broad strip of red dirt between ourselves and the stage.

The sky darkened quickly, as it does near the equator, and a flare of torches were lit around the compound. Then the first line of three drummers came out, sitting on the edge of the concrete shelf, snuggling the drums at a slight angle between their knees. Behind them, in the dark, a longer line stepped up into place behind them, holding cowbell-like instruments called *nono* and woodblocks and gourd shakers. And it was this backline that began, chinking out a steady guiding beat. The drummers cocked their heads, only listening. One of them held a drumstick crosswise in his mouth, pounding on his drum skin with the heel of his palm as if he were testing it. Then, at some unspoken signal, all three launched into a thumping, raucous cacophony.

Almost immediately, there was a flurry of movement from behind the stage and another dozen people poured out onto the sand in front of us. These were the dancers. I hadn't even realized there would be dancing. In such societies, though, there is seldom drumming without dancing. They're two sides of the same coin. At first it was five male dancers shaking spears. They sprang out into the semi-circle in front of us, elbows flying, bare feet kicking up the red dust, the looks on their faces as intimidating as hell. They were intricately synchronized, though, choreographed, though I couldn't tell if they were following the drums or if the drummers were watching them for their cues.

The drummers at Big Milly's compound in Ghana.

And as if all that weren't enough, a third group on the stage set up a sort of chanting sing-song, riffing off the rhythms with vocal counterpoint. One of the drummers looked back, flashed another white-toothed smile, and joined in the chanting, each component of the music and dance now pushing the other along, almost out of control, ripping along at a frenetic, fantastic pitch.

There are those who would call African drumming the pinnacle of rhythmic music. It's hard for a Westerner like me to count along with it, to find the downbeat of the bar. The drumming here is polyrhythmic, meaning that they don't necessarily fall into Western time signatures of 4/4 or 6/8 or whatever. The *nono* sets up the tempo then the three or four drummers at the front blast off into rhythms that are each independent of the other but each, in their own way, aligned to the *nono*. It's not something we have in the West, though some say bits of it can be found in the old-fashioned ragtime piano of the 1920s, the precursor to jazz. The name *ragtime*, in fact, actually means "time in tatters." And that's what I was hearing here. They were ripping it apart.

I don't know how they kept up the intensity. They did, though, hour after hour, driving along with a manic energy, sweat dripping down the bare torsos of the drummers as wave after wave of dancers came out.

Towards the end, others stepped up from what I'd thought was the audience. Most of these newcomers wore just jeans and T-shirts, but they stepped into the place of one or another of the drummers, sometimes almost in mid-beat. The dancers began to be replaced too. One guy stood up beside me and launched himself into the dance. He obviously knew what he was doing and quickly synchronized his moves with the others — that is until the cellphone he had in the back pocket of his jeans popped out. He kept on going and one of the drummers sprang down from the stage to retrieve it from the dust.

It struck me then that this was not so much a performance for an audience. This was not for us. This was a community getting together, doing what they loved. Everyone seemed to know the beats and the chants and the dances. They were all into it. It's hard to imagine but, really, our modern conception of "performer" and "audience" is a division that would make little sense to most of the rest of the world. Everyone here was a musician. Everyone was a dancer and a singer and a drummer. It's we who seemed to have forgotten this most elementary of facts.

In the sober light of morning, I left the compound and walked up into the village to meet a man named Simon Annoh. I found him in a crumbling concrete building not far up the road. He was well muscled but older than the drummers from the night before. Annoh is his tribal name, his Ga name, and he preferred it to his English name. Annoh was a master of the form called *kpanlogo*.

The beats I'd heard last night were kpanlogo, and it's sometimes referred to as "invented tradition." The truth is that while its roots are traditional, the singing, the dancing, and the beats all have elements that have sort of cross-pollinated with the modern world. It was invented — or at least the old forms were reinterpreted — by men such as the great Mustapha Tettey Adey.

Music doesn't stay the same, of course, and it's really hard to find something that is truly traditional and untouched. I love the story about the anthropologist Colin Turnbull. He went in to study the remarkable pygmies of the Congo rainforest. Apparently, they have some very sophisticated music, vocal harmonies and polyrhythmic drumming and more. But when he asked an elder to sing the oldest song he could think of, Turnbull thought he recognized the song. It took him a moment but it suddenly occurred to him that this isolated little Yoda was singing "Oh My Darling Clementine."

In Ghana there was a sort of golden age of reinvention in the 1960s when even here, in far-off Africa, the sounds of rock and roll were weaving their wicked spell. The new music came out of tinny little transistor radios. Grainy black-and-white televisions were showing the Watusi and the Twist. Which is funny, because those sounds and movements had actually come from here in the first place. They'd made their way across the Atlantic and had now come back the other way again.

One name that is heavily associated with kpanlogo is the American rhythm and blues player Bo Diddley. It's almost impossible to say whether the rhythms here influenced Bo Diddley or whether his kick-ass blues band actually influenced the music over here. Probably both.

Something important to understand is that Ghana as we know it, like almost all African nations, is an invention of the colonial powers of the nineteenth century. Ghana is made up of numerous peoples, Ga here, but just a few miles to the east or west, different languages and different peoples. There was a real shift in thinking in the 1950s and 60s when these "countries" got out from under their colonial status and became independent nations. There was a drive, obviously, to create a new identity, a new way of thinking about themselves.

What always remained, though, was the centrality of the drumming. Annoh led me over to a stack of drums and allowed me to choose one. I pointed at one and he reached in to retrieve it from the pile.

"What are these made out of?" I asked. It looked heavy.

"These come from the *Twene Dua*," he said. "We call it the drum tree." He rolled it over toward me. "There," he said gently, "place it between your knees. Yes, there. Now tip it up slightly. Up."

"What's this skin?" I asked. Bits of fur actually still seemed attached to it.

"Antelope. But when you take these drums to America, antelope skin will not work."

"It won't?"

"It's too dry in your country.

"And too cold."

"Yes, yes … too cold. The skins, they crack. So now, in America, they are using goat skins." He paused, thinking. "But they don't sound the same." He gave his own drum a little tap and it resonated with a high-pitched "tink." "You see?"

I tried it and nothing much came out but a dull thwap.

Annoh let forth a throaty chuckle. "Now," he said, "we begin."

For two or three hours we practised a single simple beat. He wouldn't let me go until I got it. The beat was dead easy. It was getting the right sounds out of the drum that confounded me.

With apologies to the late Bo Diddley, the beat went like this:

Diddley diddley Bo.
Diddley Bo, Diddley Bo… pause
Diddley diddley Bo
Diddley Bo, Diddley Bo

It was infectious as hell. But to do it right, you need to get three completely different sounds out of the drum, something that required three different hand positions. Two of them I could get pretty easily, but the third was a bugger.

Annoh kept stopping me. "It is like a key," he said at one point. "You get the right key, you put it in the lock and it clicks. You understand?"

I nodded, though I was really having trouble. It was the speed at which I had to change hand positions. When I finally hit it just right, Annoh's eyes lit up. He was playing along with me now, nodding at my hands like an old schoolmarm. But at the high *tink* he beamed.

Percussion instruments actually produce some of the most sonically complex sounds of any instrument. This seems counterintuitive, but it's true. A guitar string or the strings of a piano are essentially one-dimensional — a long thin line that vibrates. A drum skin is two-dimensional, a flat plane rather than a single line, so that it vibrates in a much more complex way.

After about three hours, I could hit the high *tink* fairly consistently. Then Annoh took the wind out of my sails. "Okay," he said. "That is the first part."

"What do you mean the first part?"

"That's called the 'female support.'"

I must've looked a bit taken aback because he laughed and said, "It does not mean 'female.' It's just how we say it. There is the female support beat on one side and then on the other side the male support."

I thought of the three drummers last night, all lined up. It was starting to make sense. "And the guy in the middle?" I asked.

"He is the master drummer. The drummers on both sides play a set rhythm. They are completely different but they work together."

"And the master?"

"He can play a set beat for a while, then he will improvise over the rest. He can do what he wants."

"Because he is the master."

"Listen. It is like a soccer team. Eleven players. Each has their position. Each has their job … but there is only one goal."

"Did you know Mustapha Tettey Adey?"

Annoh stopped and looked hard at me. "He is my teacher."

"You were a student of Mustapha Tettey Adey?"

"I still am."

"He is still alive?"

"Of course he is still alive."

"But …"

"He has left the attention of the world. He lives on his farm now. That is what he loves to do, next to drumming. He grows sweet potatoes and yellow yams and he knows everything about the herbs that heal. He is a very important man. Now," he raised his hands again, "shall we learn the male supporting rhythm?"

The bus station outside of Accra is not a place you want to linger in for very long. It's dirty and slightly dangerous. Teenage boys skirt through the crowds looking for opportunities — bags left unattended, a back pocket with a wallet not fully tucked in. The vendors are right behind them, hissing to get your attention. It sounds like a bed of snakes.

The ground is a sea of garbage. Tatters of paper and bits of old plastic bags flap in the puddles, like corpses in a trench. Tiny goats wander among the crowds nosing the garbage for opportunities of their own.

I clutched my scrap of a ticket and watched the buses for the signs in their windshields. When the bus for Tamale finally arrived, there was a bit of chaos and pushing and shoving, and even as we pulled out, street vendors had closed in around the bus, plying the opened windows with dishes of food. They held out plates of what looked like deep fried fish and something else that looked like gently brazier-ed cockroaches.

A big hand appeared over me and slammed the window shut. I turned to find a large white guy, clearly as much a foreigner as I was.

"Crazy, huh?" I said.

"Madness," he said, running a hand through his thick hair. "Had to push aside a couple of really mean chickens to get on."

"Are you going up to Tamale?"

"I'm going to Mole National Park."

"Me too."

"Great," he said, extending a meaty hand. "My name is Jonathan. Jonathan Bull."

The name was appropriate.

"Ever seen anything like this before?" I asked.

"Actually," he said, "I'm working in Nigeria right now. This is quite tame."

"Nigeria, what are you doing there?"

"I work in a hospital."

We were looping out of the bus station now. Even along the main street, there were street vendors walking among the lines of cars, selling what they could. "Look at this guy," I said. The man was carrying a bag of foam pieces of different sizes. "I suppose that's to stuff pillows or something."

The next man down the line had a coil of battery jumper cables looped around his elbow and Jonathan laughed. "I wonder if he sells a lot of those?"

"Can't be," I said. "These cars are all running. Barely."

"Do you see the markings on his face?" Jonathan said.

"Yeah," I said, "what is that?" I'd seen loads of men and even a few of the women with these deep crescent moon scars on their cheeks. Some had parallel crescent moons — two lines on each cheek.

"Tribal markings," Jonathan said. "Honestly, I don't know how they stave off infection."

"I read that there's something like forty-eight different languages spoken in Ghana."

"Ah, you have an interest in that?"

"Actually, I'm writing a book. I'm writing about the music of the world."

"All the music of the world?"

"Well, no, I can't cover everything. I'm trying to write about music and the brain. Why we make music."

"And why do you suppose we make music?"

"Well, there are lots of theories — I don't know. What's really clear is that every culture on Earth has music, so there has to be some sort of evolutionary reason for it. Something important — we're just not sure what."

"What are some of the theories?"

"Well, I guess the first one was that music is auditory cheesecake. It just triggers a bunch of pleasure centres in the brain."

"Do you think so?"

"Well, I'm no brain surgeon but ..."

"Ah," he said, and a strange smile crossed his lips.

"What ...?"

"Well, actually, I *am* a brain surgeon."

"You're not."

"Yes, yes, in fact I am."

"No kidding?"

"I'm volunteering in Lagos. They needed someone. Removing tumours and all that."

"Then I should just shut up."

"No, no ... it's most interesting." He stopped, thinking for a moment. "It's one of the last things to go."

"What is?"

"I mean, when a person has a stroke or a brain injury, music often seems to survive the trauma. You can have a patient who's lost the ability to speak but they can still ..."

"Still sing, right?"

"Yes. In advanced stages of Alzheimer's, the patient might not even recognize their own children, but they can still sing, quite flawlessly, a song they learned fifty years before. It's quite peculiar."

"So, what does that tell you about the brain, about music?"

"I'm really just a surgeon."

"Yes, but you're a brain surgeon."

"For the most part, I remove tumours. We open up the skull and try to take out what's not supposed to be there. Honestly, it's a bit of a gamble sometimes."

"What do you mean?"

"Well, after the surgery, we induce a coma and then when the patient wakes up, well, sometimes they're absolutely fine. Other times we'll find that the liver's not working anymore … or worse. Something completely unexpected."

"It must be difficult."

"It's a matter of millimetres, literally. Everything is so connected, it's impossible to know. Once we had a three-year-old child brought in. Fell out of a third-storey window and landed on her head."

"Oh my god."

"Well, it looked like there was extensive damage but when we cleaned it up, the child was absolutely fine. The whole skull was caved in and it was as if nothing had happened at all. Then other times, someone tips over backwards in a chair, a little bump on the head and they never recover."

Jonathan and I talked for hours. We passed little villages with round mud walls and conical thatch huts, and I thought that here was the real Africa. We passed the town of Larabanga, where there is one of those ancient mud mosques, just like you'd see in Timbuktu. After that, the bus, now all but empty except for a few other foreigners, trundled down a dirt road and at last into Mole National Park.

There's a jungle lodge in there that sits on the edge of a long escarpment. From there you can look over the canopy of trees across the park. There's nothing but wilderness for two hundred kilometres almost up to the border of Burkina Faso, and as evening came down over us I imagined all the animals out there. Lions, still, though they're increasingly rare this far west, and hippopotamus, and at least one fantastically ugly warthog that waddled right past my door as I was heading for bed.

The African dawn crept up over the ravine. A guide walked ahead of us with an ancient rifle slung over his shoulder, clomping along in gumboots. His name was Usman. He was tall and thin and wearing a floppy hat that would have looked ridiculous on anyone else.

It was just after 7 a.m. when Jonathan and I tramped after him down the escarpment and into the wilderness. We walked for about a half hour before Usman suddenly stopped, knelt, and swept a hand through the long grass. "Here," he said, and when I bent over to look, I saw a footprint as big as a dinner plate.

"Elephant?"

"A small one. He's moving to the north."

"How do you know …?"

"Look," Usman instructed. "See how the grasses are bent? An elephant will not be lifting its leg higher than it needs to. Here, his foot has bent the long grass in the direction he is going."

"I believe we have found the Sherlock Holmes of elephants," Jonathan whispered.

"How do you know it's a 'he'?" I asked Usman.

"Deeper tracks?" Jonathan reasoned. "The males would be heavier."

Usman looked from one of us to the other. Then he pointed off towards the trees.

"Look. There are no other tracks," he said patiently. "The males travel alone. They are forever bachelors."

"Forever bachelors." Jonathan chuckled.

"This is not the right word?" Usman looked confused.

"No, no … that's absolutely perfect."

"The females travel in groups," Usman went on. "Mothers will stay with their daughters for decades. As long as they live. The males," he concluded, adjusting his rifle strap, "live alone."

"Do you think he's near?" I asked.

"He will be going to a watering hole, just ahead."

A wild African elephant.

"We'll see him? We'll see an elephant?"

"Yes, it is most certain."

Usman waved his hand for us to follow and we stumbled in behind him again, watching his boots flap against his shins, his rifle clunking against his shoulder blade. "Do you … have you ever shot that thing?"

"Be quiet now. We must be quiet."

I thought I heard a bit of a crashing in the bush up ahead. Usman slowed his step, crouching just a little. Then his gaze shifted off to the left. "There," he said.

Through the trees, I could see a shimmer of water. Then I saw something big and dark. The head swivelled slowly towards us and there he was, an African elephant the size of a small garage. He lumbered forward towards us, planting each foot carefully, his trunk waving as if he were trying to catch the scent of us.

Usman signalled for us to remain still. He was watching the elephant's movements and after a moment he relaxed a bit. "Watch his tail and his ears," Usman said. "If he is waving his tail and his ears, he is calm."

Great ivory tusks thrust out from each side of his trunk. "He knows we're here. Elephants have very bad eyesight but a very good sense of smell. This one knows me. He knows I am a peaceful man."

These African elephants are the largest land animals on the planet. Whales, of course, are bigger, but the sheer weight of them would collapse their skeletons if it weren't for the support of the water. We have recently discovered that, like whales, elephants communicate with one another. They don't exactly sing and it's nothing to do with their trumpeting tusks, but they do communicate in a most unusual way.

Elephants give off ultrasonic vibrations. It seems to emanate from the bones in their skull, somewhere near their great ears. It's not "heard" through their ears, though. They "feel" these ultrasonic vibrations through their feet as a sort of rumble in the ground — something they can perceive at distances of up to five or six kilometres. As far as we know now, it's like a subsonic purring, because, as Usman told us, they purr like this when they're munching on something particularly delicious. They also purr when they're having sex — usually in the water because, well, five thousand pounds on top of you requires a little bit of support.

Elephants, despite the males being loners, are a highly social species. And it seems — seems, I say — as if they can learn to produce music. In Thailand, elephants have been trained to play simple instruments like drums and cymbals and gongs. They bang them by holding sticks in their trunks, and they're pretty good. They can keep a beat. It's even been measured, and it turns out that they can keep a fairly steady tempo going, which is more than I can say for some rock and roll drummers I know.

What they can't do is synchronize with each other. One elephant playing a drum and another beside it playing a cymbal will plug merrily along, completely oblivious to the tempo of the other. And this is a pivotal point. This is a big clue that we humans are doing something really extraordinary with our music. It's not some circus trick, you see, because we do synchronize our music, quickly and easily.

We are the only species that does this. We play together, in time with one another, syncing up exactly into one unanimous burst of sound. It's central to music — and a point I've been trying to make all along. It's not just auditory cheesecake. There's something to the idea that music, like language, not only allows us to communicate at a very deep level but it also defines us as a group. It bonds a group together in mysterious but clearly profound ways.

Elephants communicate all right, but not through music. They can express pleasure and sadness and we have even seen groups giving solace to a lone grieving mother. It's very sophisticated social behaviour but it has nothing to do with music. That one critical element, that little spark that serves to synchronize our movements and our feelings, just hasn't evolved in their brains. Nor can it be taught to them. Only humans produce and perceive music as a means of social synchronization.

Later in the day, we had another encounter with animals. Out back of our jungle lodge, the baboons were gathering. There were about twenty of them. I'd seen them in the morning. By the afternoon they'd gotten aggressive enough, or hungry enough, to come in for a raid. I was eating at a table overlooking the savannah when one of them jumped right up onto my table. Now, baboons are not small. This one was as big as a ten-year-old child. Except that this ten-year-old had biceps like Mike Tyson and a face that said, quite clearly, back away from the food and nobody's gonna get hurt here. I damn near fell off my chair, grabbing instinctively for a camera tripod I had nearby — though whether it was to protect myself or whether I thought he might try to steal it, I couldn't exactly say. I only know that I have a mental image burned into my retina of this baboon glaring at me, with half of my omelette now scooped up into his strangely human-looking hand.

Another of the guides (it wasn't Usman) came dashing out from the kitchen, yelling and screaming — which hadn't occurred to me — and the baboon blinked its squinty eyes in a sort of "so what" gesture and scampered off to share my ham omelette with his rough trade friends.

I saw them later in the evening and the scene was almost pastoral. A mother baboon had a baby riding on her back. An older male looked to be grooming a younger one, perhaps picking out pieces of my omelette from his fur.

This sort of grooming performs a very specific purpose in baboon troops. Each one has his or her turn both giving and receiving, and it serves to bond them, a sort of literal you-scratch-my-back-and-I'll-scratch yours. Interestingly enough, the famed Oxford anthropologist Robin Dunbar has proposed a vocal grooming hypothesis as the origin of both music and language. It sounds nutty but there may be something to it.

Primate groups are not large. A very large group will have at most about fifty members and the apes sort of circulate through the group, grooming one another. Baboons actually spend more time grooming one another than they do on any other single pursuit, more than hunting or eating or even sleeping.

Presumably, a million years ago, our ancestors were doing much the same thing, but in the last hundred thousand years or so, as human brains became more complex, human groupings became larger. Dunbar claims that human groups max out at about 150. It's called Dunbar's number, and sure enough, when I flipped through an anthropology textbook, there it was, Dunbar's number. What it means is that, according to him, 150 is about the largest group that a human can cognitively handle — in a very real, day-to-day, interaction sense.

Of course, this flies in the face of things like Facebook and social networking, but it has a certain truth to it. We're talking meaningful everyday interactions here, a group made up of friends, family, and work colleagues — people who you personally interact with — and that group is probably no more than 150.

However, and this is the point, Dunbar claims that number, that size of a group, is too large for the kind of tactile grooming and bonding found in primates. We just wouldn't have time to get around to everybody, and this leads to his theory that human beings had to develop a new and improved sort of social glue. What worked best was making sound, and this would have formed the basis for the development of both language and music. It's not so much the meanings that are important here (full language presumably developed later), it was just the idea of hearing the voices of others, voices we recognize and relate to. Something that tells you that you are not alone.

Honestly, I'm not so sure about this social grooming theory of music. It's a bit flaky if you ask me. On the other hand, there's no doubt that we are a highly social species and that language and music both seem to play a big part in that social cohesion. We have music at almost any social gathering — from weddings to funerals to sporting matches. It seems, somehow ... well, necessary.

Certainly, music seems to be a particularly powerful way of marking our cultural identities. And I'm not just talking about national anthems here, although they play their part. I'm talking about subgroups — the ways in which we divide ourselves up according to clothing styles and haircuts and musical tastes. You can be sure that the guy with all the piercings and the Mohawk listens to a particular type of music while the guy wearing the cowboy hat and cowboy boots probably listens to something very different.

I don't suppose it takes primate studies to tell us that. Music is one of the ways, maybe one of the most important ways, that we mark our social activities, Dunbar number or not. It's how we define ourselves as belonging to a group. It also marks, very accurately, our age. There's something special about the music of our youth, something almost magical. That's the music that most sticks with us. That's the music we will remember when we can't tie our shoelaces anymore, when we're so lost to the world that we can't even remember our own birthdays.

I said goodbye to Jonathan in the airport at Tamale. He was heading back to Nigeria and I was on my way to the Slave Forts in the south. I wished him luck with his surgery. It was a bit humbling, really. Here I am talking about the brain while he's actually opening them up. It's strange. It's almost unfathomable to imagine that a three-pound lump of grey matter houses all our emotions and our memories, all our movements and desires, everything we would consider to be the essence of a human being. But it does.

There are places on this Earth almost too terrible to comprehend. Auschwitz, the killing fields in Cambodia, and here along the shores of West Africa, the castles and forts of the slave trade. I'd seen the little round mud hut villages to the north and, but for a rusty bicycle propped up against the mud walls, they looked pretty much unchanged by the centuries. I thought when I saw them that, yes, it must have been exactly villages like this that were raided and sacked, the stunned survivors roped and chained and led south across the plains to the coast, to the roiling black waters of the Atlantic and a life — a sort of half death — beyond.

Like Dante's gates of hell, these Slave Forts stood as the last way station, the dungeon keeps where the slaves would have seen their last glimpses of Africa. This is where they had to abandon all hope.

The French and Spanish had so-called "Black Codes" that defined these slaves, not as people, but as moveable property. The Americans were just as bad. In Article One, Section Two, Paragraph Three of the American Constitution, black slaves were considered 3/5 of a person for the purposes of taxation and representation. There had been slavery, admittedly, across the whole world for thousands of years. But because, quite bluntly, skin colour was so easy a marker, the trade in African slaves had an efficiency and heartlessness that was probably not rivaled until the Nazis.

One of the largest Slave Forts is on a spit of land called Cape Coast. They call it a castle but it's not really. It's a huge whitewashed building with triangular fortifications surrounding it. The block of rooms above ground look almost like a rundown old colonial hotel. These held the offices of the European merchants and officials. Out on the fortifications, there's a sort of terrace lined with cannons that face out to sea.

The first fort here was actually Swedish, though the Swedes had come for the gold and rare timber long before the "moveable property" became a more lucrative commodity. The European powers actually fought over these forts, and this one would wind up, eventually, as British and without a doubt principally a warehouse for slaves.

On the ground level, several dark openings take you down into the holding cells.

I ducked my head and walked down one short passageway, coming out into a cave-like room that was surprisingly small — not much more than an average sized living room. It had rough stone walls and an arched brick ceiling. Only a frail wash of light came in from the courtyard doors so that I found myself alone in the echoing dark space trying to imagine what it must have been like. It's impossible though. The whole fort is whitewashed both literally and metaphorically. There is no blood, no urine or vomit. No dead bodies slumped beside you.

Outside, I asked the guard how many people might have been packed into this dungeon and he told me, almost unbelievably, that several hundred men would have been crammed in here at one time. There was a separate dungeon for the women and even smaller cells for those who caused problems. No one likely emerged from those smaller cells alive. Down another wing, they had a little museum set up with, among other things, a reconstruction of the inside of a slaving ship. The voyage across the Atlantic in those days might have taken a month if everything went just right or as much as six months if the weather and the season weren't right. This nightmare trip was called the Middle Passage because the whole thing had been set up as a triangular trading route. The ships brought material goods down from Europe to the colonies in Africa — things like guns and ammunition. These were bartered for slaves who were then shipped over to the Caribbean and North America. From there, other goods, mostly sugar and molasses, went back to Europe. It was a tidy little triangle of economic opportunity. Everything worked like clockwork.

Just not for the slaves. It's estimated that, over the long years of slavery, somewhere around two million black Africans would have died during this so-called middle passage. The last slaves came through these dungeons in 1833. That's when the British ended their slave trade, which, ironically, made things even worse for the slaves still to come. The British warships began patrolling the Caribbean looking for the slave ships of other countries. Piracy, they called it now. By the law of the high seas, they could chase down these foreign slave ships and hang the captain. Unfortunately, when these ships saw the British coming, they just dumped their slaves overboard, still in their chains, preferring to drown their helpless cargoes rather than face the justice of the British.

As I was leaving, in a sort of hallway leading into the fort, I heard music. It seemed out of place, but of course I craned around and popped into a side courtyard to see what was going on. Eight or ten men stood there, all in a row. It almost reminded me of a marching band. They were practising stepping together while playing their musical instruments. A teacher of some kind stood in front of them, like a conductor, running them through their steps. And another man stood behind them clunking out a rhythm on a cowbell. What I remember now though is that three of them had a sort of horn which, at a certain part in their choreography, they all blew into at the same time. It was just a sort of "blaat," nothing too tuneful, just two of three notes on a bone horn as long as their forearms. Four other guys had what looked like cardboard tubes covered in Christmas wrapping paper. Maybe these were training horns. I'm not quite sure.

What I know now though is that this was the ancient Akan music — maybe even older than drumming — and that the original Akan horns had been made from the tusks of elephants. None of these guys, obviously, had the traditional ivory horns. Their horns were the horns of oxen. Just bone, the colour of old fingernails.

◀⅗ LISTEN 7.2

I knew all this because I'd actually seen one of the original ivory tusk horns in the Louvre in Paris. It's just down the hall from the room where the Mona Lisa is kept. Everyone pours into the big room to see the Mona Lisa but few people go further than that. There's an extra little wing if you keep going and that houses a small ethnographic collection. And there it was, in a glass case, an ornately carved ivory horn from Ghana.

I'd like to assume that it gets a better tone than the "blaaat" of the bull horns I heard but I can't be sure. And for the sake of the elephants, I don't want to find out. Slavery might be long gone, but the slaughter of elephants for their ivory is still a troubling problem here.

Nevertheless, I lingered for a few moments, watching these guys practise their ancient steps. I don't know why they practised there in the slave fort. It would be poetic to think that it was a sort of cleansing of the place, but I don't think it was. More likely, the stone walls gave both privacy and a pretty good reverb. I watched them twirl in unison, then raise their strange horns and blaat out a discordant note, all in perfect synchronization, mimicking the steps and sounds of their ancestors, a song of the past at the gates of barbarity.

8

CUBA
MUSICAL FUSION

I FLEW INTO HAVANA AT ABOUT THE SAME TIME THAT FIDEL CASTRO relinquished power to his brother, Raúl. Things were happening in Cuba and I wanted to see it before it changed too much. Coming in from the airport, I sat hunched in the back of a taxi when up beside us pulled a great old tank of a car.

I'd expected to see a few of these old cars, I just didn't expect so many. This one pulled out in front of us and belched out a cloud of thick black smoke. "Needs a tune-up," I said and the taxi driver looked a bit surprised. I thought I might have offended him. I didn't even know he spoke English.

"No," he said in a thick accent. "Is no gasoline. She is diesel. We change the engine. Is cheaper to drive."

"What kind of car was that?" I said. "A '57 Chevy?"

"The Soviets, they no buy our sugar," he continued. "So we no buy their oil. But now," he turned to me triumphantly, "we buy and sell these cars."

"Huh?"

"Is new rule," he explained. "Before, these cars go down the family. You understand? Father to son. You cannot buy. You cannot sell."

"And now?"

"Now we sell. But she costs a lot of money." He laughed. "No one can buy it so … it is not different."

But it was, really. These are just the sort of changes that are happening. It's called, euphemistically: "*actualización del modelo socialista*." The "updating" of the socialist model. It's like tinkering away on these old Yankee cars. There's always a new way to keep it running, a new bumper to shine, a new horn to wire into the system. But sooner or later, you're going to have a whole new car.

I'd come to Havana, of course, to experience the fantastic Cuban music scene and I'd had a stroke of tremendous good fortune. I was going to meet with a man named Alberto Salazar Rodriquez. Apparently, he's quite a mover and shaker here. A friend of a friend in Montreal knew somebody who knew somebody and gradually I was put in touch with Alberto. We emailed a few times, and even that was a part of the changing times. It's more or less illegal to have your own Internet connection here. For that matter, there are almost no cellphones either. They're not technically illegal, they're just so damn expensive that no one can really afford them. It took me awhile to realize what was strange about Havana — and that was it. No one carried a cellphone. No one at all. Except Alberto.

I didn't know what to expect of him. He'd described himself as a "white Cuban," which struck me as an odd thing to say. We were to meet in the lobby of the Hotel Saratoga in Havana Veija, and when I arrived, well, the description certainly helped. The man who got up from the couch looking apprehensively at me was young and white. He was shorter than me but he had a dark, handsome Mediterranean look and he sported a hip little goatee. His English was perfect and he struck me immediately as the kind of entrepreneur who was going to surf the coming tide of capitalism and really do quite well with it all.

Alberto, I'd been told, was the manager for several top acts here and, as it turns out, he would spend the next week weaving me in and out of music venues, getting me into places that no tourist would ever see. This was going to be a crash course in Latin American music. This was going to be the real thing, and it was going to be a whole lot of fun.

We walked out onto the street, the Paseo di Marti, and just down the road we came to a familiar looking building. "El Capitolio," said

Alberto pointing up at the neoclassical columns as we walked past. The capitol building.

"Hey," I said, "that sure looks like ..."

"Yes?"

"... like the Capitol Building in Washington, D.C."

"They are identical ... except that ours is two metres higher."

I looked at Alberto and he looked at me, to see how I would take it. Then we both started to chuckle. "The Americans don't know this," he continued. A big old Chrysler rumbled past us. "I don't think they will like it."

I was beginning to like this guy.

"Come," he said, "I am taking you first to EGREM."

EGREM is the holy grail for music here. It's the state-owned recording studio. In North America, we know it for the Buena Vista Social Club. That's a remarkable story on its own. Ry Cooder had gone down to make a different documentary and discovered these old musicians — and I mean old — in their eighties and nineties. They'd been band leaders from the 40s and early 50s — before the revolution — kind of Cuban versions of Nat King Cole or Duke Ellington. Cooder brought them together again to play, and play they did, astonishing the world all the way from the recording of their album in the studio here to a spellbinding concert in Carnegie Hall. That took some paperwork, let me tell you. Post-revolution Cubans don't easily get visas to the United States.

We crossed over the Avenida de Italia and into the barrios of Centro Havana. They were narrow streets with crumbling apartment buildings, but rather than the concrete blocks of Eastern Europe, these buildings were really old — two or three hundred years old. They were colonial Spanish architecture with wrought iron railings and intricate stonework, covered in the soot and dirt of unkempt centuries. A few kids played stickball down one street. A man was bent over the open hood of one of the old clunkers, diddling with the battery.

"Now," said Alberto, as we got closer. "This music is rough. It is called rumba."

"Rumba?"

"Yes, but not the rumba you are thinking. This is not the dance of the ballroom. This is something stronger, so don't be alarmed."

"Why should I be alarmed?"

"It is not dangerous. It's very safe there. They are good people."

"But what do you mean, alarmed?"

A giant of a doorman guarded the entrance. He was about six foot two and muscled like a prize fighter. He smiled warmly when he saw Alberto, though. They slapped hands in a sort of jive handshake and we got waved right in. Alberto seemed to be a bit of a celebrity here. Through a throng of handshakes and backslaps we passed into a little courtyard at the side of the big brick building. There was a low stage there and a few tables and chairs. I looked around and realized what Alberto was trying to tell me. The crowd was entirely black. He and I were the only white guys, and he wasn't sure I'd be okay with that. I guess he didn't know me very well.

A couple of dozen people sat around the plastic tables. Quite a few of them had been drinking heavily, and a sticky puddle of half-dried rum was on the table we sat down at. A man beside me eyed me sleepily, wobbly drunk, but he flashed me a big grin just as the musicians piled up onto the stage.

The wall behind them was papered with EGREM album covers. The stage was long and thin and lined with drums, and whatever this was going to be, it was going to be mostly drumming. Three men sat behind an assortment of conga drums. Then there were two guys to the right of them, one with a set of wooden claves in his hand while the other held a drum stick. On a metal pole in front of him was a wood block. These two started the rhythm and I instantly thought of Africa. It was exactly the same. The clave and the woodblock set up the rhythm and in a bar or two the drums came crashing in, each thumping to their own beat but each syncopated with the others. I leaned in to Alberto. "This," I began. "This is African."

"Yes," he said. "This is rumba. There's another form called *ton*. Ton became the tango," he said. "All Latin music comes from these rhythms — the mambo, the bolero, the salsa ... it all starts here."

"Really?"

"We call this recording studio La Matrix de la Musica Cubana."

"Matrix?"

Alberto held his hands on his stomach. "Where a mother holds her baby."

"The womb?"

Rumba at the EGREM studio.

"Yes, yes, the womb ... or no, maybe 'cradle' is a better translation in English. This is the cradle of Cuban music."

🔊 **LISTEN 8.1**

We turned back to the drumming, and it was at about this point that the singers came forward. I have to say that the drummers were all black but the singers were white. When I mentioned this to Alberto he laughed. "Music here," he said, "does not have a skin colour."

I liked that. Music doesn't have a skin colour.

Cuba is a surprising little island. The Spanish already had seven cities here while the rest of the New World was still a vast uncharted wilderness for the Europeans. Christopher Columbus landed on the northeast coast of Cuba on October 28, 1492. In fact, they buried him here in the cathedral of the greatest of the seven cities, Havana. Eventually they moved his remains back to Spain (to Seville) when they'd realized his terrible mistake. This was not India and the Far East after all. This was something completely different.

Still, Cuba turned out to be quite profitable for the Spanish. By the mid-nineteenth century there were 400,000 slaves working the sugar cane plantations here. And this cruel slavery lasted until 1886, making it the last place on Earth to formally abolish the slave trade.

Over the centuries, these sugar plantations rang with music. The British slavers to the north, it seems, were very particular about separating their slaves, isolating individuals from their tribal groups. They feared rebellions, of course, so they turned to a Tower of Babel solution. The British slavers deliberately mixed the peoples of different tribes so that they could not speak to one another and hatch any plans for escape.

The Spanish, on the other hand, did not separate the individuals from their tribes. They brought whole villages, almost intact, from Africa to Cuba. And what this meant was that the peoples kept not only their languages but also their music, the rhythms and dances and chants of their ancestral homes.

In North America, the peculiarities of the British slave trade meant that the social context of music was lost — and that is, the rhythms. But even there, the singing remained. You can sing on your own even if you've lost every other member of your community. Black spirituals can be traced right back to the British slave ships, and in the book *Deep Blues*, the author and musicologist Robert Palmer managed to trace back the flatted thirds of the blues scale to the *griots*, a class of travelling singers who'd wandered West Africa a couple of hundred years ago. He traced a direct line from this griot singing to the songs of the early bluesmen of Mississippi around the turn of the century. And this gave birth to not only the blues but eventually jazz and even rock and roll.

Particular musical styles sometimes blaze a trail across the world like this. In Cuba, the African rhythms were predominant, and those grew into Latin grooves. There was one more component to it. One more slice of ancestry.

Alberto leaned in to me a few bars later. "Listen to that," he shouted over the drums, "that singing. It comes from the flamenco tradition."

"Flamenco? No kidding?" I thought about that. It did sound like the *quejillo* of Seville — the complaint singing. These singers were doing a sort of call and response thing over the beat. It was simple, usually only a couple of notes in a scale. If this was based on the "complaint" singing of flamenco and the rhythms were African, then I was probably hearing some of the world's first real fusion music. Spanish and African. Like chocolate and peanut butter.

One of my favourite theories is the theory of memes. Memes? Well, they're related to genes. Kind of. The idea comes from the famed British biologist and evolutionist Richard Dawkins. What Dawkins figured was this: ideas seem to function just like genes. They replicate themselves, literally being passed from one mind to another, just as DNA replicates itself. Good concepts, Dawkins thought, might be sort of like dominant genes.

Dawkins had been looking at a series of studies on how birdcalls are transferred from adults to their young and how that call might be perpetuated over many generations. And he began to think about how similar this was, first to genes and then finally, inevitably, to the ways in which human behaviours are replicated. The more he thought about it, the more he imagined that cultural ideas not only replicate themselves but are subject, just like genes, to environmental influences and pressures. Some ideas might be recessive memes, just like blue eyes or left-handedness are recessive genes. They could be outmuscled by dominant memes — for example, the way in which the English language is supplanting less spoken languages around the world. And he imagined that these memes, like genes, could also mutate and change over time. It all began to get very fascinating.

The invention of the alphabet is a good example of a meme. As a writing system, it's beautifully simple and it has spread, over the millennia, through all but a handful of languages. Dawkins — though he's very controversial here — even suggested that something as abstract as a belief in life after death might be a kind of complex meme. I don't know about that but I could see in Cuba that the rhythms from Africa and the singing of flamenco had memed over to the New World. I was hearing the proof right in front of me. It mutated a little and, as Alberto was telling me, it then became the basis for most of what we now call Latin music. Now surely that's a textbook example of memes.

The memes of African music travelled in the holds of slave ships, over the dark Atlantic. It's pretty much indisputable. The Spanish brought their own "music of the people," and there you have it. That's exactly what I was hearing in front of me.

I thought I had it all figured out. And then almost exactly when I began thinking of the dancing in Africa, out came two dancers — who had nothing to do with the dancing of Africa.

There was a man and a woman, strutting like flamenco dancers. Flamenco, though, is always a solo dance. So that's not right either. This was different. These two were tantalizing each other with overtly sexual movements. The young man, dressed all in snazzy white with his collar upturned, strutted like a rooster. He jerked and swivelled across the stage, often thrusting his hips out like a male stripper. He was all over the stage, puffing out his chest, moving in towards the woman then pulling away from her again, teasingly.

The woman flapped a large red scarf in front of her torso like a shower towel. It was silk with an almost Chinese patterning on it, but it was a lurid red. She struck a bashful stance, holding the scarf in front of her, and then she lifted it slowly, seductively, as if she were lifting up her dress. Then she gave a big throaty laugh and started grinding her hips while the guy gyrated around her, strutting like a young James Brown. Really, these two were oozing hormones.

Darwin would like this, I thought.

The band was chugging away behind them, thumping out these driving rhythms. The singers were almost chanting and everything grew to a fever pitch. The crowd was on its feet now, some dancing too, and I had to remind myself that it was not dangerous. That there was nothing for a skinny white guy to be alarmed about.

Alberto stood up.

"Where are you going?" I asked desperately.

"Rum," he said. "We're going to need more rum."

I met Albert again the next morning. Again we just walked. The sun was hotter that day and he told me a little of the history of the island. One of his favourite places was Viñales, famous for its cigars. Before the Spanish and before the slaves, the indigenous people here, the Tainos, became the first peoples on Earth to harvest and smoke tobacco. How's that for an idea that has spread around the world?

Then, of course, Christopher Columbus arrived. Alberto pointed out a fountain just down the street from El Capitolio. It was called the Font du Indie, the fountain of India. "That's for Columbus," he said.

"I don't get it."

"Columbus thought he'd found India. So we have obliged his mistake." Alberto chuckled.

He took me down a street that could have been in suburban Los Angeles. It looked just like that, well, maybe with hints of South Central L.A. We walked in to the yard of a house called Jardines de la Jiribilla. It looked like it was set up for a wedding with rows of white plastic chairs — all very garden party.

"The concert today," he explained, "is *trova*. It comes from your word *troubadour*."

At the front were four chairs and an equal number of microphones. A strange-looking acoustic guitar was leaning up against one of the chairs. It looked like it only had three strings.

Before the concert started, a man walked in and there seemed to be a number of photographers circling around him. He was plainly dressed — in fact, he was just wearing a red-checked shirt and casual slacks. He slid down the rows and sat almost directly in front of us. He turned once to look at the crowd sitting behind him. Alberto stiffened slightly.

"Who's that?" I whispered when the man had turned back around. I thought I saw his gaze light on me a little longer than it should have.

"I will tell you later," Alberto hissed, pressing a hand down onto my arm. "Later."

Four musicians came out. In the middle was Tony Avila, a young black man. He wore a jaunty flat cap and was clearly the star there, a singer-songwriter of real talent. He said a few things to the crowd in Spanish and everyone seemed to titter a little. Chuckles rippled around me.

"What? What is he saying?"

"He is making a joke. It is nothing."

Avila strummed a few chords and then began to play. To his left was a percussionist with a big congo drum and a whole array of other smaller drums around him. To Avila's right was a backup singer who played various shakers. And to the far right was a man who played the strange guitar. It was all very beautiful and heartfelt and very Spanish-sounding. *Ah*, I thought, *here's where the flamenco had landed.* They all sat on chairs in a row, facing us just like the musicians in the flamenco bar in Seville. There was the impassioned singing. There was the fiery guitar playing.

They played some old songs, including one, I think, even from the 1920s, an old folk tune from the island. Alberto leaned over and told me that these old songs of trova were the beginnings of the *bolero*. Put a little rhythm to it, a little 2/4 beat and there you have it.

The band played for forty-five minutes or so, gradually working their way up in to Tony Avila's own compositions. They were good. Something like a Spanish James Taylor. Or maybe even Simon and Garfunkel.

◀᷇ LISTEN 8.2

At the break, I asked Alberto about the strange-looking guitar off on the right. "Come," he said. "Let me show you." We went up and had a quick look at it. It actually did have six strings, but they were funnelled down into three double strings — like half a 12-string guitar. I'd already heard how the guy, and he was quite extraordinary, used it to solo above the chords of Avila's guitar.

"It is called a *tres*," Alberto said.

"That's a reasonable name."

"Did you hear? Because of the strings, it sounds a little like a mandolin. It stands out, above the main guitar." Behind us now, the man in the red-checkered shirt had stood up. He was moving through the crowd shaking hands. I glanced over at him.

"So who is that? He looks important."

"That," whispered Alberto. "That is the vice-president."

"The vice president of Cuba? Holy crap."

"He is the vice-president of Culture. A very powerful man." I could see all the photographers lining up the handshaking in their shots. Just then he looked over at me again. He was mostly bald and maybe a bit gaunt, but definitely a cloud of authority was emanating from him. In fact, he looked for all the world like Vladimir Putin of Russia. I bet they'd be friends anyway. Sharing hints on how to keep the Americans out of the country.

He looked at me again, just a sort of glancing blow, but I thought I saw his eyes narrow. "Alberto," I said. "Am I allowed to be here?"

"Don't worry. It is not a problem."

Tourists in Cuba are supposed to carry their visas at all times. I had mine dutifully tucked into a pocket. Never thought I'd need it, but now my hand wobbled down into the pocket just to make sure it was there. Just in case.

We sat down again when the musicians came out to do a second set. Tony Avila joked with the crowd. "What's he saying?" I was pretty much tugging on Alberto's sleeve now.

"He is telling a story about when he went jogging. He asks the crowd, 'What do you think when you see a white man running? Jogging, right? But, he says, when you see a black man running ...'"

I laughed, a bit behind the others. One or two people turned to look at me, but not Vladimir. He was enjoying the jokes too. This was nuevo trova — compositions of Tony Avila's own that were, what shall we say, provocative. Apparently in trova you can say a lot that's quite controversial — even political. It's all very cleverly masked in euphemisms. You can say political things but only in a very roundabout way, and everyone, of course, knows exactly what you're talking about.

This is how it goes when there are no cellphones and almost no Internet. Alberto told me it costs about a day's wages to make a single call on a cellphone, so it's just not worth it. The newspapers and radios are all strictly controlled, so the one true means of saying what you want to say is through music.

It's been this way since Fidel Castro, Che Guevara, and a handful of others landed on the shores of Cuba in 1957 and, much to everyone's surprise, eventually took over the country.

Che Guevara has gone on to iconic status, but there's a funny story about him here. Believe it or not, he was not only completely tone deaf but rhythm deaf as well. This is an incredibly rare condition. There are loads of people who can't carry a tune but that doesn't mean that they're tone deaf. True tone deafness means that a person can't even tell the difference between "Happy Birthday" and "The Star Spangled Banner," let alone sing the two songs in tune. And rhythm deafness is even more singular.

Poor Che, who was a doctor himself, couldn't make out anything of music, though he'd trained himself to dance. On the occasion of his twenty-fourth birthday, a party was held that went on till three in the morning. The band was playing Peruvian waltzes, Argentinian tangos (where, in fact, he was born), and Cuban mambos and chachacha. Che Guevara had cleverly arranged that his friend would prod him when a tango was played, since he fancied himself quite a good tango dancer. At one point in the evening his friend, seeing a shapely young nurse across the room, tapped Che on the shoulder to point the girl out to him. Che, misinterpreting it, grabbed the girl and lit out onto the dance floor in an elegant, passionate slow tango — while the band raced through a bouncy Brazilian shora.

Ironic, then, that this founding father of über-musical Cuba should be so completely out of sync with basic pitches and rhythms. It's strange, isn't it? Certainly, while most people in modern societies are not musicians, pretty much everyone is an expert at listening to music. And we have only to feel sorrow for those who cannot understand it at all.

On my second last night in Havana, Alberto took me to the appropriately named Karl Marx Theatre. Leaving my hotel, I asked the cab driver if he knew where it was. "Everybody in Cuba knows where the Karl Marx Theatre is," he laughed. I met Alberto and his beautiful wife on a dark corner across the street.

We'd hatched a bit of a plan, you see. Alberto had bought a ticket for me in local pesos — one hundredth of the price I'd pay — so I had to pass myself off as Cuban to get in. It wasn't going to be easy. I'd only been in the country for a few days and I was still pasty Canadian winter white. "If there's trouble at the door what you'll do is have a five-peso tourist currency bill ready to give the ticket taker. That should stop her from saying anything." I was a bit worried, since there seemed to be a lot of police about. "If that doesn't work," Alberto went on, "you'll just have to pay the whole fare." This would be the same as about thirty U.S. dollars — again, about a month's salary for the average Cuban.

"When we get near the doors," Alberto said, pushing me forward, "you go first." I imagined that this was not very brave advice, but I trundled on ahead of them and when I came to the door, I just kept my head lowered. I flipped my ticket out at the usher but I carefully avoided eye contact. She took it and the crowd pushed in behind me before she had a chance to really register me. As Alberto came in behind me I gave a half turn and sort of nodded, feeling like a Cold War spy.

What I'd be seeing tonight was truly something no foreigners would be seeing. I'd had the luck to be in Havana on the anniversary concert for EGREM studios. It just so happened that they would have, playing live at the Karl Marx Theatre, all the best musicians in modern Cuba and it would be a sort of travelogue through the musical history of Cuba.

The theatre held five thousand people. Five thousand wildly dancing, enthusiastic Cubans, it would turn out. The theatre was actually built just before the revolution and thus, from the American point of view, stolen from its owners, though they were likely Mafia anyway. It had been renovated over the years but to me it was still Cuba — kind of worn and scruffy with uncomfortable seats that clanged up behind you to fold up when you stood.

The ushers wore dresses like 1950s stewardesses, herding us to our seats. The lights dimmed and onto the stage came all the descendants of the slave memes of Africa and the flamenco memes of Spain. It was flashy and the level of musicianship was extraordinary. Most of the bands played various shades of Latin fusion and a lot of it sounded like big band salsa: crushing horn sections and thumping percussion. There was an all-saxophone band called, logically enough, Habanasax. Funny thing is that all five of them were music professors from the Institute of Arts and Culture. They played like no professors I know.

There was even a sort of teen boy band: David Calzado and His Charanga Habanera. When they came out, all the women in the audience kind of lost their minds. Even the stiff-starched ushers were dancing in the aisles. They played a form called *timba*, which is a zoomed up version of salsa (you see how things keep mutating?). Alberto was grinning from ear to ear, whispering into my ear what each new act was, how he knew that trumpet player or the singer over there with the growly voice. At one band, he leaned over to tell me about a particular song. "That's a really good one," he said. It's called 'Kill My Television.'"

At one point I asked him if any of the guys from the Buena Vista Social Club would be playing and he shook his head and said that, no, most of them were dead now. Most of them had already been in their nineties ten years ago. "But look up behind you," he said. A couple rows back, just up a little bit and to the left was a large man with a huge cowboy hat. I don't know why, but the hat always reminded me of the big yellow one the man in the Curious George books used to wear — a big ten gallon thing. This man sat there radiant. "He's one of them," Alberto said. "That's the guitar player from the Buena Vista Social Club."

"Oh yeah," I said, recognizing him. I felt like I was in the presence of royalty. He didn't play at all, just sat their lording over the proceedings like a king.

For the grand finale, the stage filled up with an all-star line-up of musicians from several of the bands. They played like the gods of Latin American music that they were, percussion section laying down an insanely infectious beat, trumpet sections on fire. The audience was on its feet and roaring.

Alberto grabbed my shoulder. "We should go," he said, "before the crowds."

"Before they trample us?"

Alberto looked at me strangely. This doesn't happen in Cuba. The wild crowd, as soon as they hit the street, will return to order right away. People don't even speed here — not even the taxi drivers. They are too wary of the police to try anything so ill-advised.

I followed him out into the hot Havana night. It had been a hell of a run but it was time to say goodbye. There's no way I would have been able to see half of what I'd seen without Alberto's help. This was his world and I'd been fortunate enough for a few days to have front-row seats to some of the finest musicians in Cuba. It was astonishing. This little island was a sort of ground zero for music. It was music that spilled over with joy, music that swung and bumped to cadences that were the very best of memes.

The music we call Latin American encompasses a huge range of styles and moods. Some twenty countries — a continent and a half — claim some form of it for their own. It's getting so it's quite hard to say that any one given thing is common amongst the various forms — maybe a beat that, even in the slow songs, swings and struts in a way that other music doesn't. Much of it is almost inseparable from its dance as well, from formal ballroom styles to the martial arts tumbling of capoeira. Really, the one thing we can say with assurance is it's a combination of musical DNAs and something greater than the sum of those parts. It's had an influence around the globe, infusing everything from classical to jazz to pop with its infectious beats.

I had a morning to kill before I left, so I set off walking down into the streets of Habana Viejo, the oldest part of the city. The whole area is a World Heritage Site and certainly one of the oldest, if not the oldest, urban centre in the western hemisphere.

Down the winding streets of the old city, I heard music. And there, coming up the street towards me, was a sort of marching circus. Two or three Latin beauties swung towards me on stilts, each of them dressed like Las Vegas showgirls. Behind them marched a cracking good percussion section and at the tail a man in a fedora, also on stilts, blasting away on a trumpet. It was a roving busker show with the women on stilts reaching down for you to throw a few spare pesos in the satchels they carried. This was pure spectacle, a show put on for the tourists, but all the same, it was a celebration and outburst of joy and skill, and rhinestoned leotards.

◀୧ LISTEN 8.3

The party moved down the street amongst a crowd of onlookers, me included, past an old Franciscan monastery, and finally down to the old fort, a Renaissance fortress built in 1590. This music, I could tell, was very much an invented tradition. It was for the tourists and did not have the authenticity of the rumba or the trova performances I'd seen. But did it matter?

They were still thumping out fantastic rhythms. They were grooving off of one another, playing as a single unit and enthralling the people that trailed out after them. Music does this. That's the most important thing it does. We sync ourselves in joyful unison.

We humans are completely hardwired to sync up with metrical beats. Some surprising results have turned up in studies of the human ability to follow beats. It turns out that when we tap our finger along with a metronome beat, we are incredibly accurate, tapping right on the beat. We are also effortlessly able to tap out a beat above the tempo or below it, in half time or double time.

What's even more amazing is that when we tap along with a human-made beat and not a metronome or a drum machine, we actually tap our fingers a few milliseconds ahead of the beat. Something in our brain recognizes that this is not machine-made. Some other part of our brain gets engaged and we anticipate the beat rather than just react to it.

I can't overstate the importance of this. We know when we're listening to another human being even if we can't see him or her — even if it's just coming out through headphones. This is not the same to the brain as a machine-made sound or the random thumps of nature. Our brains leap to the human meter in a way that is probably one of the defining characteristics of our species. Our brains light up across the auditory cortex, the motor cortex, and subcortical systems in the basal ganglia. Even imagining a human rhythm or beat will activate these areas. It's almost as if it is a special process to alert us to the existence of another human being. It's profound and remarkable and something that is at the very heart of understanding why music has such a powerful hold over us.

This is the groove. This is the driving force that causes us to tap our toes and clap our hands. This is what makes us dance. This is the connection.

9

JAMAICA
STIRRING IT UP AT BOB MARLEY'S HOUSE

THE ZION BUS TRUNDLED UP FERN GULLY AND INTO THE MOUNTAINS of Jamaica. Neville, the driver, honked his chrome horns around the tight bends, warning oncoming drivers that we were coming. Many years before, this same Zion Bus had been a country bus with squawking chickens and sacks of coffee beans. Now it was decorated in graffiti and filled with pilgrims off to see Nine Mile, the birthplace and final resting place of the first international superstar to come out of the Third World: the great Bob Marley.

Eli was our "ductor." At first I thought he was saying "doctor" and I thought it had something to do with being Rastafarian, something to do, maybe, with the "herb" they all smoked. Actually, "ductor" meant the bus conductor. As the bus edged up the narrow road, three thousand feet above sea level, Eli spoke into a microphone, crackling through makeshift speakers that were hanging by a wire from the roof. "Bob, he be just a country boy," Eli said. Outside, tropical forests whirled past the occasional clapboard village. "Born all de way out here — miles and miles from Kingston. Rastafari!"

They were handing out rum on the bus. It was ten o'clock in the morning and already ferociously hot. I took a bottle of water instead.

Eli put on a Marley tune. "Dis one for Rita, his wife. He work his magic, yes he did."

Eli started singing along through the tinny speakers. "One love, one heart ... let's get together and feel all right."

We all sat in our seats, squirming, smiling affectedly at other passengers, acting as if we were having a riotously good time. The bus wound its way up the narrow roads and finally out into the middle of Jamaica, into a landscape of wild buckling green hills.

Out here, just to the west of the Blue Mountains, famous for some of the finest coffee beans in the world, they grew a different kind of crop. Here and there, outside the bumping bus, we could see patches of marijuana growing as high as a person.

"About two thousand people live in Nine Mile," the 'ductor continued. "Ninety-eight percent of dem be farmers — and most of de farmers grow de weed. Rastafari!"

We pulled into the town of Nine Mile with a plaintive scatter of young boys running after the bus, hands out for money. Jamaica is not a rich country. It has one of the highest murder rates in the world, but that's mostly down in the poorer sections of Kingston, areas like Trenchtown — exactly where Marley and his Wailers first worked out their sound.

A set of high iron gates swung open and the bus turned into the compound built around Marley's birthplace. Here, cut into one of the walls, is the infamous "meditation window," a low-slung, small-shuttered opening where you can buy dope. Two dodgy-looking men were down there offering up bags and long, tapered joints, like tiny white traffic cones. One of these firecrackers cost fifteen U.S. dollars, which I thought a little steep. Not that I have a benchmark, but it just seemed, well, a bit unreasonable. Many in our party bought the things and promptly lit them up with mischievous grins. It's the only place in Jamaica where it's actually legal to buy and smoke it. I conservatively bought a can of Coke, which seemed to slightly confuse the men in the window. There was a certain commotion while they fluttered about looking for change and then, unable to come up with it, one of the men held up a small round cake. "You want a piece of cake?" he asked.

"You mean instead of change?"

"Yeah."

The meditation window at Bob Marley's house.

And figuring I wouldn't get any change, I took a small wedge of the stuff. Now, I should've known better. I wolfed it down with my Coke and by the last bite I think it had sunk in that there was probably more than just flour in this "cake." We'd been herded up to the entrance where we were to meet our guide, and he came out in a blaze of "look at me" confidence. A big tri-coloured Rastafarian toque was piled high over his dreadlocks and he had a certain swagger and inimitable stoned chuckle. "My mother call me Curtis," he began. "But everyone else call me … Crazy." He burst into laughter, a melodic guffawing that descended in even notes and which, I had to admit, was infectious.

I was starting to feel something from the cake. It was roiling around inside me. A bit of an edge. A bit of anxiety. It all might have been good fun had not the oldest member of our Zion Bus group promptly keeled over. I'd watched him bogarting his traffic cone of a joint, and now without a warning he just collapsed like a sandcastle. His wife, a middle-aged Brit, panicked a bit but Crazy had seen all this before. A combination of the hot sun, the altitude, and of course the marijuana. It turned out the man hadn't had a toke since the 1980s and he certainly wasn't prepared for the stuff here. No matter, Crazy brought him a glass of water with a squirt of syrup in it, and that seemed to do the trick. It balanced his electrolytes, or whatever it was, and he continued on at the tail end of the group, his eyes as wide as saucers, obviously stoned out of his mind.

I was getting pretty buzzed myself. Crazy was scampering around, pointing out this and that, though we had not come any further than the stairs up out of the parking lot.

He ushered us into a long room. It had one of Bob Marley's guitars up on the wall and in a corner was a rickety old piano, which I assumed Marley had used to write a few of his songs. All along the walls were the gold records he'd been awarded for sales in the be-jillions.

It was a cocky young dreadlocked youth that strutted into the Island Records offices in London in 1972. No one had heard anything like this kind of music before, and something about the rawness of it, the earthiness of it, kept thumping through the thoughts of Island Records owner Chris Blackwell.

Everyone told him to stay away from this rough band. No one wanted to hear this Third World roots stuff. It was the time of the epic concept albums like those of Pink Floyd and Bowie's *The Rise and Fall of Ziggy Stardust and the Spiders from Mars*. Who wanted to hear anything from a forgotten little island in the Caribbean?

Blackwell lent them four thousand English pounds and all but wrote off the money. He never expected to see them again. But Marley and his Wailers took the advance and went into the studio. They came out a month later with a searing new sound and an album called *Catch a Fire*.

And catch it did. Reggae spread through the world music scene like a rush of blood to the head. It's an unbelievably infectious little meme with a beat that plays quite contrary to rock and roll. The guitar has a choppy little upswing strum where the backbeat of the drum would usually go. Only the whole thing was in half time so that it had a lilting, lazy, almost hypnotic feel. Everything about it was different, and here was a man, a prophet in dreadlocks, swaying, singing with a little crackle in his voice, "Stir it up, little darling, stir it up."

Crazy led us out and over to a tiny two-room shack. This was where Bob Marley had grown up. It was his grandparents' place but the little bed in the back was his. "Bob's father was white," Crazy began when we entered. I didn't know that. "Norval Sinclair Marley. He got a young black girl pregnant and den he up and left." We looked at Bob Marley's tiny bed in a simple whitewashed tiny room. "Bob's mother, she buried up not far from Bob." He pointed up a garden stone pathway. "She was dark … like coffee. Bob's father was like milk." There were a couple of stoned giggles around the group and Crazy's whole face lit up in anticipation of his punchline. "So Bob was — cappuccino. Haw. Haw. Haw."

Much more of this hilarity ensued. Corny, really, but when followed by Crazy's unrestrained guffaw, really quite funny. "Speaking of beds," he kept on, "Bob had eleven children … by a few different women. Maybe as many as nineteen. We call dem DNA children. You know what dat means?" Again his face scrunched up mischievously. "Daddy Not Available. Haw Haw Haw.

Crazy brought us outside to another little spot, a sort of courtyard where, in the middle, a flat rock was gaily painted in the colours of the Jamaican flag. "Dis be Bob's pillow," Crazy said reverentially. "He even talk about it in his song, 'Talkin' Blues.'" When he was a tatty boy, he lay right here, his head on de rock, dreamin' 'bout de times to come."

Crazy took the tour group off into some other room but I lagged behind. I was really quite stoned and I didn't really want to talk to anyone. When I had the chance I slipped back out the doorway and went back to the rock pillow. Only for a moment, because I thought I might get in trouble, I lay down on the flagstones and put my head back on the rock. It nestled in there nicely and a fierce hot blue sky rocked above me. My poor brain, I've got to say, was slopping around like so much mushroom soup. No one was around but I just kept thinking I was going to get in trouble, so I only stayed a moment. Then I scurried back up and ran off to catch up with the group.

The active ingredient in marijuana is THC, or more accurately delta-9-tetrahydrocannabinol. It does a number on your short-term memory but does tend to heighten your senses. You get the munchies because food tastes so good. Sex is pretty great and music, well, music just sounds fantastic.

Cannabinoids, actually, are naturally occurring chemicals found in the brain. One type of cannabinoid receptor is found in the basal ganglia of the limbic system, and it is here that we produce our sense of euphoria.

It's here that we get the chills down the back of our spine when something moves us.

It's complicated, of course. There's always a Byzantine interplay of neurochemicals flooding across our synapses, not to mention an equally complex adjusting of uptake and inhibition levels in the neural receptors. Sometimes it's hard to know whether the neurochemicals are actually responsible for our actions or whether our actions, like listening to music, are triggering the neurochemicals. It's a bit of a chicken and egg situation.

Clearly, music has been tangled up with chemicals both natural and self-induced since the dawn of time. Here in Jamaica, in the heartland of reggae, there's a whole religion riding on the sweet waves of marijuana smoke.

The Rastafarian religion is a sort of offshoot of Christianity that originated in Jamaica in the 1930s. There's no clear-cut set of church beliefs, but basically they believe that Haile Selassie (the emperor of Ethiopia from 1930 to 1975) was the new messiah. By tradition, Selassie claimed the ancestry of both King Solomon and the Queen of Sheba. Most importantly, however, the Lion of Africa was a black who fought hard against the colonial powers (Italy in this case), leading his people and his country to real independence.

That may sound bizarre, but it speaks to the idea that Jamaicans are very conscious of their African roots. And really, Rastafarianism is as much a lifestyle as it is a religion. Most of them do not drink alcohol and many are vegetarian. It's about simplicity and it's certainly about equality of peoples. Crazy talked, quite sincerely, about the idea of the exodus of slaves out of Africa being kind of the same as Moses leading the Israelites out of Egypt. Only Moses, as far as we know, didn't have dreadlocks. And again, we don't know — I'm just saying — but he probably didn't smoke dope.

Crazy sure did. And so did Bob Marley, who was perhaps the world's most famous Rastafarian. In fact, the tight connection between reggae and marijuana brings up the oft-quoted idea that music itself is a kind of drug. Steven Pinker called music "a cocktail of recreational drugs that we ingest through the ear to stimulate a mass of pleasure circuits." That was his auditory cheesecake idea, and there's at least an element of truth about it.

Music does trigger the release of dopamine into our systems, just like other more tangible rewards, like sex or drugs or, well, like rock and roll. And not only is dopamine released when we're listening to our favourite music, but studies show it can even be released when we're just anticipating listening to a particular piece of music. In particular, dopamine is released into an area called the nucleus accumbens. It's the area in the brain that has been associated with addictions — all kinds of addictions.

Music, from the symphonies of Beethoven to the pop tunes of the Beatles, has what we call "hooks." These contagious little pieces of melody or chord structures or rhythms seem to root right into our brains and cling there. And songs with particularly tenacious hooks often wind up as "ear worms," music that we just can't get out of our heads.

Oliver Sacks, the famous neurosurgeon, claims that ear worms are typically between fifteen and twenty seconds long — a mere fragment of the song, probably the bit containing the hook. This is partly because our working memory, our short-term memory, that is, basically loops around such fragments of time, and because music itself is usually built in 8- or 16-bar sequences of about this length.

There is a way to get this sometimes-annoying ear worm out of your head, and that's to deliberately break the loop. If you can, you have to sing the song the whole way through. Where the loop would end and naturally start over, you have to push on through to the next line and on to the end of the song. I haven't tried it, but the next time you do get ABBA, say, stuck in your brain, you might be able to do an exorcism on it by playing (however painfully) the song all the way through in your mind.

Anyway, the point is that music does in fact have many of the hallmarks of an addictive drug. We crave music. It seems to enhance our lives, lighting up our pleasure centres like a lab rat pressing on a bar.

Reggae, of all musical forms, seems a good example of the intoxicating nature of music. It lays way back on the strict metrical beat. It's languorous, drifting along like clouds on a summer day. Marley too, if you listen carefully, plays really loosely with his vocal phrasings. He's singing from the heart, you can hear that for sure. It's almost like he's in the room, talking to you personally.

Somehow, he touched a chord in people all over the world. His music transcended culture and class. I've heard Marley in Tibet and along the

Red Sea in Egypt. I've heard him in coffee shops in New York and outside of mosques in Istanbul. It's universal.

Crazy led us through the slaughtering heat up to Bob Marley's grave. It's a mausoleum, actually, about the size of a small house, and just outside the entrance they'd painted the words "Jah — Love." I've got to say that old Crazy gave a very inspired speech up there. One of the girls in the group was an immaculately dressed young black woman from the States somewhere. Crazy zeroed in on her. "Hey, fashion Rasta," he called out to her. "You know why I wear de dreadlocks? People think it's because we don't wash it. Nah. We just don't comb it, dat's all. We let it be." He took off his high Rasta toque and his dreadlocks bounced down around his shoulders.

"If you just leave your hair and let it grow," he continued, "everyone gets de dreadlocks. White, black, Chinese, it make no difference. One love …" he said, looking at each of us in turn. "One heart. We are all de same."

We went in through the doors of the vault. Candles were flickering on a little shelf in the front. There were a lot of notes tucked here and there and a sort of wall that formed the actual sarcophagus of Marley.

It was stifling in there. We were crammed in there pretty good, so no one stayed for very long. Just a few silent prayers and then back out into the sun. Crazy gathered us together in the courtyard out front, grinning lopsidedly.

"Now," he said, "who wanna sing wit me?" We'd all sat down on the low concrete wall there and Crazy sat down next to me.

I put my hand up slowly. I don't know why. "All right," Crazy said, turning to me. "What we sing, den?"

"'Redemption Song'?" I suggested meekly. I thought everyone was looking at me now and it was the only song I could think of.

"Oh pirates yes they rob I," he began, and I joined in right away. For some reason all the words came to me. "How long shall they kill our prophet … " We went through the whole thing, exactly as it had been on the record.

Crazy looked at me with something like pride when we finished. "Cappuccino," I said, pointing at him and then pointing at my own chest. But nobody laughed.

◀€ LISTEN 9.1

One of the single most interesting findings about the brain and music has been that of the neurohormone called oxytocin. It's a most remarkable hormone, this oxytocin, and it's released only under some very specific conditions.

One of these conditions is singing together. It won't work if you're singing by yourself in the shower. You have to be with others, producing music together, synchronizing your mood, in effect, to the others around you.

Oxytocin seems to engender feelings of contentment. We know, for example, that it is released in great gushes when a mother is lactating, serving apparently to build a bond between her and her baby. In the animal kingdom, oxytocin is exactly the neurohormone that enables the phenomenon of "imprinting." When little goslings waddle in a line after their mother, and when they finally take to the air in the famous flying "V", this is the oxytocin imprinting the infants on the mother.

Why human singing should cause this same gush of hormones is a bit unclear, but it has the same emotional effect. It reduces anxiety and works to create a connection between people, a measurable, lasting, physiological bond. In terms of drugs, it is one of the active ingredients in MDMA — the street drug ecstasy. With it, all of a sudden you feel very close to the people around you and, I suspect, the action of dancing together further reinforces all this oxytocin uptake.

So, what is it with music and all this chemistry? What is it about the auditory cheesecake idea that just won't go away? Well, first of all, as I said, let's be careful about which one causes which. We probably don't have the rush of oxytocin first and then run to find our reggae records. In this case, it's the music first that triggers the rush of neurochemicals.

Music is absolutely a social stimulant. It's used in every major ritual of our lives. We sing "Happy Birthday" when we bring in the candle-lit cake, we sing carols at Christmas, we bugle out the Last Post on Remembrance Day and sing "Auld Lang Syne" at the New Year.

We play music at weddings and celebrations. And music will probably be played to mark our deaths. Just up above us was the grave of Bob Marley and, though it hadn't occurred to me at the time, "Redemption Song," the song Crazy and I had just sung together, was actually one of the very last songs that Bob Marley wrote. Most accounts now say that he knew he was dying when he wrote it.

In 1978 he was playing soccer, his third great love behind his wife Rita and his music. He stubbed a toe quite badly, and when a doctor took a look at it, he saw something much more grave than a stubbed toe. I'd often heard that Marley died of lung cancer. Others say it was a brain tumour. That wasn't it at all. It was a melanoma under the toenail. Skin cancer, of all things. It was a form known as acral lentiginous melanoma, which is rare in that it is not linked to sun exposure. It's also thought to be a form that particularly strikes black populations.

Marley continued touring and recording. He refused chemotherapy, accepting the verdict as a part of his Rastafarian faith. In 1981 he collapsed in Central Park in New York. By this time the cancer had already spread to his lungs and, yes, his brain, and he decided to fly back to Jamaica for the end. He didn't make it, dying in a Miami hospital room at the age of only thirty-six.

So let's be clear here. When Crazy and I sang "Redemption Song," it was for a purpose. It wasn't for the rush of chemicals — though that is a nice side dish for sure. It was to mark something. It was a nod to a man's life. It was a little social ritual that we played out. And for me, it will be what I most remember about this strange pilgrimage to Nine Mile.

Crazy walked with us back out to the bus park. He just kind of stood there as we filed out, but just as I passed him, he stopped me. His red-rimmed brown eyes bored into me and he brought up his hand, balled into a fist, knuckles pointed at about the height of my chest. I knew what he meant, though, so I brought my fist up too and we fist-bumped as I'd seen the locals do — just lightly touching our knuckles together. All the time his eyes were on me. "Respect," he said and nodded slightly. There was no guffaw. He simply turned and loped back up the lane to meet up with his next tour group.

On the ride home, everyone sat in exactly the same seats as before. Exactly. And everyone studiously avoided everyone else's eyes. We were all coming down, I guess. Squirrelling a little. Lost in our own jagged little thoughts.

The islands of the Caribbean sweep out into the green Atlantic like a necklace. Furthest out into the Atlantic is the teardrop shape of Barbados. I'd come here to see something called Crop Over, a big festival that marked the end of the sugar cane harvest.

Barbados was built on sugar cane. Well, that and rum — lots of rum — which they make from the sugar cane after the harvest. In July all of Barbados goes crazy over this Crop Over thing. They've been doing it since at least 1780.

It's muggy in the summer there, the front end of the hurricane season, and the work of bringing in the cane (once done by slaves) is tortuously hard. So the end of harvest is something worth celebrating.

I got a taxi driver to take me past some of the cane fields. Honestly, there's not a lot of them left. Tourism is the big moneymaker now. The southwestern coastline of Barbados is called the Gold Coast. Further to the north, though, they've invented something even better. Like in credit cards, it's now called the Platinum Coast.

I wouldn't even have known we were passing sugar cane fields if the cab driver hadn't slowed down to point out the plants. Just a field of bushes, really. I'm not sure how far along this particular field was, but the cabbie told me that they now actually get two harvests a year.

I was staying down at St. Lawrence Gap, a little strip of beach just down from the capital of Bridgetown. In the morning I saw the fishermen taking in their catch, and in the afternoon as I was wandering up the beach, I heard the sound of a steel drum band drifting out of a faded pink hotel.

When I came up closer, there they were. Five elderly men who wouldn't have looked out of place in a little New Orleans club were plinking away at the steel drums under a roofed shelter. They had a little sign set up. Beneath the symbol of Neptune's trident was written "The Barbados Steel Orchestra."

There was a swimming pool half full of tourists just across the cement, so the drummers were clanging out some popular tunes. They played the Beatles — "Ob-la-di, Ob-la-da" — and it didn't sound out of place. The notes glittered in the Caribbean sun, flashing like sparkles, and you couldn't help but get caught up in the exuberance of it. Then they did, of all things, Beethoven's Fifth Symphony — or at least the first bits. The long notes trilled under their mallets, and even this seemed to shimmer happily in the sunshine.

When they took a break, I went over to talk to one of the men. He was tall and thin and completely bald. His eyes were a bit bloodshot and I'm guessing he was well over sixty. He could've walked in from right off of the set of the *Shawshank Redemption*.

"I liked the Beatles stuff," I said, and he nodded in acknowledgement.

"Do you play the more traditional stuff too?"

He looked up at me, pointing a long, spindly finger. "You want to hear calypso?"

"Yeah, yeah, calypso."

He shook his head slowly. "Calypso is not for de pan. You have to watch de Pick-O-De-Crop."

I had. Pick-O-De-Crop is the calypso competition that coincides each year with Crop Over. The best calypso singers in Barbados face off with new songs, usually composed especially for the competition and usually some kind of social commentary. Last year was a song about the troubles in Haiti. The winner this year was a man named Mighty Gabby, and when I said the name, the old man lit up.

"Yeah, Mighty Gabby, he win more than a few years."

"But you guys don't play calypso?"

"De pan is not for calypso, but we can play it. We learn their melodies, just play that."

"And are your steel drums …"

"Pan, we call dem pan."

"Are your pan drums really made from oil barrels?"

He chuckled. "In World War Two, you know, de German submarines were dippin' in here and there." He swept his hand out towards the ocean. "Barbados is de furthest east of any of da Caribbean Islands, so de Americans came down here and set up their navy bases all along here. Here and in Trinidad too. All 'long the docks, they set down their fifty-five-gallon oil drums. And when they was empty, the sailors just filled dem with trash and left dem. They didn't need dem. Took 'em awhile to notice some of their trash cans gone missing." He chuckled then, a deep, throaty laugh.

"And you made them into drums?"

"More than drums. Look at dem. We got altos and tenors and bass pan."

"You always call them 'pan'?"

"Pan, yeah, dat's what we say down here. Mine's de alto. Usually it's de one carryin' de melody." He stood up and took me over to the stage they had set up. His alto was about five inches deep and had a silvery shine. "This one," he said, "cost a thousand U.S. dollars."

"So they're not cut from oil drums anymore?"

"No, no, these ones are specially made now."

Along the metal playing surface were eight flattened spots in a circle. There were less of these flat spots on the big bass pan — the full oil drum size — and a few more, maybe twelve spots, on another one beside that. The steel drum is the only instrument in the world built around the cycle of fifths. You'll see charts of the cycle of fifths in books on music theory — how in the key of C, for example, you'll also have the prominent fifth note of G but then how the fifth for G is D and how you can make a sort of colour wheel for them all. It's a neat little map of how key signatures all work with each other. The pan drums are actually set up like this chart so that you just move diagonally across the circle to the fifth. It's not like a piano keyboard at all and it's funny, in fact, that no other instruments have ever developed in this way. It's so straightforward and simple.

"We used to have to tune these ourselves," he continued. "We'd bang dem out with hammers. Get de shape and size just right or the note won't play right." He tapped at one. It pinged richly.

"You hear dat?" he said, cocking his ear down towards the pan. "Up until now, there wasn't any recording equipment good enough to catch all the ..."

"The harmonics?"

"Yeah, the harmonics." He pinged it again and I could hear it was a complex tangle of overtones. Something between the clang of a bell and the clip of a cowbell. And that was just one note. Nowadays, they are specially tuned so that even the more prominent overtones are tuned, not just the main note. I don't know how they do that, but they do, and if it's tuned right, the sound plinks like a sparkle of sun on the ocean.

"Now look," he said, holding his mallet loose in his hand. "It's from de wrist." He flopped his wrist loosely like the broken neck of a bird. "Hear dat?" he said, cocking his head down to the pan drum. "Dat's right."

What he was showing me was an example of cross modal perception. There's long been a debate over the way in which percussionists hold their various sticks. And, more importantly, whether it actually makes a difference to the sound.

The answer is yes ... and no. In watching footage of a performance, even in slow motion, the gesture used in striking the surface does indeed affect the sound — to the performer and the audience. But if you take away the picture in the video and just listen to the audio, there is no sound difference between this "gesture" and a more standard one. It turns out the visual perception of the music really does change the way our brain perceives the sound. Music, in this way, is cross modal. There's even research into the facial expressions of performers. And, yes, when a performer scrunches up his or her face with the emotion of the note they're hitting, the audience very tangibly hears that.

It's all about the "feel" of music — which, if you think about it, is another form of cross modal perception. We feel music. And that overall groove or "feel" is critical. It's the x-factor that gives you chills down the back of your spine. It's what makes music especially and essentially human. It's the THC in the drug we call music.

When they got up to play again, the man I'd been talking to said something to the others, and they launched into a bouncing little melody. Out across the beach, the rhythms splashed with the surf and the melodies belonged to the sunshine. They were playing calypso now and the man on the alto pan, I never did learn his name, winked down at me and smiled.

◀ᴈ LISTEN 9.2

The Grand Kadooment was to be on the Friday. I had no idea what that meant. *What the hell's a Kadooment, let alone a grand one?* Some people told me that it meant a big to-do. Others called it a big ruckus or a big commotion.

It's really the social event of the year, one big blowout of a party marking the last day of Crop Over.

I went into Bridgetown not really knowing any of this. The thing was to start at the National Stadium and I thought maybe it would be a kind of a parade. Well, by the time the first float went by, I knew I wasn't in Kansas anymore.

For one thing, there was a little truck wobbling along between the floats. This was the Cockspur Rum truck. They were handing out free rum all day. Even at 9:30 in the morning, pretty much everyone had a plastic cup of the stuff, sloshing it down.

There were, I guess, about a dozen floats; all dolled up big flatbed trucks. Live bands were playing on some of them. One had a great steel drum band. But lots of others just had big speakers and they were playing music from the dance clubs.

Behind each float came a throng of dancing people, almost all of them in costume. The ones behind the pan float were quite elaborate, as in Carnival in Rio or Mardi Gras in New Orleans. One woman was dressed up as what I can only describe as a giant dragonfly with gossamer wings ten feet high floating out behind her. A man was dressed as a sailboat, complete with fishing nets and dangling fish.

Most of the people, though, had simpler costumes. The men wore yellow plastic shorts and brightly coloured top hats. The women wore sequined bikinis of silver and gold with loops and draping beads. On their heads they wore feather boa tiaras, great fake feathers that bounced as the women pranced behind the floats. Almost everyone was slip-sloppy drunk and dancing their hearts out, shaking their backsides in ways that would certainly embarrass them on a normal day.

I nestled in for a while behind one particular float. It was blasting out modern dance tunes from speakers the size of refrigerators. Behind it danced a throng of twenty-somethings. It seemed largely young ladies. All were wearing either green or yellow bikinis and all were pretty intoxicated. A virtual gold mine for any young man. All inhibitions seemed to have been lost in a fog of rum and music. At one point we passed a police station at the side of the road, and three of the young women climbed up on the cement wall that surrounded it, dancing wildly like go-go girls. I wandered along with them trying to keep in mind that I was writing a serious tome on music, trying to see the swinging hips and ample bosoms in the guise of an anthropologist. I'll admit I wasn't all that successful.

There was a raw sexual tension in the air. Actually, not tension, that's what was so interesting. It was just out there, fully liberated, a sort of drunken joy in the flaunting of sexuality.

◀᠅ LISTEN 9.3

Sex, as Darwin or Freud — or any university co-ed — could tell you, is as pervasive as breathing, as ever-present as our heartbeats. It's a gush of hormones and chemicals that, once we reach puberty, is never far off. In fact, it's the magic potion of oxytocin that once again rears its head in the act of sex. Though we've seen that oxytocin is released when singing together and probably dancing together, though we've noted its effects in bonding a mother to its child and vice versa, the purpose of oxytocin in humans is primarily related to sexual intercourse. It has nothing to do with impregnation or getting the boy's swimmers going in a straight line.

No, oxytocin's main effect is to bond people together. It's very rare in the animal kingdom for females and males to mate for life, but we humans — along with only a handful of other species — at least try. And much of this may be accounted for by oxytocin.

But let me say again that you can't put the cart before the horse. In the case of music, it's the music itself and the social rituals that are wrapped around it that cause the gushes of things like oxytocin or dopamine or endorphins or any of several dozen other neurochemicals. Clearly, music takes our basic auditory perceptions and uses them to its own purposes. It appropriates all sorts of brain functions, even enlisting our basic neurochemical gushes to enhance and maintain its devious powers. And why? Because music is all about creating the social animal. It enhances our rituals and celebrations and spectacles to bond us in groups that will remain with us for the rest of our lives.

Crop Over in Barbados.

Anyway, there I was traipsing along with all these young beauties. There were some guys, too, but they were also in ridiculous plastic green costumes, with plastic top hats. I was wearing my usual clothes and I remember at one point a very pretty girl coming up to me. "Why aren't you revellin'?" she said, straight out.

"I'm, ahh ... what?"

"Revellin', revellin'."

"I'm just listening to the music."

"You don't listen to it." She looked at me as though I were an idiot. "You have to go into it. You have to go revellin'. You have to dance. You have to drink."

"Excuse me?"

"You can't stand off by the side. You have to be a part of it."

She danced out into the throngs behind another of the floats, and I thought that she actually had a pretty good point. I wasn't a part of it.

Feeling defeated, I stepped off into the crowds that were now starting to line the streets. The floats were winding down toward Spring Garden Road, where it all ends. And more reasonable people were coming out to watch the whole drunken mess as if it really were just a parade.

Spring Garden Road runs along the ocean front. The savvy locals there had set up little booths to sell more rum and beer, though the dancing crowds were slowly drifting off in clumps and knots. It was still not much more than the middle of the afternoon and the Barbados sun was screaming down on us. I headed for the taxis to take me back to St. Lawrence Gap, my ears still echoing from the blasting speakers, my mind woozy with heat and pheromones and the many miles I'd walked.

I was thinking I should have danced.

10

THE MAYANS
COUNTING OUT TIME

I FLEW NORTH FROM SAN SALVADOR OVER A TOWERING VOLCANO CALLED Quetzaltepec. We went over the border and into Guatemala, out past the lakes and towns of the south up to the far northern reaches of the Petén, where nothing but deep green jungle stretches almost unbroken all the way up to Mexico.

Buried here in the vines and twisting roots are the ruins of whole cities, of temples and palaces and standing stones — markers of time from the greatest civilization of the western hemisphere. This is the lost world of the Maya.

I had been here once before so I was really excited about seeing the ruins of Tikal again. It's at the centre of the great mystery of the Mayans. They vanished, almost overnight, leaving the city to the creeping forest. No one really knows why. And now I had come just as their "long count," the ancient Mayan calendar, was about to run out.

The plane landed at a little place called Flores and then it was another hour by Land Rover to the jungle lodge, a long wooden building cut out of a clearing in the deep jungle. I was met there by Jose Antonio Ortiz. He goes by his middle name, Antonio, which was his father's name, and rightfully so because his father was one of the original archeologists working on the dig here from 1956 to 1969. In fact, Antonio the father, in true Indiana Jones style, actually discovered one of the temples: Temple Six, the Temple of the Inscriptions.

Antonio, the son, grew up in the jungle here. As a little boy he played in the ruins while his father worked, uncovering the city. Now even the younger Antonio is a gruff old man closing in on sixty. He's wiry and grizzled, with a voice like Rod Stewart after a couple of packs of cigarettes and a bathtub of rum. But he knows every little corner of the ruins here. He knows the wildlife and the red dirt trails between the temples and, most of all, he knows the glyphs. The Mayan civilization was the only one in the western hemisphere to develop its own writing system; strange, bulbous glyphs unlike anything else on Earth.

I sat with Antonio near the kitchen of the jungle lodge. The place had been built for the archeologists, and up on the wall to the left were yellowing newspaper clippings showing photos of his father and the uncovering of the great temples with machetes and axes. To the right was a copy of a Mayan mural, almost entirely in red, the colour of blood.

The mural itself showed two men. One held what looked like a mask in his hand. He seemed to be offering it to the other.

"What's that?" I asked.

Antonio looked up to where I was pointing. His English was perfect, and in a smoky voice he said, "It's a severed human head."

"Oh my god."

Antonio laughed. "A captive. Look closely at the shape of the skull. It's the head of a royal captive."

I bent forward but I couldn't really see what he was talking about.

"This is a ritual scene. Look, the man in the cloak is a high priest. He's giving the head of the enemy to the king. There are stelae that talk of this."

"Stelae?"

"Standing stones. All the important events, the coronation of a new king, the capture of an important enemy, all these were all marked with standing stones."

I knew about this, of course. The Mayans were completely obsessed with marking time. The city of Tikal reached its height long before

A Mayan fresco at Tikal.

Columbus sailed from Spain, before even the Vikings capped the northern reaches of Labrador. They built vast temples and left murals and glazed pottery that showed a society as alien and strange as any in history. They could predict eclipses of the sun and the moon with incredible precision. They developed a calendar called the Long Count that marked every day for almost five thousand years. Their writings tell us that they believed in cycles of creation and destruction — all the more ironic when you know that they monumentally failed to predict their own destruction, a societal collapse as catastrophic and lightning-fast as any the world has yet experienced.

The funny thing is that their so-called Long Count ended more than a thousand years after their own demise. December 21, 2012, was the last day in their figuring and there was, of course, all sorts of speculation about the end of the world. If you're reading this now, you know that didn't quite happen. So what is all this Long Count stuff and who were these strange people?

"Look carefully at their skulls," Antonio went on. I eyed the mural dutifully. There was something odd about the men in the picture.

"The king," said Antonio, "had piercings and tattoos all over him. He would have had his teeth inlaid with jade. But we know these are noble men because of their skulls."

I looked again. The backs of the heads of the men seemed to bulge out grotesquely. The king grimaced and sneered out at me across the centuries.

"The ruling class had their skulls shaped as infants," Antonio explained. "They strapped them to cradleboards then bent another board down onto their foreheads."

"Their heads were shaped like cones?"

"Yes, like cones."

Who the hell were these people?

Antonio looked at me and chuckled throatily. "It's called cranial deformation."

God, I thought, *piercings and tattoos are one thing, but having your actual skull elongated. That's way out there.*

"There's a ritual," continued Antonio, "where the king would have a hole cut in his tongue. Then they yanked a rope through it. This rope, it was woven with thorns, maybe pieces of sharp obsidian."

"My god! Why?"

"So the king would have a spirit vision. The word is not "king." That's not right. In Mayan it's called *ajaw* or *ah'kin*. A little bit different. *Kin* is the word for sun, so they were like gods. Not just kings. Everything revolved around them."

"What's this vision thing?"

"Well, the blood from the tongue dripped down onto a cloth. Then the cloth was burned in a special jar and the king would see visions in the smoke that came up. Prophecies."

"But they didn't see their own end coming?"

"No," he said, rising. "No, they didn't."

I thought for a moment I might have offended him, but he only looked at his watch.

"We'll go out there tomorrow," he said. "Before the dawn."

All this talk about skulls reminded me of something called altriciality.

Much of human behaviour probably arises because of the altriciality of our species. So, let me explain. Several million years ago, two things happened to make humankind the species it is today. The first was that we started to stand upright. It didn't happen overnight. Geneticists now believe that it takes about five thousand years for a gene to spread throughout a population. So this rewiring took a long time. Our entire physiology — our spines and our muscles — had to evolve. Our pelvic structures, especially, got smaller and lighter. The pelvis of a four-footed creature can be more massive because it has a lot more support. Once you raise it up and put it on only two legs, well, it has to be lighter and smaller. What that means is that in the female of the species the birth canal becomes much narrower.

So, that's the first thing. The second is that our brains, and in particular our frontal lobes, got a lot bigger. These are the areas where we form plans and make goals. It's where we sort out the possible consequences of our current actions and, essentially, do the things that make us human.

The problem with all this is that these two developments are in direct opposition to each other. You can't have a smaller birth canal and bigger-headed babies. That just doesn't work.

The only possible evolutionary solution was to increase the altriciality of our species. Altriciality is the length of time it takes from the birth of an individual to the point at which they can survive on their own. This is carefully measured in different species. Many mammals will be standing up within minutes of their birth — wobbly, perhaps, but standing. Birds are kicked out of the nest and fly away on their own within weeks. Humans, though, humans take a lot more time.

As it happens, humans have by far the longest period of altriciality for any species on the planet. And it's basically because we're all born prematurely — before our heads get too big for the birth canal.

This is another example, then, of a side effect of evolution — an exaptation — that has had massive social ramifications. With this long altrical period, mothers had to stay longer with their helpless infants. This, in turn, meant that the men had to stick around to provide and protect them and, if that doesn't sound too sexist, it probably accounts for the formation of family units. And it doesn't stop there. Family structures were not enough to really take care of these children, so humans started banding together into small tribes, small hunting and gathering tribes of no more than Dunbar's number.

This is an important point. Everything that we are as humans — all those long years together, huddled around cooking fires, hunting and gathering, and waiting for our babies to get old enough to take care of themselves — all that time accounts for our social structures and the rise of things like cave paintings and language and, yes, music.

It goes right back to the womb. Now, let me deal here with music in the womb. There's a lot written about that. We are told, for example, that you are supposed to play Mozart to your unborn baby. It will make it smarter. This, unfortunately, is hogwash. A baby does have the full apparatus to hear by about the twenty-fifth week of gestation (at the earliest) and it will do things like startle at the sound of a slamming door. The higher frequencies of sound, though, are completely lost in the murk of amniotic fluid, so a clear perception of something like a Mozart piano concerto would be next to impossible.

On the other hand, babies are very conscious of their mother's heartbeat. They are probably aware, too, of the sound of her voice. It would be largely unintelligible phonetically, but a baby does perhaps hear the general contours — the prosody of language — high and sharp sounds when stressed, longer vowels and more gentle issuances when relaxed. And this leaves an indelible imprint on the unborn child.

At only two weeks after birth, a baby clearly recognizes the sound of its own mother's voice, long before it recognizes her face. Babies, in fact, are born with most of the fundamentals of music already hardwired into their tiny brains. Soon after birth they can recognize melodic contours in general terms and they can certainly discriminate different rhythms. By two months they can distinguish between pleasant intervals (a major third for example) and dissonance like the Tristan chord. They know when something is out of tune.

What's most important, though, is that all through this long period of altriciality, mothers are constantly with their babies, cooing to them, singing lullabies, speaking to them in soft and elegantly shaped prosodies. This is true across all cultures and without a doubt it forms the bedrock for both their later language development and musical ability.

By seven months old, infants can remember pieces of music for two weeks (a piece by Mozart was, in fact, used for these tests) and distinguish it from other pieces. At about a year, a child will start accurately synchronizing to music — that is, clapping or tapping in time and dancing — not just wiggling randomly. By this age, in fact, they may have all the abilities of music recognition opened to a musically untrained adult. By the age of three, children may make up their own songs. They can create variations on songs they've heard. By the time they're five they're attuned to complex things like key changes and by seven they're already quite fossilized in their appreciation of the particular rhythms and melodic patterns of their own culture. It's not that they hear "foreign music" as unpleasant or unlistenable, but it's already become different. It's the music of others. Not ours.

And all this is because of altriciality.

Antonio knocked on my door the next morning at exactly 4 a.m. Outside it was pitch dark and all I could see was his flashlight beam dancing across the jungle foliage outside my door. It had rained heavily in the night. I'd heard it thrashing down on my roof and now, though the rain had stopped, a thick mist hung in the air, occluding the stars and the moon. "Time to go," came Antonio's grizzled voice. He turned and clomped off towards the jungle. There was a single lane, wide enough for a Jeep, that burrowed into the trees, but Antonio wasn't heading for that. Instead, he stopped and waited for me. He told me to keep close and then ploughed off into the dark foliage to the west of the lodge.

Wet leaves brushed up against my face and there was a musty, sweet earthen smell kicking up all around us. Not even the insects had woken up yet, so there was an eerie silence in the dark jungle, something I had not experienced before, just the clump of my rubber boots on the wet mulch of a thin red-dirt trail.

Antonio tramped into the darkness and I struggled to keep up with him. What little trail I could see beneath my feet suddenly ended. "Down here," Antonio said, veering right, and I followed his flashlight beam. He strode off the trail another ten or twenty metres and then came up against something large looming out of the darkness. "Look at this," he said, and he was already tipping his flashlight across it. "In the daytime you can't read this. It's too weathered."

We were standing beside a stelae, one of the stone markers, as big as a surfboard. "There," he said, and he held the flashlight up at the side of the standing stone, its beam angling across the surface of the rock like a train headlight on a winter night. And across the stone, I could see, in the shadows created by the beam, the writing — the bubble-like glyphs of the ancient Mayans.

"What is it?" I asked.

"The end of a *katun*," he rasped.

"A what?"

"These stones all mark dates. This one is the end of a katun, a twenty-year cycle. There, you can see the bars and dots. That's the Long Count date. It works out to 396 C.E."

The flashlight etched out the glyphs.

"And there are the glyphs for the name of the king. This stelae was erected by Nun Yax Ayin."

"An important one?" I asked, but Antonio was already stomping off into the darkness again. I should have known that they were all import-ant. The ruler was everything in the Mayan city states. I've read that the whole city was like an extended royal household, with circles radiating out, further and further from the real power. Only about ten percent of Tikal has been excavated, really just the central temple complexes, and far out into the jungle would have been the compounds of peasants — of soldiers and craftsmen and farmers.

Antonio was really cooking along now. The sky was just starting to lighten and I could make out shapes. We passed by the central acropolis and I could just make out the dark shapes of the temples rearing up into the sky. We came out onto some wider pathways and I heard the first of the birds begin to croak out their greetings to the dawn.

Antonio kept stopping to wait, hurrying me along with his look. Not too much further we came up to a rise covered in scrubby bushes and ferns. Up ahead of us was a set of wooden steps, edging up into the darkness. This was Temple Four, the highest of all the temples at Tikal. The roof comb crests out at about sixty metres above the jungle floor (the height of a twenty-storey building) so that for two thousand years this was the highest building in all of the Americas.

It still takes quite a few lung-crunching minutes to climb the wobbling wooden steps to the top platform, just below the doors into the temple proper. Those are sealed off with chicken wire, though there's not much to see inside anyway — just bare rock rooms, unadorned but once upon a time the hallowed ceremonial places of the kings.

We sat down at the original stone steps, facing out towards the endless jungle. In front of us the dawn was breaking. A coati, the Central American version of a raccoon, snuffled up a few steps below us and I wondered what had brought it this high above its jungle floor home. Then, out in the mist, the roar of a howler monkey, rolling almost like thunder, drifted across the jungle. "The sun is coming up," Antonio whispered, shifting on the hard rock seat. Far off to the east we could just start to see the temple combs of the other great temples of Tikal, rising up out of the canopy like tombstones. We sat up there for a long time, watching a great red sun rise above the jungle, the mists whirling and dissipating in its glare. Beneath us, the world was coming alive with the raucous calls of parrots and the thrum of uncountable insects. A family of spider monkeys crashed through the trees beneath us and Antonio told me about the long history of the Mayans here.

"The stelae we looked at," he bent in towards me, still almost whispering, "that is from the early classic period. None of these temples were here yet."

"What did you say, the year three hundred and something?"

"Give or take. There were smaller temples then. They are underneath the bigger ones now." He pointed at one in the distance. "The Temple of the Jaguar is the tomb of a king."

"They're tombs?"

"No, most of them are not. But symbolically they represent the king. Many of them are just built over the temples of their fathers — or grandfathers. If you dig into one, you will find smaller temples beneath it."

"Like those Russian dolls."

"Exactly — one inside the other. The Mayan Long Count, it begins on August 11, 3114 B.C.E."

"That early?"

"There was nothing here then. Just jungle."

"Then why ...?"

"We don't know. There were earlier civilizations — Olmec to the north — but there was nothing here until after the birth of Christ. Early on there is a pre-classic stage, maybe just wooden buildings, but slowly the Mayans were becoming more and more powerful, harvesting corn, building their cities And then about 200 C.E., this begins the classic era. Soon, Tikal here became the greatest city in the western hemisphere. One hundred thousand people."

"And then they collapsed."

Antonio turned on me. His grey eyes were almost sad. "Not yet," he said in his gruff voice. "They had a whole golden age ahead of them still. Look, out there. You can still see it."

The jungle canopy, a lush green carpet, spread out to the far horizon. A mist still swept around it, clearing now in the rising sun, and off to the west, a kilometre away, the great buildings of the central plaza, the Temple of the Jaguar and the Temple of Masks, rose up above the canopy like knifepoints, like the shoulders of mountains.

We came down from the temple about an hour later and Antonio took me across to an area called the Plaza of Seven Temples. He stopped in what looked like a small ravine. Up on both sides of us, scrub-covered hills sloped up maybe double our height.

"Do you know what this is?" he said, stretching his arms wide.

I looked around. There was nothing to see.

"This is one of their ball courts."

"Wow," I said. I knew that the Mayans revelled in their ball game. It was one of their most important rituals. A volleyball-sized solid rubber ball was bounced off the hips and knees of the players up against these sloping walls. They couldn't touch the ball with their hands or kick it with their feet, and they wore elaborate wooden braces to help bounce the ball. The post-classic courts to the north seem to have stone hoops, almost like a sideways basketball net, but down here in Tikal there were no such hoops, and we really don't know how it all would have been scored.

What we do know is that the game had massive religious overtones. The court floor was itself a symbolic entrance to the underworld, the home of the gods of death.

And I was standing right on top of it.

"Ah …" I said, lifting a foot tentatively.

"There are five ball courts at Tikal," Antonio went on. "Three of them are in this plaza."

I'd actually seen a reenactment of the Mayan ball game up at a place called Xcaret. They had the king come out — an actor with a normally shaped head, I'm afraid — and he was draped in the replica of a jaguar pelt with loops of jade and turquoise and a big, fine head-dress. They carried him in on a litter surrounded by high priests and guards. The whole thing was really impressive and there was music playing — that I remember — with a lot of drumming and thumping and a mournful, echoing flute.

After they carried the king out, the music stopped and he called out something in the Mayan tongue. Then ball players came out in a solemn single file to take up their positions in the vast modern reconstruction. Five players were on each side and they did have some skills. They had to. You try bouncing a heavy rubber ball off of your hip, up a wide slope and, yes, in this case, through a stone circle. When the first ball went through, the crowd went nuts.

◀ LISTEN 10.1

I wondered at the time how authentic all this re-creation was. Music, especially, is the most ephemeral of the arts. Before Edison began to record sounds on wax disks not much more than a hundred years ago, all the music of the world literally vanished into thin air as soon as it was over. So is there any way to know what Mayan music might have sounded like? Here's a society as strange as any we know, completely isolated and untouched by any other civilization — east or west — so how can we possibly hope to know what kind of music they played?

As it turns out, we do have some pretty good ideas about it. First of all, loads and loads of musical instruments have turned up in the archeological digs. There are also murals and ceramics and even glyphs that clearly show how important music was to their ceremonies and rituals.

Some of the instruments we've found can still be played, so, like King Tut's trumpets, even if we don't exactly know the melodies, we do know the sounds and that's a pretty good start. Drums, as in most societies, played a prominent role. There were also lots of flutes and something called an ocarina. Ocarinas are ceramic and circular, looking almost like teapots. They're glorified whistles, really, with maybe two or three holes for different pitches. These ocarinas have been found in abundance, and because they were cheap to make and easy to play, it's thought that they were probably the instruments of the lower classes. Flutes, and we have some that are beautifully carved and decorated, were probably used by the higher classes. It's a simple formula; implements of any kind in archeological digs can usually be attributed to a certain social class. It comes from the costliness of the materials involved, the workmanship, and, especially in the case of music, the difficulty involved in playing the instruments. Instruments that are hard to play, that would have taken years to master, probably indicate a class of professional musicians employed by the higher, more powerful classes.

In the Mayan wall murals — and there are some really fantastic ones at Bonampak a hundred kilometres to the south — there are whole orchestras. They show as many as twelve men playing together on drums and flutes and rattles with one of the men, called a *holhop*, acting as a sort of conductor. And that's pretty close to what I saw and heard at Xcaret.

But what were their melodies? I keep thinking that surely a culture as way out there as this one, well, wouldn't their music be just as strange? Well, not necessarily. One of the really interesting finds we have is an elaborate bone flute, clearly something from the noble classes. It is still playable and when the researchers tried it, it sounded out a perfect C major scale — the exact "do, re, mi, fa, so" that we hear in all our modern Western music.

There really are some natural constraints on what music can be. There are exceptions, of course, but the seven-note scale (eight with the octave) is found all over the world. It seems to be a basic property of auditory physics. And it's not unlike the ball game, if you think about it. For the ancient Mayans — for all their strange ways of being — the ball game is still dependent on the way the ball bounces and arcs. It's still all about the angles and the principles of gravity. It can't be anything but. And the same is true for music.

There is some astonishing new research coming out about the development of the human brain. It turns out that not everything in the brain gets set during our so-called period of altriciality. As children grow, things seem to be nicely falling into place, and then at about the age of twelve, kaboom, two more sweeping changes take place.

It's not what you're thinking. I'm not talking about teenage hormones here. I'm talking strictly about a change in the brain and how it's wired. At puberty, the axons of the neurons — the branches that send signals on to the next neuron — start to become sheathed in myelin. This process starts in the base of the brain, and then in slow waves, over many years, gradually encompasses the entire brain. The process comes to a close when we're about twenty-three years old, with the myelin sheathing appearing, finally, in the all-important, decision making, consequence-understanding frontal lobes.

This myelin, basically a white fatty material, greatly accelerates the speed of neural firing. If our brains were computers, I heard one researcher say, it's as if the bandwidth has been drastically improved, from some whining old 90s dial-up modem to a high-speed super connection.

But there's a downside. Once a neuron gets encased in myelin, it is much more difficult to form new connections. In fact, connections that are rarely used atrophy at this point. They wither and die. It's part of the reason why we have critical periods in learning. It's partly why we are able to so easily learn new languages before puberty. Or take up a new sport. Or become proficient on a musical instrument. We can learn these new skills later in life — after this myelination has taken place — but it's a lot harder.

The second major change in the teenage brain explains even more about their sometimes alarming behaviour. Once again, starting at about age twelve, the brain starts gushing out oxytocin. Oxytocin, you will remember, is the "affiliative neuropeptide" that has to do with bonding, with imprinting and making strong social connections. Initially in life, these rushes happen between a newborn and its mother. In the teenage brain, this second infusion of oxytocin is thought to be associated with the process of peer bonding. It's an evolutionary adaptation that shifts the young adult away from his family bonds to new and stronger social connections with his own peers. And as any parent knows, this striving for independence accounts for a lot of their teenager's seemingly surly behaviour. It's biochemical. It's the brain changing.

This explains a lot of things. In music, we all know that the music of our youth — and especially the music we hear between the ages of twelve and twenty-three — carries a special place in our hearts. We can be quite specific on those ages now. There are now countless studies, even cross-cultural studies, that all point back to these processes of myelination and the re-emergence of oxytocin in the rewiring of the teenage brain. During this time, our brains are narrowing down and strengthening our cultural identities, losing the ability to take up other languages and another culture's music, for example. At the same time, we are bonding with our peers, and, in another example of exaptation, we are bonding — rather strongly — with the markers of this time in our life. The oxytocin seems to have the side effect of bonding us, quite strongly, to the books we read, the movies we watch, and, most of all, the music we listen to at this time in our lives.

Later that same afternoon, I set off on my own with a map to guide me. I wanted to see the Temple of Inscriptions. It's pretty far from the rest of the ruins, off in a direction you wouldn't expect. So I traipsed off down the path and soon found myself quite alone with no one around for miles. I kept going and going, thinking that this couldn't be right, but after a lot of trudging through the stifling heat with a sticky patina of sweat on my back, I came around a bend and saw a hill mostly covered in foliage. It wasn't a hill, of course, but a partially restored temple.

The Temple of Inscriptions is remarkable in that the back of the roof comb is carved with one of the longest pieces of text we have from the Mayans. In one hundred and eighty-six massive glyphs, it tells the two-thousand-year history of the city of Tikal. This is what Antonio's father had discovered. A pretty good find by anyone's measure.

I stood there, my hand cupped above my forehead, trying to make out the glyphs, but in truth they were severely weathered and barely stand out any more. The second last glyph names one of the last great kings of Tikal, and the very last glyph talks of an unnamed king long after the temple was already complete. And then there is no more.

Around the front of the temple, the stone steps are still largely covered in sod and small shrubs. But there is a stelae out front of the steps — one of the best-preserved stelae in all of Tikal. It shows a bound captive from the endless wars — probably from the neighbouring city of Caracol. One thing we do know is that this endless warfare between the city states was a part of the reason for the Mayan collapse. The other reason was ecological collapse. Jungle soil can only sustain corn crops for so long, and a population base of one hundred thousand people means a lot of hungry mouths.

We can't know exactly what happened here at the end, but there's lots of speculation. It's likely that the ruling classes lived blissfully on through the warning signs. They would have had the best of the food. They would have had the best of the living spaces, so it didn't really occur to them that everything was coming to a crashing end.

As things tightened up, the great majority of people — the peasants, so to speak — would have felt it the worst. And in time, they may well have had enough. Warfare is one thing and ecological troubles another, but in the end it may have been the disparity between the classes that finally did it. A social uprising is the only thing that could account for such a sudden and complete collapse.

I'd seen the rituals of the kings — or their reconstructions anyway — up at Xcaret, but I remember now that outside of where they'd put on the show, I came across a more humble troupe of Mayan musicians. It was an entirely simple affair, just five or six guys playing together in a grove of trees.

I could see that three of them were playing ocarinas, the ceramic instruments that are now thought to have been the hallmark of the peasant classes. The only difference was they were thumping on them like drums rather than playing them like whistles. There were others playing wooden drums and one or two playing simple flutes. I stopped to listen and I remember at the time feeling as if I had just stepped back in time.

The men here were bare-chested for the most part. A few wore head-dresses, but they were nothing like the wicker fantasias that the rulers had worn. No, they were more simply adorned and the music they played was pretty and uncomplicated.

Could it be that this was music of the ancient Mayans?

Well, we have at least one more remarkable piece of evidence. There is a written account from one of the first Westerners ever to meet the Mayan people. This was a man named Diego de Landa, and in the year 1566 he wrote of a group of Mayan musicians. Up in the Yucatán there were still remnants of a post-classic phase, and here is exactly what he wrote about their music:

> They have little drums which they play with the hand,
> and another drum made of hollow wood with a heavy
> and sad sound. They beat it with rather a long stick with
> a certain gum from a tree at the end of it, and they have
> long thin trumpets of hollow wood with long twisted
> gourds at the ends.

And the music I heard? Well, there was something heavy and sad about it, all right. Far from the palaces and temples of the kings, I imagined that these men were playing for themselves, just for the pleasure of hearing. It was as close to real as I was going to get. As close to hearing their lost music as anyone on this Earth will ever get to hear.

◀ᴇ   LISTEN 10.2

The city of Tikal fell back into the jungle sometime after our year 869. That is the last date they recorded on their standing stones. The collapse was sharp and sudden. A generation or two at most lingered on in the ruins before disappearing back into the endless jungle, leaving the palaces and reservoirs and temples to the twisting vines and yabbering monkeys.

I spent three more days at Tikal, sometimes with Antonio but mostly on my own, walking up and down the gritty stone surfaces of the temple steps, wandering the pathways beneath the dappling jungle canopy. Emeralds and jades sparkled in the sun splashes of the high branches, and around my heavy boots olive green roots and vines wound like snakes. All around me was a sweet, earthy scent and always, from dawn to dusk, a cacophony of thrumming insects and raucous birdcall.

I walked, sometimes all day, my clothes sticking to me, a sheen of sweat on my forehead and on the back of my neck. I wandered and wandered and lost myself in the glimpses of ancient ruins, a broken standing stone lost in the vines, a crumbling wall half buried under earth the colour of rust, and the great temples standing silent against the centuries.

We humans have no organ to perceive time. It's a remarkable fact when you think about it. We have senses that take in the world in a thousand different smells and sights and tastes. But none of these record time.

Neurophysiologists now talk of something called "the perceptual present." This is the very real world we live in, this present. Behind it, the past stretches away back to our own births and the long train of DNA that has led up to us. The future too lies just out of sight, a great mystery that we are always desperately trying to predict.

But our realities are in the here and now. The "perceptual present" is a stretch of time anywhere from half a second to about ten seconds. This has been measured. Commonly it's about two seconds, a little window that keeps shuffling along with our consciousness. And it is in this present that we perceive everything — including music.

Now that's strange, because no piece of music is two seconds long. So there's a lot more than our ears at work here. Our auditory cortices are busy monitoring the present, parsing out the vertical in the right cortex and the horizontal — more or less — in the left. But other parts of our brains are busy, busy, neatly summing up what has already been heard in the piece. The neural circuitry of memory is very much at play. We think we hear a full passage in our minds, but we don't really. Our brains have made it seamless, but our real perception is still in that tiny window of the present and all the rest is in our memories. Our basal ganglia, the sequence engine in our brain, is probably keeping track of the beat, while still other parts of our brain — likely parts of the frontal lobes — are anticipating what will come next.

And in our doddering old age, when our own minds begin to collapse around us like Mayan ruins, when words fail us, when even the faces of our own children become unfamiliar, it is interesting to note that music is still left to us. It may have to do with the fact that music is widely divested through the human brain, more so than almost any other single human pursuit. It's an exaptation from a whole number of neural networks, from memory to emotion, from movement to our construction of the social self. It is something fired hard in the first few years of our lives. And even as death closes over us, it is still there, playing resolutely along in our fading mind. A last fragile whiff of something at the very centre of who we are.

PART THREE
RITUALS OF SOUND

11

THE SOUTH PACIFIC
THE SINGING OF WHALES

I SAW WHALES FOR THE FIRST TIME OFF THE PANHANDLE OF ALASKA. We were flying out to Haida Gwaii to see the ancient totem poles of the Haida people. Our Cessna float plane glided out over the steel grey ocean, mountains rearing up ahead of us and the whole of the Pacific beyond them. "There," said the pilot, looking down over his side window. He banked the plane and dropped a thousand feet to skim over the water. A black shape crested up below us, then another beside it. "Those are humpbacks," he said, turning to me with a grin. "Some of the largest whales on the planet."

The whales dipped back under the dark waters of the Hecate Straits. This was feeding season for them, but it would not be long before they began their great migration, slipping out into open ocean, coursing five thousand kilometres to their southern breeding grounds.

I imagined them, as big as dirigibles, gliding a hundred metres beneath the surface. I could picture a cathedral shaft of light angling down across their mountainous backs, down through the milky green waters. A burst of silver bubbles would sparkle out of their blowholes and, though we couldn't hear it above, it would be the call of a mother to her calf, sounding her voice out across the cold and silent depths.

Sound carries through water four times faster than it carries through air, so it shouldn't have come as a surprise that whales sing. But it did. It wasn't until 1971 that we discovered the songs of the humpback whales. And that's when we realized we were not the only musicians on the planet.

We can tell a lot from other species. Remember the elephants and the fact that they can't sync rhythmically with each other? That's important and it tells as much about us as it does about them. We've been using animals to define ourselves for a long time. For many years it was thought that humans could be differentiated from the rest of the world's animals by the fact that no other species made tools. Then, in 1960, Jane Goodall's work with chimpanzees in the wilds of Tanzania blew that one out of the water. The chimps not only made simple tools, they also planned their use, seeing even before they were fashioned what might be needed, how that implement could be constructed, and then actually using it for that purpose. So that definition of humanity was out.

Others have tried to define our species by our use of language. But then there was Koko the gorilla and her acquisition of sign language. And Koko was not just mimicking things. She actually made up sentences and produced ideas, like naming her pet kitten, and that could not be accounted for by simply repeating what she saw the researchers doing.

So that left us with music. For a while there was a lot of interest in songbirds. Darwin, for one, presumed that because songbirds were singing to attract mates, then that must be the basis for human music as well. It was all about sexual selection. Well, clearly that's not all there is to music and the consensus now is that what birds are doing is instinctual and not really like human music at all.

But what the humpback whales do is very much like what we do. And not just in singing. Humpback whales also make social sounds that are probably analogous to language. These are just short grunts and cries, nothing more than the briefest and most simple of communications. A "wop" sort of sound is used by a mother who is locating her calf. It's a basic "Where are you now?" utterance. The "thwop" sound, meanwhile, is used when a male is locating another male, and something called a grunt train is used when different pods are joining up during the great migration.

Humpback whales in singing position. (Courtesy of Dr. Louis M. Herman/NOAA)

But none of this is whale song. The songs of the humpbacks are complex and lengthy, truly one of the most remarkable phenomena in all the animal kingdom. Their songs consist of different themes, like a symphony, and the songs they sing can go on for as long as twenty minutes. The whales make an exact sequence of sounds — a grunt and then a long, descending squeal and then a rhythmic bellowing, for example. They repeat this a few times in exactly the same sequence, and then all these repeats form, for lack of a better word, a "theme." Each full whale song is made up of five to seven of these themes. There's nothing random about this. They know what they're doing. It's planned and ordered and structured and very much the sign of a higher intelligence.

◀ ⦔ **LISTEN 11.1**

What really makes it different from birdsong is that it has at least three hierarchical levels. No other creatures but humans do this. Essentially, this is how both language and music work. In language, we use phonemes — the single sounds of vowels and consonants — and build them up to make words. That's one level. We pattern these into sentences using grammatical rules. We know now, in fact, that our brains are hardwired to generate perfectly grammatical sentences, at least in our mother tongue. And that's the second level. Finally, we pattern these sentences into whole ideas — telling a story or a joke, outlining an argument, whatever it is — a feat of three hierarchical levels which allows us to communicate pretty much any thought, no matter how complex.

So that's language, and it's fairly straightforward. But we also do this with music. We start with individual pitches and build them up into a second hierarchical level of melodic phrases. Then we go up to a third level, arranging these phrases into the verses and choruses and bridges that make up a whole song. Professional musicians pick up new songs easily because they've become very good at chunking out all this information. They'll pick out the underlying chord pattern in a sixteen-bar melodic structure and be quite adept at filling in the melody — even improvising variations that fit perfectly. All of it is structured hierarchically. Our great big human brains are really good at that, and apparently so are whale brains.

There is a lot of overlap between language and music. They seem to have come from the same evolutionary path. So what exactly is the difference? More importantly, why is there a difference? Why should we have these two separate systems?

Within the auditory cortex, both domains seem to have each staked out their land claims. We know this absolutely because in stroke victims it's not unusual for a patient to suffer the loss of language (aphasia) but completely retain all of their musical abilities. The reverse is true as well — it's possible to lose your musical abilities but retain language.

Even humpback whale brains seem to have this distinction between language and music. Their social communications, such as the call of a mother to locate her calf, are brief and relatively simple. They are clearly utterances that involve a relaying of information. Music doesn't do that. And whale song, in particular, is something much more sublime.

So why? Why is it we need two separate systems of auditory production?

I saw the whales again in the dying days of December. I was out on a fishing boat in the Hawaiian Islands between Lanai and Molokai and Maui. Okay, I won't lie. It was a stag party. A nephew of mine was getting married and we'd planned a sort of pirate party for him out there on the water. We'd all donned pirate hats and were drinking beer and "ahoy mate-ing" one another. We were enjoying the sunshine and only half fishing and when one of us passed by another — maybe on the way to get another beer — we'd laugh and growl out a "yar," and say "shiver me timbers" or some such nonsense.

But every few minutes, someone would point off to the horizon and there would be a humpback whale, pretty far off, breaching the metal green waters. We'd just see a black hump appear and a splash of frothing spray and we'd hoot and holler, "Thar she blows."

This was the same population of humpbacks I'd seen off of Alaska. Humpbacks live throughout the world's seas — many different populations like different cultures or different nations. They all have their set migration routes, Australia to the Antarctic, Bermuda to the Grand Banks. The population I kept seeing spend their summers in the krill-filled waters off the coast of British Columbia and Alaska while they spend their winters down here, always exactly in the area between these three Hawaiian islands.

There's a sort of mini continental shelf here, a sandy floor three hundred metres down. It's bathed in tropical sun and the water is still and clear and more or less undisturbed by winds or storms or rain. These are the mating grounds of this particular population. This is where they come to frolic and make babies. And this is where they sing.

The songs can be heard over a good hundred and fifty kilometres of ocean, maybe more in the days before shipping lanes and the noise pollution of propellers. I've heard that you can sometimes hear them yourself if you're snorkelling in a quiet bay, though many of the frequencies are low and down near the very bottom of our human range of hearing.

I saw a whale, later, from the shore. It seemed to be moving with real purpose, maybe four hundred metres out from the beach and parallel to it. I watched it as it went past a sea kayaker. I'm not even sure that he saw the black bulge of its back going by. Then, ploughing straight ahead, and staying near the surface, I saw it pass by a sailboat, not ten metres off its port side. Someone was standing on the deck and I could see her head swivel in amazement. She yelled something and then I could see that someone else was in the water, just swimming up to the back of the boat, from where I guess they'd launched themselves for a swim. And then the whale was gone, breaching, its tail fins rising up one last time before submerging back into the depths.

One strange thing about the whale song is that it's only the males that do it. And they only sing here in the mating grounds. They don't sing in the northern feeding grounds so, obviously, there is something Darwinian about it all. At first glance, it would seem that these songs are simply "displays," either to gain the attention of an impressionable female or to ward off a male competitor. That's a part of it, for sure, but then why all the complexity? Why the themes and why the length? Why not a simple grunt or two and get on with it?

Well, truly, we don't know yet. There's something going on and we're still trying to get to the bottom of it. Another curious thing is that sometimes — but not always — the singing is associated with a pair of males who seem to be working together. It may be that they're somehow coordinating their efforts in corralling and blocking a desirable female. Another idea is that the song is a sort of sonar. The complexity of all the frequencies may give the males an exact reading on how far away they are from another male, how big that other male is, and just what direction he's heading. Not necessarily in terms of aggression or territoriality, but more like a sort of air traffic control — well, if you're going that way, then I'll go this way.

But we still think there's more to it than that. These are not primitive sounds. They're structured and rich and we can't help but think there's an element of aesthetic pleasure in putting it all together.

We met the rest of the wedding party that night for a Hawaiian *luau* in the old town of Lahaina. A luau, of course, is the traditional feast, usually involving a pig that's been roasted on hot coals all day in a pit dug in the sand. There's also *poi*, a traditional foodstuff that seems to have the consistency and taste of wallpaper paste. There's all kinds of fish too and, in these modern days, lots of alcohol.

In the old days there had to be a reason for the celebration. A luau was held to mark an event, a wedding or a birthday, for example. They were parties and there were performances and dancing.

Ours was a bit of a tourist affair, and after eating, the program of events said there'd be a performance of traditional Hawaiian music. I braced myself and got ready for some hula dancing, for some grass skirts and tacky ukulele music.

In fact, that's not exactly what happened. Actually, not at all.

What they did perform was called *Hula Kahiko*, an ancient art form of drumming and chants and, yes, a little bit of hip-swaying dance. It was the real traditional music and the first thing they performed was a sort of homage to their ancestors who came up in outrigger canoes from Tahiti some thousand years before. The chants are a sort of oral history for a language that had no written system up until the arrival of the missionaries. And we know now that the oral history is pretty much true. The first settlers of Hawaii came up from Tahiti and the Marquesas and would have crossed some three thousand kilometres of open ocean in canoes, relying mostly on star maps.

The drumming was ferocious and the dancing was graceful. There are schools that pass down these traditions and, according to the ancient ways, if a single mistake is made in the performance — one dancer out of step, one drum beat smacking before it's time — it's all rendered invalid. It's unlucky and disrespectful to make a mistake, so the performance here was really quite impressive.

After the homage to the ancestors, a lone man came out onto the stage. He was elderly, his long grey hair tied back with banana leaves. He had a huge tattoo on his shoulder that looked like a Polynesian star map, and he sat down beside a drum called an *ipu*. This is a thoroughly Hawaiian invention. It's made from two calabash gourds fastened together, a big one and a smaller one on top. The old man played it by bumping it on the ground, which produces a low, resonant thump, while at the same time slapping on the side of it with his open hand, which gave a sort of pinging thwap. He syncopated these two into a rhythm and chanted over top of it a traditional love song filled with all those lovely Polynesian vowel sounds.

◀⧼ **LISTEN 11.2**

There's little doubt that the first music was simply the human voice, intoning out sounds at a time when maybe music and language weren't that greatly differentiated. And I was hearing the echo of that here. It was just a slight heightening of the prosody and rhythm that is inherent in language anyway. And chanting in the Hawaiian language — a language filled with breathy vowels — is like no other.

Language and music, as I said, have taken over different bits of auditory real estate in the brain. It may sound counterintuitive, but basically language has commandeered our perception of timbre — of the sound of sound — and that's because language, at its base, is phonetic. Each phoneme (each letter in the alphabet in simple terms) actually represents a certain timbre produced by the vocal folds in our larynx. Vowels are a pure vocal sound formed by shaping the back of our throats with our musculature. Try it — a, e, i, o, u — you can feel it in your throat, how it changes slightly to make each one. Consonants are no more than the final shaping of those sounds by our lips and tongue and teeth. It's all timbre. This is at the root of how we make languages — any language.

So, language has carved out timbre as its foundation. Music, on the other hand, uses pitch and rhythm. But that still doesn't give us any reason as to why the two should be separate. And that's the chief question here.

Language, obviously, has to do with the transmission of meaning. But music is a hard one. The partial answer at least is that it reinforces social bonds. It's like a language of affect, a language of emotion if you prefer, and it helps us to understand others, to synchronize ourselves with others. That's the theory I've been playing out, and it has its merits and certainly its proofs, but it doesn't seem to be the whole answer. It doesn't seem as obvious as our need for language and the communication of meaning. Defining music as a means for bonding us into groups simply doesn't explain the power of it. There's got to be more.

The later parts of the performance at the luau were what I'd been expecting. It was a modern hula dance — grass skirts, coconut bras, ukuleles — the works. It's another example of what's called "invented tradition." In Hawaiian, this form is *auana*, which means to "drift" or "wander" and what that means is that it's drifted away from the more traditional dances and chants. Oh, some of the same components are there, the wiggling hips and gentle hand movements, open hands lapping like waves, but it's all been pretty much made up in the last hundred years or so. I'd seen a hula dance performance over on the heavily touristed Waikiki Beach and I remember that one of the songs they sang was in English and had to do with a Jeep ride up into the mountains. Now, correct me if I'm wrong, but I don't believe the Jeep was a traditional form of transport for the ancient Polynesians, nor, I think, did they speak English.

So, anyway, this was what I was expecting. And I've got nothing against it. The musicians and dancers were clearly professional. The instruments were modern — including even a steel guitar — and although the flowers were plastic the performers were still putting their hearts into it, and the crowd seemed to like it.

Music and dance do this — actually, language does too. They drift away from the original. They change with the times. They meet foreign influences and incorporate them. There's nothing wrong with it. There's no reason, particularly, to be purists about tradition. Things change. Ironically, it's the way things have always been.

A couple of nights later, after the boys had put away their pirate games and the women had held their bridal shower, we all met for the wedding. It was exquisite. Out on a promontory, above the crashing sea, my nephew and his new wife said their time-honoured vows. She was in white. He was in a tux. There were real flowers and the father walked the bride in to the serenade of a guitar player who played the most amazing song. It was the Hawaiian version of "Over the Rainbow." At least a few people in the audience started daubing their eyes. Tears were flowing now. The total effect of the ceremony, the setting, the music, and, of course, our happiness for these two young people was all creating, well, something as close to magic as we are able to experience in this life.

I don't know if you've heard this version of "Over the Rainbow." It was first done by a man who has become pretty much a legend on the islands, Israel Kamakawiwoʻole. He had to have been at least three hundred pounds — a huge guy — and I don't even know how he got his hands around that little ukulele, but he had the voice of a deep baritone angel, and something about it, his particular take on the song, just worked. It's an extraordinary adaptation and beautifully suited to a wedding.

The most important moments of our life are almost always accompanied by song: birthdays, weddings, funerals, all the rituals that mark our passing through this life. For each, there are certain words we say and things we do. There are certain clothes we wear and ways we move. We have birthday candles and Christmas trees and wedding rings. All of them are part of the complex cultural rites we've developed over the centuries. We change it up sometimes — have everyone go off to Hawaii for the ceremony, for instance — but at its heart the ritual is the same. We are celebrating the same essential fact, the same essential moment in one's life.

And over it all is music. Language can't do this. Language has to be listened to and focused on for it to sink in. Music, meanwhile, has this fantastic ability to work in conjunction with other things. It can be laid on top of a visual or a movement or a taste. We can drive a car and listen to music quite easily, though we now know it's not a good idea to talk on a cellphone. Music works with other things — that's one of its essential properties. So it works with our rituals. In fact, it works beautifully.

The islands around Tahiti are the single most beautiful place I've ever been. That's what I was thinking as I stepped off the ferry. I'd been hop-scotching from one island to another and had just crossed a narrow strait called the Sea of the Moon. Behind me was Moorea and ahead of me were the mountains of Tahiti, rearing up out of a bright turquoise lagoon. It was like someone had taken a bolt of thick green felt and just draped it over the entire island. Only the upper peaks of the mountains scissored up through the greenery like shards of black glass.

These islands, the French Society Islands, are at the heart of Polynesian culture today. I'd come to see the celebrations called Hieva I Tahiti, a month-long affair of dancing and music and canoe races that celebrates the traditional ways. In Papeete, the clapboard town that serves as the capital, I got onto the public transport simply called Le Truck. They're basically pickup trucks with seats in the back.

We trundled down a road strewn with fallen palm fronds. It was breezy here and the truck swayed with the winds, chugging down along the south coast of Tahiti Nui. On board was Sylvia, a woman from

Switzerland. I got talking to her. This was the best place on Earth, so she'd decided, one way or another, that she was just going to move here.

She had a fascination with Polynesian culture, and we talked in the back of the truck about their history. The Polynesians were great seafarers. They crossed pretty much the entire Pacific Ocean in outrigger canoes, navigating thousands of kilometres of open ocean with nothing more than star maps and their knowledge of cloud patterns and sea currents.

"You know the star maps?" she said.

"There's one on Oahu, carved in stone like a giant compass."

"This I have not seen."

"There's a hut there," I said, "where they keep a reconstruction of one of their ocean crossing canoes. They call it Iosepha. I think that was the name."

"It is big?"

"It's kind of a catamaran, you know..." I put my hands side by side to show the double hull. "I don't know, maybe twenty metres long. Pretty big."

"They would have pigs aboard," she said. "And coconuts. They would have to travel for a long way."

"The people who built the Iosepha actually sailed it from Tahiti to Hawaii. Three thousand kilometres. Just like their ancestors. It took twenty-seven days."

"And no GPS?"

"Nothing. I guess they had some elders on board. Just the ancient ways."

"It is quite remarkable."

"It is. It is."

The truck lurched to a stop at the side of the highway. I didn't see much there but the driver called "Arahurahu Marae," and that was our stop all right. We hopped out of the back and walked down a little path into the forest. There, at the entrance, was a tiki, a carved statue of a head, about the size of a person. Sylvia gave a little squeal of delight.

"She is just like the ones on Rapa Nui."

"Rapa Nui?"

"Easter Island. You see?"

"Oh yeah." It did look like one of those big bug-eyed stone heads from Easter Island. That, in fact, was as far east as the Polynesians made it. They'd spread out over fifteen million square kilometres from New Zealand to Rapa Nui — just thirty-five hundred kilometres off the coast of Chile. There's been talk that the Polynesians reached South America, but really there's no evidence of it. The silent statues of Easter Island seem to be the end of their travels.

Even in Tahiti, there's not a whole lot left to see of the original culture. But there are some places and one of them is here at Arahurahu Marae. *Marae* are ancient ceremonial sites. When we walked down to it, past the tiki, it was nothing more than a raised platform of rocks maybe the size of a tennis court. It had seen animal sacrifices, and once Captain Cook witnessed a human sacrifice on the marae, an offering to Oro, the god of war. Some poor captive was brought up and his head was cleaved in with an axe. Strangely enough, Cook's own head would get bashed in just a few months later on the shores of the big island of Hawaii to the north. That was his third and final journey to the South Pacific, an ignoble end to a great explorer.

There was going to be a performance here tonight as part of the Hieva I Tahiti, but we had some time to kill so we wandered down to the nearby beach. There was no one there. Just a stretch of white sand and the long, unbroken horizon where the turquoise sea met a cerulean sky.

"Do you speak Tahitian?" I asked. "I mean, if you want to live here."

"I am from Geneva. I am French."

"Yes, but …"

"I know, I know. You will tell me how the French tested their atomic bombs here at Bikini Atoll."

"It's not so far from here."

"I am not French."

"But you just said …"

"I am Swiss. I speak French and many other languages. I speak your English."

"It's true. My French is not very good."

"It's a shame."

"It's true. But I only wondered if you had an interest in …"

"I will learn Tahitian. I am learning already."

"Apparently," I said, "all the Polynesian languages are fairly similar. The Tahitians call themselves Maohi. The New Zealanders are Maori. It's pretty close."

"Pretty close. Like France and Switzerland," she laughed.

"But …"

"I am only making a joke with you."

"Oh."

"We must go back now, I think. The show, she will be starting."

In the time we'd been gone, they'd set up some long wooden benches. The torches had been lit and they flickered now in a line around the marae. The place had begun to fill up and as the sun set down through the foliage, the tropical twilight clapping to a quick close, the crowd hushed and the ceremony began.

It was the reconstruction of a meeting of two peoples. A canoe had come down from the Marquesas Islands to the northwest. They'd come to marry off a girl from one of their *ariki* — their noble families — to another family on Tahiti. The girl was carried in on the shoulders of a giant Marquesian warrior like a father would carry a four-year-old. Others carried offerings, like trade goods, coconuts, weavings, and roast meat. The Tahitian man she was to be married to wore the *maro-ura*. This is a sort of waist band of red feathers reserved only for the highest ranking chiefs.

As they carried her in, the high priest launched into a chant to invoke the presence of the gods. I didn't know the meaning of the words but there it was again, the prosody that exists between language and music. The sing-song of vowels and the rhythmic patterns of the prose. There were drums, too. And then, finally, there was singing called *himene tarava*. The singers sat over by a thatch hut at the edge of the marae. The high priest was standing now, performing hand gestures, and the singers opened their voices and filled the air. At the end of some of the phrases, I noticed, they let the note glide down. I recognized that. The old man at the Hawaiian luau had sung that way. It was a sort of meme, I guess, an accent or characteristic of Polynesian music. Something that marked the music of this place, the music of these people.

I thought again about our rituals. I thought about my nephew's wedding in Maui. Was this one really so different? There was the pageantry and protocols. There was the clothing and the food — but most of all there was the music.

When it was all over, the crowds disappeared and a few people lined up for Le Truck. Under a blanket of stars Sylvia and I rode all the way back to the north coast of Tahiti, jumbling along in the back with a mother, a grandmother, and her kids. None of them spoke English. The children chirped happily in a mixture of French and Polynesian and the mother's head bobbed sleepily under a straw hat the size of a dinner platter. To our left, the ocean came into view, dark now with a shimmering strip of light coming down across the water from the moon. There were whales out there, I thought, though the time for their singing was over.

They don't like to talk about it, but there were once cannibals on the islands of Fiji. This was the furthest west I'd be going on this trip. I'd flown in from Western Samoa and I could see the island of Vanua Levu out the little airplane window to the north. There are two main islands here, though there are hundreds of smaller ones trailing along in an archipelago. In a few more minutes, the plane glided down to land on the largest of the islands, Viti Levu.

The Polynesians had been here (it was one of the first island chains they came to) and although traces of them remain genetically and culturally, they have largely been supplanted by a Melanesian people, darker in skin colour and related to the islanders of Papua New Guinea and possibly, though more distantly, the Australian Aboriginal peoples. At any rate, these Melanesians were fierce, war-like people who, yes, did occasionally feast on human meat. One Fijian chief named Ratu Udre Udre consumed some 872 people, a number we know from a pile of rocks he kept as a record of his, ah, dinners.

Many of the entrees were apparently enemies fallen in battle. But other ceremonial occasions demanded sacrifices too. A chief's long-house usually had a body buried under each corner post, and when a new canoe was built, it was rolled out along the beach on human rollers who were crushed by its weight. All this was supposed to bring good luck. And it was so far out of whack with European mores that early explorers like Captain Cook completely avoided the isles. They were called the Cannibal Isles, and for a long time not a whole lot was known about them.

Today the islanders call those days the "Time of the Devil." And this tells you that the missionaries did finally get a foothold on the place. A few got roasted in the process, but they eventually changed almost everything, from the food to the clothing to the music.

I stayed a day in a place called New Town just by the airport and then made my way out to a little slice of heaven called Beachcomber Island. There are all sorts of these lagoon-fringed paradises just off the main island. They filmed the movie *Castaway* out here, and these little islands are pretty much exactly what you would think of when you imagine being stranded on a desert island. They're edged with powdery white sand and have a grove of palm trees in the middle. Beachcomber Island was about the size of a neighbourhood park back home. You could walk around the whole circumference in maybe twenty minutes.

Even as I stepped off the boat, the *Tui Tai* — an old double-masted schooner that looked like something out of *The African Queen* — I saw two middle-aged Fijian women smashing the hell out of something on the beach. They were both banging away with clubs and when I wandered over they looked up at me with frazzly hair and ragged clothes. But they both smiled and laughed. One of them held up a long stringy piece of meat. It was an octopus (which I would taste later that night) and they were tenderizing it. Clobbering it for all they were worth.

I spent my days there snorkelling and, well, yeah, beachcombing. Under the water I saw brain coral and schools of neon fish darting like fluorescent tubes at a rave party. I saw spider crabs and a starfish that looked as if it were made out of blue foam rubber. It curled one of its starry tentacles as I drifted past, and though I stopped to listen a few times, I did not hear the whales underwater, just the whispering of surf and the slosh of water around my prying ears.

There would be a different humpback whale population off of these shores, but the rules of their songs would be much the same. Only the males sing, and every male in the population sings the same song. Over time, slight changes will appear, but the thing is, these alterations — a grunt here in bar number three — will be taken up by the entire male population. And over several years, like the invented traditions in human music, the song of an entire population will eventually change quite radically. Though, in lockstep fashion, they will all keep to the same song.

My question is, why? If whale song is only meant as a sexual display, then why would they sing the same song? If that were the case, wouldn't they be trying to outdo each other with their vocal pyrotechnics? No, this concentration on maintaining the "song" is the beginning of cultural thought. It shows intelligence and patience and purpose.

On Beachcomber Island, every Tuesday night, they put on a bit of a cultural show. It's just put on by the cleaning staff mostly, indigenous Fijians, big mountainous men and women like the ones I'd seen pounding the octopus. They must have hired some of them in part for their musical abilities, because they really could sing and dance. In fact, Fiji is one of those cultures where they have a word that encompasses both dance and music. It's *meke* (the name for a ritual performance, really), where the dancers and musicians are all very much a part of one single thing.

In the back, three or four men sat down behind their drums. Well, they're not really drums, I guess, because they don't have a skin. The most traditional percussion instrument is a *lali*. It's kind of like a huge wood block the size of a small coffee table. It's carved out of solid hardwood and played with sticks. In the old days, the lali was used to call people together to announce births and deaths and warn of enemies approaching.

The other main piece of percussion is the *derua*. They're tubes of bamboo that you hold upright and tamp down on the ground. They're different lengths so they set up this ringing plunk that's really quite nice. Over all this is the singing, and even in the warrior dances, the vocals are rich in harmony.

One of the first mekes was a warrior dance. There were two big, barrel-chested guys. They wore scimitar-like teeth necklaces and they came out swinging war clubs like baseball bats. Behind them two drummers thunked out a rhythm and sang a sort of two-part harmony chant. The warriors stomped and whooped and googled out their eyes like Muhammad Ali staring you down in the boxing ring.

In the middle, the tempo slowed and the warriors went into a sort of skulking lope, as if they were sneaking up behind you in the jungle. Then the drummers cracked into form again and the dancers swung their clubs wildly, ready to smash in brains and bones. Finally, like a rock band drummer crashing to a halt, they stopped frozen in their final pose, one of them looking directly into my eyes, staring me down. It was intimidating as hell.

◀ᴇ LISTEN 11.3

It goes without saying that all this was very much like the *haka* in New Zealand. You've probably seen it before. The All Blacks, the rugby team, are famous for performing it just before a match, right in front of the other team. They slap their knees and chests and bug out their eyes, a lot like the warrior dance in Fiji.

The thing is, the warrior dancing I saw in Fiji is Melanesian, and the Maori haka in New Zealand is Polynesian. It's a powerful meme. Intimidation and martial displays are very useful tools. Like the mock charges of elephants or grizzly bears, you can sometimes get the result you want without any real violence happening at all. And it's perhaps no surprise then that we find this ritualized in music as well.

Maybe the whales were doing this but I still think it's more. Whales have a rudimentary culture. There are different populations of humpbacks with entirely different migration routes, and these serve as something like "nations" of whales. One of the most astounding pieces of research I came across was from Dr. Ellen Garland and her colleagues at the University of Queensland in Australia. They studied 745 humpback whale songs from six different whale populations. They spanned an eleven-year period and what they found surprised them to no end. The whale songs (like memes) actually jumped populations. It may be that a single whale crossed to a new population and brought along his former culture's song with him, or it may be that the males of one population can actually hear the others just at the borders of their own territory — and they simply like what they hear.

For some reason, these songs get transmitted from west to east across the Pacific, following the same course as the Polynesian migrations. That's probably a coincidence, but the point is that the complex whale songs, like a video that's gone viral, seem to migrate across populations, out across the broad Pacific, passing from population to population, from nation to nation. It's kind of like Bob Marley's reggae phrasings sweeping around the world or the minuets of Mozart being played in China.

Clearly, these whales are conscious of the aesthetics of what they're doing. Their songs have something to do with mating, no doubt — either impressing a female or warding off a competitor — but that's only the start. It has become something more ceremonial. Something ritualized and sophisticated.

At the end of the evening on Beachcomber Island, a number of women came out. They had big black dots painted on their cheeks. I recognized the two women I'd first seen when I arrived. They all lined up and without accompaniment began to sing one of the most beautiful songs I've ever heard.

It's called "Isa Lei," and if I understand right, it's the Fijian song of farewell. These women were in rags. They were barefoot and yet they sang in three- and four-part harmonies. In counterpoint and polyphony. It was as gorgeous as any cathedral choir. It was solemn and, as a farewell should be, winsome and poignant. And there on that tropical beach, once more, I felt the chills run down my spine at the sheer beauty of the music. The women smiled shyly when they'd finished to an enthusiastic round of applause, then they ducked back into the kitchens to scour the big cooking pots and get ready for the next day's catch. I was left only with the magic. With the soul-stirring elegance of what they'd just sung.

12

BALI

THE DANCE OF SPIRITS

WHEN A BABY IS BORN IN BALI, IT IS NOT CONSIDERED HUMAN. INSTEAD, they are seen as spirits, tiny gods, who have descended from the heavens. When the little god is twelve days old, a shrine of bananas and flowers is placed by its cradle. At forty-two days a ceremony is held to cleanse the child's mother. For the first ninety days of a child's life in Bali, its feet are never allowed to touch the ground. It is carried everywhere. The ground in Bali, you see, is the domain of demons.

Everything here is either the domain of gods or demons. When I first came into the town of Ubud, I was struck by how many mangy dogs there were roaming the streets. They looked a little vicious, and I thought that they just needed good homes, maybe a little food. Well, they weren't going to get it here because dogs, in the peculiarities of Balinese Hinduism, are most definitely demons.

I'd landed in Dempassar in the evening after a bruising marathon of a flight, so I didn't see much on the trip up to Ubud. My mind was a jet-lagged blur. In the morning I drank a cup of coffee that was half grounds, a powerful muddy slurry. It didn't really help. I only made it a few steps out onto the sidewalk before I stepped down onto something with a crunch.

Shit, I thought. I looked down and there was a little square of woven banana leaves, now flattened. It had contained a mound of rice and some flower petals. This was a *canang*, a ritual offering. They were all down the sidewalks and all over the town of Ubud, on street corners and on mailboxes, in doorways and in phone booths, on almost any flat surface that would hold them.

The ones on the ground were meant to placate the demons. The ones higher up were for the more beneficent spirits. A dog trundled up the sidewalk towards me, eyeing the scattered rice. That'd be his best meal for the day, so I stepped away and let the tight ecosystem of Balinese deities run its natural course.

On the 105th day of a child's life, the body and spirit are deemed to have become finally and inextricably bound together, and on this propitious day the baby receives a name and its feet are allowed to touch the Earth for the first time. A child's first birthday is celebrated at 210 days, when the baby's hair is finally cut and an offering is made to announce that the child is a part of the village.

Much later, when a child enters puberty, his or her canine teeth are filed down flat. The sharp canine teeth are considered the mark of demons, you see, though the thought passed my mind that perhaps teenagers the world over really are evil incarnate.

I wandered down Monkey Forest Road, past shops filled with woven mats and wood carvings. The workmanship was incredible. One carving was of a twisting dragon, huge, the size of a couch, and it had all the polished perfection of a Michelangelo. I'd heard about this already. Bali is a land of artists. Every village has its own specialty, such as batiks and delicate hand-painted eggs. And everywhere there is the plonking and chiming of gamelan, a music like no other on the planet.

I walked along, still in a tropical haze. Mopeds clocked by me, belching out smoke. The pavement was hot and uneven. A few shopkeepers called out to me. "Only looking," they said. "Only looking."

I thought that was my line.

At the bottom of the street, the pavement swung off to the left out into the countryside, but right at the bend there was a patch of forest and a big sign that said "Monkey Forest Sanctuary."

I went in, and there were monkeys all right — long-tailed macaques with beards and tufts of whiskers like wizened old men. They were nasty little critters though, and after I saw them in action I felt sure they had a much better claim to the demon moniker than either teenagers or the poor dogs. They leapt at a pair of Japanese tourists, pulling at the man's camera strap and running off with the girl's water bottle. Outside the front gate, there's a stand where you can buy bananas to feed to these little ninjas. It's a big mistake. The monkeys congregate just inside the gate and mob anyone who's carrying anything vaguely banana-like.

Past the entrance, they're not so bad. A cobblestone pathway leads down into the forest and soon you are in the quiet of the trees. Every village in Bali has three distinct temples. It depends on where they are, compass-wise, in relation to the village. Down in the Monkey Forest Sanctuary sits one of the big temples, the Pura Dalem temple. This means the temple of the dead.

Balinese Hinduism has all the complex pantheon of Hindu gods, of course. There was a statue of Ganesh, the elephant-headed god, and the temple itself was dedicated to Durga the inaccessible, a female goddess associated with death. The Balinese also have a lot of their own, sometimes animist deities. Here at the temple of death, there's a figure called Rangda, a sort of witch monster, a manifestation of Durga, and she's devouring two children, cramming the innocents into her mouth. She's set up near the entrance to the temple, and the idea is to scare off the evil spirits. It didn't seem to work on the monkeys. I saw a workman with a trowel, diligently working at some mortar on a retaining wall. Off to the side, he'd propped his bicycle up against the wall, and every few minutes a monkey would swing down and bite into his bicycle seat, ripping off tufts of yellow foam. The workman would rise from his work and yell and the monkey would scamper away. A minute later it would be back, clambering down the wall and onto the bicycle for another go at the apparently delicious bicycle seat foam.

I walked around the side of the temple. The sculptures here are extraordinary. They're old (bits of this temple date back more than seven hundred years) but the detailing is fantastic. All over the temple, carvings of turtles and curling serpents and scowling bloated faces were locked in stone.

Towards the back, a wide courtyard butted up against the forest. The temple entrance there was guarded by two colossal statues, one of a wild boar, the other of a lioness. In front of them, on the ground, a man sat in a sarong. He had long black hair and, unaccountably, he held in his hands a didgeridoo. At first I thought it was a bamboo flute — I'd seen those here in the shops — but when he put the didgeridoo to his lips, there was no mistaking it. He was clearly Balinese, so why he was sounding out an Australian Aboriginal didgeridoo in this most holy of places, I'm not sure. He sat facing the statued animals as if lulling them into compliance. He sat with one leg tucked beneath him and the other stretched out so that the tip of the long didgeridoo rested on the toes of his upturned foot. The low drone drifted over the ancient stones, rolling and humming and buzzing like the breath of the gods.

"Writing about music," Elvis Costello is reported to have said, "is like dancing about architecture." Well, okay then. Let's dance.

Under a scimitar moon, I walked one evening up to the Ubud Palace. In the twilight, I could see it glimmering in the distance. They'd set up lanterns along the cinnamon-coloured walls and I could hear the tentative chiming of the gamelan orchestra players just nestling into their positions. Tonight was to be a performance of the Legong Dance, a story of love and kidnapping and a monkey god, all coming from the ancient Sanskrit epic the *Ramayana*.

I found myself a place to sit in an open space in front of one of the main gates to the palace. On either side of the gate was a row of musicians, already seated in front of their instruments. To the right was a row of instruments called *saron,* an instrument of shining metal bars, like gold bars stolen from a bank. The bars were actually bronze. They were set into polished wooden frames, like a xylophone embedded in a coffee table, and each musician sat on the ground behind his own saron, a strip of silk folded around his forehead like a piece of origami. All four men bonged out a sequence of notes in unison. They struck the bars with wooden hammers in their right hands and with their left deftly pinched the sound off again with a thumb and forefinger.

The four saron would all be made and tuned by the same master craftsman. They are all tuned together with each bronze bar being tuned to the corresponding bar in the next saron, shaving down the cast bronze, bevelling the edges so that they ring in an exact way together. In fact, they are tuned ever so slightly off from each other. This is done so precisely that the sound actually shimmers slightly. It's part of what makes gamelan unlike anything else on Earth. There is a perfection to everything, a precision that only comes from the most accomplished of artists.

The musicians clanged out repeating sets of motifs just a few notes long, simple pentatonic motifs filled with languid major sevenths. The motifs repeated and built and tumbled into the next pattern, deep gongs like staccato cathedral bells and high tinkling notes like wine glasses struck with a spoon. And all of it in exact lockstep pattern, repeating and building in a hypnotic construction of notes.

Sitting across from them, facing the saron row so that they frame each other like a mirror, are the *tromping* players. Tromping look like rows of upended brass kettles with knobs on top. The knobs are struck with a stick wrapped in rope. Five men sat here, the same silk headwraps on their foreheads, six or ten gong kettles on the ground in front of each, and they struck their tromping in counterpoint to the themes being set up across from them by the saron players.

Add a few cymbals for emphasis and a man playing a *kĕndang*, a double-headed wooden drum, tucked in the back — and actually a sort of conductor for the whole affair — and this makes up the full gamelan orchestra. It's a clockwork symphony of gongs, a typewriter flurry of clangs and bongs and clinks surging in simple five- and six-note patterns like waves cresting and burbling up onto the shore in a wash of seafoam.

◀⧽ LISTEN 12.1

Behind the musicians was the ornate gatehouse of the Ubud Palace. Several centuries ago this was once the royal residence. Six simple steps led up to a double wooden door, intricately carved with weaving vines and flower blossoms. Above the door, two storeys tall, rose a three-tiered confectionary of chiselled stone. The shapes, though all carved from stone, were organic, curving and swirling and rippling like cloth. Just above the wooden doors was the leering snout of a demon spirit and to either side of the steps the squatting sculptures of monkey gods, their midsections wrapped in checkered cloth, their foreheads covered with the same silken wraps as the musicians.

The gamelan clanked and washed over the walls for some moments before, at an unseen signal, the wooden doors burst opened and down the steps came the dancers. Four men stepped into the yard, their feet splayed, their shoulders hunched up, their eyes darting back and forth like flittering birds.

All these movements are part of the unique vocabulary of Balinese dance. This one was a *baris,* a marching warrior dance. Timed to the drum, the warriors grimaced and flicked their eyes and brought their knees up and to the side, holding a leg at a right angle before stomping down and lurching forward again. Their faces were heavy in makeup and they wore strips of cloth that dangled and danced with their movements. Their hands especially, fingers separated and arched back, curved further than human fingers should go.

At another signal from the drummer, the music stopped suddenly and the dancers held their place, though their eyes still flickered and their hands still fluttered. All these movements — a certain lurching glance, a flipping of the hand, a raised knee — all are tied to specific rhythmic structures in the music. They are the visual equivalent of the gongs and chimes sounding out around them. Even the curls and swirls in the stonework behind them reflected the intricacy of the dance and music. It's all one.

The warriors frog-marched off the stage, the gamelan petered out, and the stage cleared at last for the Legong dancers. This is what I'd come to see. Surprisingly, the principal dancers in the Legong are two girls who have not yet even reached puberty. The girls train for this role almost as soon as they are born. Gamelan music is played for babies when they are still in the womb. Then mothers, who were Legong dancers them-selves, upon seeing that they have had a baby girl, begin to show them the flickering eye movement, called *sĕlĕdet.* And the baby girls, as babies do, mirror the gestures much as they would a smile. As soon as the baby girls can walk, their mothers show them the basic moves, the arching of the fingers, the raised foot, the tilt of the head.

By the age of seven, the real formal training begins. When they are eleven or twelve, they are dancing in performances like this one, master dancers already, artisans of the highest standard. By the time they're fourteen, most Legong dancers have already retired. Imagine that.

Legong dancer in Bali.

The dance goes on for almost an hour, every step memorized, or deeper, every step and gesture becoming a part of the dancer's very being. Music and dance are intertwined here. Balance and a sense of movement, as I've said, are functions of the human ear, and the fluidity of a series of movements is lodged deep in the basal ganglia where automaticity is attained — the same kind of automatic complex muscle movements that allow us to walk or chew or ride a bike. They're tied, intimately, to the rhythms of our world. They are a part of music.

Throughout the story being told, the young Legong dancers take on several roles, miming different characters with the specific dance motifs that mark that character — something that every Balinese person in the audience would know but something that left me in confusion at times. The weight pressed more heavily on the right foot meant, at one point, that a different character was being portrayed.

A certain jingling in the fingers is called *jĕriring*. A wide-eyed darting glance is a *dadĕling*. It's an alphabet of gestures and positions, a semiotics of movement that ties directly in to what the music is doing. It ties in with the clothing and the makeup. It ties in with the gates of the Ubud Palace behind the dancers, and of course it ties in with the story they are telling.

In the end, good wins over evil and the kidnapped maiden is returned to her true love. The music rippling behind the story was unlike any I'd heard before and the movements of the dancers were strange and fantastically eccentric, but the story had a familiar, universal theme. It ended in happiness.

The gamelan sighed and clapped the lovers' happy reunion and the tropical night stilled at last, the performance done, and the shining scimitar of the moon walked me back to my room on the Monkey Forest Road.

The bemo trundled up into the volcanic hills. It was packed with people — a dilapidated minivan really, serving as a sort of cross-country taxi. We left from the Frog Pond Inn in Ubud and our driver was a young Balinese guy who'd for some reason taken the name Johnny and learned the harmonica. He wore his hair in a long ponytail and when we got out on the road he brought out his harmonica. He played a few little licks he'd made up himself, vaguely blues-like and not too bad, and then he turned to us with a broad smile. On the dashboard he had a little Hindu shrine that bounced as he drove. Taped to the passenger side mirror was a loop of red flowers. The mirror itself had been smashed off in some "a little too close" incident, so I assumed the flowers were meant to placate the mirror gods, the demons of traffic. Maybe, I thought, he should focus a little more on the road and a little less on the harmonica, but I let that go. He seemed a friendly guy.

Soon enough, the villages dropped away and we came up into the verdant central hills of Bali, where rice paddy terraces were carved into every slope. Everything was green and lush. The locals compare these hills to emeralds and say that the terraces are the cuts of a master jeweller. When the paddies are filled with water, they reflect the sky. They shimmer and sparkle.

Finally our bemo wound its way up a series of switchbacks with us heaving first one way and then the other in the bench seats in the back. My hand was pressed against the ceiling in a vain attempt at anchorage but the others had their cheeks alternately flattened up against the side windows and then up against me. We crested the rim of a volcano and a narrow winding roadway lined its rim. In the cauldron, a great lake sat still in the sun. "This," Johnny announced, "is holy lake. Lake Batur."

He pulled down a side road that led to the lake's edge. It was tranquil out there. No boats broke its surface and no villages lined its shore. Johnny pulled to a stop to let us out for photos. "Here," he said, before we'd got the doors opened. "Here is Pura Ulun Danu Batur temple."

Out on a promontory in front of us was a stupa, like a Japanese pagoda. It was different from the other temples I'd seen. "Water ceremony goes on here," Johnny explained.

"The water ceremony?"

"One time a year. The *subak* all come."

I'd heard of these subak. They are century-old organizations who control the rice production. One subak can oversee several villages and hundreds of rice paddies, essentially all the outflow from a single water source. These subak meet to plan dams and irrigation canals. They coordinate the planting and the harvesting of the rice, and all of it is woven around a meticulous calendar of gods and spirits. The religion here is called Agama Hindu Dharma, where *Agama* literally means water — the water religion. And the water goddess, Dewi Danu, is said to live here in Lake Batur.

"The priest, he make a water bottle," Johnny went on, pointing to the bottle lodged tightly between my knees. "Little water for each." He held up his hands, giving us a measure.

"A bottle?"

"No, not so much like this. It is bamboo."

"A cannister?"

"Yes, yes … like this. Bamboo jar fill with holy water. The subak have one for each."

"So," I said, "the priests give a bamboo container of holy water.…" I felt like I was supplying subtitles "… to each chief of the subak. It's ceremonial."

"Yes, it not enough for rice paddy … to fill. It is ceremony. Only ceremony."

"From here? From this lake?"

"Yes, exactly here."

All of Bali runs by this sort of clockwork of the gods, a ceremony and ritual for everything. A god and spirit for everything. They have the rice production down to a fine art. And there is more than enough for everyone. Funny enough, the World Bank tried to ply more fertilizer-friendly, pest-resistant rice hybrids on Bali in the 1990s. It was an utter disaster. The fertilizer washed down the streams and out into the ocean, destroying much of the island's natural coral reefs. And the production was not as high anyway. People went hungry for the first time in centuries.

The Balinese themselves had already developed the perfect system. They knew the cycles and they knew the soil. And I suppose they knew the gods. It took a while but the World Bank finally backed off and things are back now to the ways they'd developed over the centuries.

Margaret Mead, the famed anthropologist, came here in 1936. In her writings she offered the observation that such a remarkable culture could only have arisen in a place where the essentials of life are readily obtained. It's an old idea and, I suppose, a basic truth. All the ancient civilizations — the first towns and cities — naturally arose in places where the soil was good, the water supply ample, and the foodstuffs easily obtained.

And so it is on Bali. For a thousand years, the rice terraces ensured that the basic necessities were met. An intricate, perfect system of water management and rice harvest evolved and with this abundance of food came a culture rich in art. To this day, to an extent that is unrivalled anywhere else on Earth, Bali is an island of artists. In every village and tiny hamlet there are musicians and dancers, silversmiths and textile artists, woodcarvers and painters, and many of them are working at levels of sophistication and craftsmanship that are easily the equal of any classically trained artist in the West.

In these hills too are the villages of the bronze masters. The manufacture of the bronze gamelan takes place here. The precise mixture of the bronze — mostly copper and tin with smatterings of lead, zinc, arsenic, and silver — is a carefully guarded secret. The molten bronze is cast into the slabs of saron and the kettle shapes of the tromping.

Unlike almost anywhere else on Earth, the notes of the Balinese scales do not match the seven white notes and five black notes that the physics of wave frequency dictate. Instead, there are two scales here, an octave divided equally by five notes called *slendro* and one closer to ours, an octave divided equally by seven called a *pelog*. In Ubud I had heard slendro, and with all the harmonics of bronze and the way they are tuned to shimmer with each other, it sounded to me pretty close to the pentatonic scales found in China or Vietnam. It's not, though. By the old Greek method it's closer to an Aeolian scale with its prominent major seventh note, something that was rarely heard in the West until just over a hundred years ago.

A gamelan orchestra played at the Paris Exposition in 1889. A young Claude Debussy heard the strange tones and became enraptured, incorporating the wistful major sevenths and circular wave-like rhythms into his own compositions. Soon all of Europe was listening and the tiny island of Bali became the focus of musicologists and anthropologists from all around the world.

Tourism followed to such an extent that it's bred a sort of demonic intensity. It's a little hard to ignore sometimes. We climbed back into the bemo and Johnny took us east and up still further to the highest point on Bali. This is the volcano called Gunung Agung. The peak is at 10,308 feet (3,142 metres) so we're not talking any small potatoes here. This really is a fearsome mountain, and it's still active. It last blew its top in 1963.

There's a temple up on its slope, the mother of all temples, the largest and most important in all of Bali, the Pura Besakih. In 1963, when the molten lava began to stream down the mountain, a white hot river snapping and sparking, it suddenly split into two streams and wound around the temple, missing it by mere metres, leaving it completely unscathed. The Balinese look upon this as a sort of miracle. The gods, obviously, had spared the temple.

If only the gods spared it now. Even as we came into the parking lot, our bemo was attacked by hawkers and touts. I've never seen anything quite like it. We were mobbed. One woman threw a wooden carving in the slightly opened window, claiming that if we touched it we had bought it. We threw it out again.

Johnny seemed to find the whole thing quite funny. He pulled up a bit further and we managed to get out. We never did get up to the temple, though. There were booths where we had to pay an entrance fee, then past them we were surrounded by more wildly aggressive guides who insisted we could not go further without hiring one of them ... or all of them. We tried to make a break for it, and I remember that one of our crew started singing the *Mission Impossible* theme ... Dum Dum, Da Da, Dum Dum. It was madness. We finally gave up and slouched back to the bemo. Johnny was chuckling in the front seat, waiting for us.

I was a bit angry. "What's with these people?" I asked him. "Don't they want us to see the temple?"

"Oh yes."

"Then why are they making it so difficult? Look at them." There were still five or six of them hovering around our bemo, urging us — quite aggressively — to come out and hire them. "Why don't they get real jobs?"

"They have real jobs."

"They have too much time on their hands. Look at them." All up the pathway were dozens and dozens of so-called guides, sitting in any shade they could find, waiting to pounce on the next busload of tourists. "Why don't they learn a craft like the others?"

"Ah, sir, they know their art. They are very good at it."

"They're just sitting there."

"No, sir." Johnny beamed. "This is their job. They are harvesting the white coconuts."

"What?"

"They are harvesting the white coconuts."

I looked blank.

"You," Johnny laughed. "You are a white coconut."

On the way back down south, Johnny played a bit more on the harmonica. Then he got bored and put on a CD. It was Bob Marley. We passed back through the rice terraces, down past villages called Tegak and Klungkung. We wheeled past a place called the Temple of the Crazy Buffalo and all the time the bemo shook to the bass notes of reggae. All the time, Bob Marley's voice crackled and eased us. "Don't worry, 'bout a thing. Every little thing is gonna be all right." And it was. Our vanload of white coconuts wove down the mountain roads, back down through the lush rice terraces and off towards the coast.

In the evening, in the purple dusk, a fishermen walked knee-deep out in the surf holding a lantern high above his head. He paced slowly, a circle of light bobbing around him, looking down into the dark water for octopus or maybe sea cucumber. Across the bay behind him, the peaks of Gunung Agung rose up out of the ocean, floating in the darkening sky.

Things ran at a much gentler pace here in Sanur. A long beach stretched out around the bay. In the morning, the kids skipped across the sand and flew multi-coloured kites. The kites came in shapes you'd not expect. One was a ship, three masts and sails in a rainbow of colours. There were birds and fish and dragons and turtles all bobbing at the end of long strings, dancing in the breezes coming up across the South China Sea.

I'd come back down to the south to see a performance called the *kecak*. I bought my tickets from a guy on the street and he rode along beside me on his bicycle to show me the way.

The kecak is utterly unlike gamelan. It's a chant, a purely vocal arrangement of about a hundred men's voices. It was originally used to induce a trance-like state for a religious rite called *sanghyang*. The idea was that, in this trance, a priest would be able to directly communicate with the gods and demons. It's not so unusual. I've seen these sorts of trance rituals, or the remnants of them anyway, all over the world. From Tibetan monasteries in the high Himalayas to the great plains of North America, altered states of consciousness are aroused, often through music, to put yourself in touch with the spiritual world.

The brain does have triggers, usually consistent, repetitive patterns — lights, pitches, words, movements — that induce neural oscillations, more popularly known as brain waves. And music, more than any other art, bears repetition in its chord structures, its melodic motifs, and obviously its rhythms. We'll listen to a specific song hundreds if not thousands of times and, if we like it, we won't get tired of it. That's not true of watching a movie or reading a book. It's a particularly interesting property of music and one of the main reasons why music lends itself so well to spiritual rituals. There is something about repetition that puts you into what a professional athlete might call the zone. Professional musicians feel this too. They'd be lost if they thought too much about each note and every finger movement. It would all come to a crashing, embarrassing halt. So, music, and in particular rhythmic chanting, really does have properties that alter our consciousness. And certainly, I've not heard anything quite as bewitching as the swell and flow of the kecak.

In reality, though, it's only the chant itself that's left over from the old sanghyang ritual. Nowadays, the kecak is a performance — an almost theatrical production — that has little in common with its original purpose. In another example of "invented tradition" a foreigner, a German painter named Walter Spies, got together with a local musician and created the spectacle that we see and hear today. Walter Spies had come to live in Bali in the 1930s. He was fascinated by Balinese culture and especially some of their more exotic rituals, and it was he who orchestrated the splicing of the kecak chant with a story from the *Ramayana*.

When I arrived there was a torch flaming in the centre of a large, flat yard. Something like a hundred men came marching in, wearing checkered sarongs and chanting a sort of chuk, chuk, chuk rhythm. They sat in concentric circles, cross-legged around the torch, and quieted while a man in a white suit spattered drops of water over them in a blessing. The chanting started up again. There were a few dancers, vaguely Legong-like, but what I most remember is a man in a monkey suit hopping amongst them. I couldn't really tell what or how the *Ramayana* story fit in with the chanting, but there you go. Another white coconut trying to work it all out.

The kecak chant.

The men stayed seated for the most part, though they bowed forward and backward and sometimes, like a wave cheer through a stadium, leaned sideways into each other, rippling with movement. "Chuk, chuk, chukka, chuk chuk, chukka, chuk, chuk," they went. It was all the same syllable, a hundred voices clacking out a rhythm. It was hypnotic and the sound swelled and surged. A few of the men began an alternating chant with a different sound that was almost gong-like, a nasally "go, go, go" that came exactly on the backbeat, the offbeat, to the chuk, chuk, chuking. Then high above that a lone male voice brought up a chant, something like a wailing. It was a bit guttural and followed a simple melody. But all of it worked together, forming an intricate, almost rapturous rhythm.

They rocked back and forth, sometimes extending their arms in front of them, waving their fingers like leaves in the breeze. They swayed and chanted and at times half rose to their feet, only to sit back down again and continue their rocking.

 **LISTEN 12.2**

The whole thing was entirely vocal. There wasn't a single instrument to be heard — not even a drum. Chants, of course, may well be the most ancient art form we have, the very ancestor of both language and music. It keeps coming up, doesn't it? The differences between the two, where they overlap and where they create their own possibilities. One of the most important differences is a very simple one. Language is turn-taking; one person speaks at a time while the rest listen. Music, even if it's very language-like, as in chanting, is more often done in unison. This might not seem like such a big deal, but it's actually pretty important. It's one of the fundamental qualities that separates music — and dance, I might add — from other human endeavours. Music and dance are performed in synchronization with other people. They are communal.

Even the audience become involved. We are seduced by rhythms like the kecak. We are aware of the movements of the men, of their waving hands and their heaving chests. We are acutely aware of the expressions on their faces. Humans are particularly adept at reading faces, and it all creates a sort of collage in our minds. We enter the music, emotionally, just as the performers themselves do.

There is some research now suggesting that there's a special kind of brain neuron called a mirror neuron. This mirror neuron system, though still a little controversial, suggests that we have mechanisms that imitate what another person is doing. For a millisecond or so, our own faces will mirror the face of someone we see in distress or bowled over in laughter. Yawns are a particularly good example of how this works. The infectiousness of yawns has been tested in cultures around the globe. We start to spontaneously yawn when we see another doing it, and it doesn't matter a fig if we're actually tired or not. It even turns out that we more readily yawn when the other yawner is a person known to us. There's more of a delay for a stranger's yawn.

This idea of mirror neurons was first noted by Italian scientists only a few years ago. They'd been doing studies with monkeys, and apparently left the electrodes in one monkey's brain, sort of accidentally. They were already into the next round of tests, you know, one of those things where they put the bananas just a little out of reach but have a stick there on the floor. The smart monkey is supposed to figure out that he can get the bananas by picking up the stick and reaching for them with it. In this case, the forgotten monkey, the one with the electrodes still implanted in his brain, watched all this and all the motor neurons of his brain reacted just as if he himself were the one figuring it out. The motor pathways in his brain were firing just as if he were actually reaching for the banana with the stick.

That sent a good ripple through the scientific community, and the search is on for these mysterious little neurons. The thought now is that mirror neurons might have developed as a way to accelerate learning new things. For example, it might partially account for how infants learn their mother tongue so quickly and apparently effortlessly. Babies watch how the mother shapes words with her mouth — lip reading, so to speak — and the baby's motor neurons are then replicating the whole range of small and highly complex muscle movements around their own lips and tongues.

It's also thought to be a mechanism by which we learn to empathize with others. When we see someone in pain, it's more than just seeing them. Our own brains are producing at least a little of some of the same responses they are feeling. Our own facial muscles, if only for a few milliseconds, pull themselves into the same expression.

And if that's right, then this might explain something of how music affects us. Music seems to tap into these neural networks of automatic motor control and emotion. Whether we are the actual performer of the music or whether we are in the audience listening and watching, we become totally lost in the music. We are enveloped by it. It fills us up and takes us over completely.

As T.S. Eliot wrote, "You are the music, while the music lasts." And I can't think of anything more true.

When a person dies in Bali, his body is burned and the spirit is chased away from the village. Despite how that sounds, it's actually a pretty joyful affair. Hindu belief is that the spirit will be reincarnated and if the life lived has been a good one, then the spirit will come back in a higher form, a higher caste, and a better position in life. So there's no cause for sorrow.

August is the peak time for cremations. Often in the smaller villages, they'll bury a body, no matter when the person dies, and just wait until there are enough deaths in the village to warrant a big spectacle. These funeral rites are expensive and often a number of families will pool their dead bodies together to make up one big fantastic funeral.

I'd seen a poster for this and, just like the other performances here, went to buy myself a ticket. All that seemed very strange, but there was a point to it. Once again, I was packed into a bemo and driven off down the dusty roads to the centre of Bali. I was dropped off in some unnamed village with a promise to pick me up later. I had no idea where I was or what I was supposed to be doing.

Down the road came a long procession of women. They wore beautiful silk sarongs, their best obviously, and on their heads they carried ritual offerings, baskets of flowers and bananas and little sculptures of coloured rice. I stepped off to the side, and behind them, tottering like drunken stilt walkers, came the funeral platforms. Each one was a good two storeys high, fashioned of bamboo and papier mâché. Each one was shouldered by eight or ten village men and underneath, the effigy of a mythical beast held the white shroud of a body. One of the towers was a stylistic lion, a reference I think to the man's caste, and strangely, another man, I assume a close relative, straddled the lion figure, riding it like a merry-go-round pony. Every hundred metres or so, the men carrying the platform would gruntingly circle it around three times, slowly, creaking under the weight. This was to confuse the spirits of the deceased. Spirits, you see, are a bit bewildered by their own deaths. They don't really realize they're dead yet and they want to return to their houses, so the spinning confuses them and in their dizzy confusion sends them reeling off in the direction they're meant to go. All the men wore black T-shirts and dark sarongs so that the spirits wouldn't recognize them. All the spirit would see would be the strange attire of the tourist crowds — the Bermuda shorts, the blue jeans of backpackers, and all the gaudy assortment of clothes that we white coconuts had brought, unwittingly, to this ritual of death. This would scare the hell out of the spirits and chase them off to the next world.

Behind the funeral platforms came the gonging, clinking chimes of a marching gamelan orchestra. Ingeniously, they'd fashioned a sort of scaffolding of bamboo that held up their various tromping and bronze saron bars. They were like a gamelan marching band. The cremation music, called Gamelan Angklung, sounds much like the Legong dances except that it's just a little bit sweeter and a little more delicate. This is only because they've left behind the largest of the gongs. The cast bronze is just too heavy to carry, so all those cathedral bell reverberations, the deep booming clangs of the largest of the gamelan, are gone. The sound here is more tinkly, more like wind chimes and doorbells. The playing, too, was a little less extravagant. There was none of the virtuoso runs I'd heard in Ubud. This was not a time to show off.

Still, they clanged the shrouded remains off to the funeral pyres. I'd slipped in behind the whole procession now and we moved out of the village and off to a garbage-strewn field. Up on a slight hill, they'd set up the pyres and these too were in animal shapes. They were like wooden kilns, something halfway between a tiny log cabin and the wooden horse of Troy. I didn't see them lift the bodies from the platforms and get them into the ovens. They were already lit when I arrived, and I craned my head over the crowds, only to see the slow drift of oily smoke coming up off the pyre.

The smoke spiralled up through the treetops. The sun shot through it, flickering and dancing. The gamelan had gone quiet now and only the murmuring of the crowd and the crackling of the fire played the soul on out of this world, up into the air, stepping lightly across lifetimes to its final rest.

13

INDIA
THE PULL OF EMOTIONS

WE HAD JUST GOT ON THE OVERNIGHT TRAIN IN NEW DELHI WHEN THE transvestite slapped me. A host of touts came down the aisles before the train pulled out of the station, selling everything from chai tea to tomato soup. I'd already sat down, arranging my things, when a strange voice came from above me. "Baksheesh," it insisted. The hand was out. It was a woman, but something was off about her. Drunk, I thought, or stoned, but there was more — a squareness in the chin and badly overdone makeup. I said "No," as I'd already said a hundred times that day, and she glared down at me.

"No," she mimicked, her face tightening in disdain. Then she wound up and bitch-slapped me.

"What the hell was that?" I said, rubbing my chin. She, or he, was already stumbling off down the aisle.

Bhanu was sitting beside me. He was our tour guide. "A eunuch," said Bhanu. He'd hardly looked up at all. For a guide, Bhanu didn't talk much. He wore a sort of Crocodile Dundee hat and a hunting vest that made him look adventurous, but he was unusually distant. How he'd got a job as a guide, I don't know, but he was leading a few of us, mostly Australians, down to the holy city of Varanasi.

"A eunuch?" I pressed.

"He is Hijras caste. That mean he is transvestite or gay or, some time, they kidnap the boy child and they …" Bhanu made a snipping motion with his fingers.

"They castrate them?"

"Yes, it is possible."

"This is a caste?"

"One caste, yes. Not so important. They are living to themselves. Sometime they are uninvited singers at weddings. Sometime they are begging."

"And sometimes they are slapping foreigners."

"In India you will see too much surprise." Bhanu's head bobbed apologetically and he turned away again.

There were four in our little group, three young women from Australia and me. None of them had known each other before but they were sure as hell having a good laugh at my expense now, wishing they'd had their cameras out for the Slap. Others would join us in Varanasi but for now it was Amie, a nurse from Perth, Dom, a young surfer and lifeguard who'd come up to do volunteer work, and Jess from Melbourne.

"What about you, Bhanu?" Amie asked.

"What about me?"

"Are you married yet?"

"No, not yet."

"It'll be an arranged marriage?" Dom broke in. "I mean, when it happens."

"Yes. Probably." He looked unhappy. "I think we should set up the beds now," he said. "We arrive in Varanasi at six. Too much early."

Night closed over us. There were no more eunuchs, though all night porters came down the aisles selling snacks and more chai. The Indian national railway is the single biggest employer in the world. More people work on the trains here than, say, the entire population of Toronto or Seattle. India is filled with numbers like this. One point two billion people now. It's almost impossible to fathom.

The train station at Varanasi was a seething mass of humanity. The platforms were strewn with garbage and hundreds of beggars slept on the bare pavement. Crossing over a bridge between platforms, I walked by a pile of plastic bags. In it something moved. A human head turned up to me. He had no arms and no legs. Just a torso and a face looking up at me pleadingly.

It was a haunting, startling beginning to things and a bit hard to reconcile with what I had expected of Varanasi. It is, after all, one of the holiest of places for Hindus. As every guide will insist on telling you, it's the oldest continuously inhabited city on Earth. From a thousand silver braided streams, the Ganges River comes cascading down from the high Himalaya Mountains. By the time it reaches Varanasi, it's as wide as the Mississippi. To bathe in its waters is to free yourself of sin and to be cremated there, to have your ashes swept into the river, is to end the cycle of lives. "It's like Mecca," Bhanu told us. "Every Hindu should come here to bathe one time in their life."

We arrived at the end of the monsoons and the river was running high. It was also a holy month. Hindus have a lunar calendar, much like Muslims, except that every three years they add a month — a leap month, I guess you call it — and it was on this propitious month that we came into the crazy, dirty maze of streets that is Varanasi.

We settled into our hotel, an old colonial relic, and after sleeping a bit more, Bhanu gathered us together for our orientation. Two tuk tuks appeared. They were painted green and yellow like three-wheeled little bees, their engines no more powerful than lawnmowers. We tucked ourselves into their metal shells and plunged down into the city.

The streets were choked with traffic. Everything about India is loud. The tuk tuks honked and beeped, weaving between the slower rickshaws pedalling through the streets. We had to swerve suddenly to avoid cars and other tuk tuks, and, once, a camel pulling a wooden cart. Motorcycles veered up onto the sidewalks beside us. There was no order, just chaos and the endless braying of horns. A policeman stood in the midst of it, wielding a bamboo cane. Every once in a while, he would whap at the back of a rickshaw, though it did little to hurry it along. There was just too much traffic, too many people, and lolling through the whole sorry mess came the lumbering sacred cows, shambling along as if they were out grazing in a field, oblivious to the cacophony all around them.

The tuk tuks let us out at some nameless square and Bhanu walked out into the middle of the traffic. We followed like goslings following their mother goose. I was terrified, trying to keep track of all the vehicles surging in and around me, and at the same time watching where I stepped. The pavement was uneven. Unmarked holes appeared, enough to snap an ankle, and cow paddies the size of dinner plates smouldered on the cracked cement. All manner of filth banked up against the curbs and walls like the snow drifts of hell.

We walked on and the afternoon faded, shadowing into an eerie twilight.

"Where are we going?" I yelled up at Bhanu.

"Now we are going to the ghats," he said without turning.

The ghats were the platforms along the river itself. There are about a hundred of them lining the Ganges. Most have a temple above them, and the ghat itself, a platform the size of your living room, sits over a set of crumbling steps that lead down to the brown and fetid water.

Just as it darkened completely, we veered off the busy streets and into the warren of alleyways that form the oldest part of the city. Many of the pathways are no wider than your two arms outstretched, but the motorcycles still come choking down them, honking as you press yourself up against the crumbling walls.

In the recesses and shops that lined the alleys, we could see old men sitting lotus-like on the cement floors, silhouettes dimly lit by butter candles. A bull came lolling in from another alleyway, and we had to press ourselves up against a wall once more, letting it move by us like a slow motion running of the Pamplona bulls. The alleys wove this way and that, and were it not for Bhanu, we would have been lost in minutes.

In the distance I heard a bell tolling. I could smell smoke, too, though I still couldn't see anything. It had grown very dark. At last, the alley opened up and large black shapes were all around us. The smell of garbage and cow shit was taken over by something sweeter. I put my hand out to touch one of the shapes. It was a whole tree trunk lying on its side. Entire trees were piled up there like the debris of a hurricane.

"Sandalwood," said Bhanu. "It is used for the burning."

We turned into the concrete shell of a building and went up a set of inner steps. Again, eyes stared out at us from the darkness but we continued to climb, three or four levels above the street. At the top was a cement terrace and from there we could look down over the black

Ganges. The bell was tolling down below us now and chanting was rising up. At one end of the terrace, clouds of smoke were billowing up over the lip of the wall. A Hindu holy man stood behind us. He was old. He had a great white beard and around his waist was a wrap of rags. He had no shirt or shoes. He just stood there eyeing us.

"You cannot take photos here," said Bhanu. He indicated the holy man, whose job, I think, was to enforce this one simple rule.

Another group of foreigners was already up there and their tour guide waved us over, gathering us all together. This guide's name was Singh and his group would parallel ours for the next couple of weeks. He was the antithesis of Bhanu, lively and gregarious.

"Any caste may be cremated here," Singh began in close to perfect English. "It does not matter. But the wood is expensive and it takes three or four hours to burn a body fully. A rich family can afford enough wood. A poor family cannot and what is left unburned goes into the river too. About 250 bodies are burned every day. Please, no pictures, but you can look ... over here."

Some of the people in our group pulled their shirt collars up over the mouths and noses. Down below us, four bodies were burning, quite close to each other. The flames were already huge, bonfire height, and I couldn't really see much through the smoke. A chanting was coming up but it was so hot that the mourners around the bodies had backed off a ways. There was another holy man down there leading the ceremony and at the very edge of things a few scurrying untouchables whose job it was to carry and cut the wood and, finally, to sweep the ashes off into the river when it was all over. I turned back, my eyes watering, trying not to cough.

Bhanu stood far off away from the rest of us. We could only see the tip of a lit cigarette under the brim of his hat. "What's with Bhanu?" I said.

"He's kind of mysterious," Amie offered. "Like a secret agent or something."

Singh was watching us, and when most of us had pulled away from the wall, he signalled for us to gather around him again. "Listen," he said. "Holy men are not burned. They are already pure and their bodies are buried. This is also true of pregnant women — because they hold purity in their wombs. And those that are bitten by snakes."

"Snakes?"

"The snake is the symbol of Shiva. People bitten by snakes have already been touched by a god. They do not need to be purified by fire."

"What about the untouchables?" someone asked.

Singh smiled. "Listen," he said. "I will tell you a story. The untouchables are the lowest caste. In the villages they do not live in the same parts as the rest. They cannot drink from the same water. But once, here in Varanasi, the principal of a very important private school came to arrange the cremation of his wife. It is difficult to arrange sometimes, you must be knowing someone. Many people are wishing to be burned here. And at this time, it was not possible. Too many bodies. He could not arrange it. Too full."

Bhanu's cigarette went out. I think even he was listening now.

"But one of the untouchables recognized this man," said Singh. "The untouchable said to the principal, 'I will arrange for your wife, if you will take my son into your school.'

"'That is impossible,' said the principal.

"'You wish a cremation,' said the untouchable, 'and it is not possible. I wish my son to go to a good school, it is not possible. But together, it is possible.' And so it was done." Singh paused and even Bhanu came in closer. "They say the son went on to become the best student. They say he went to the best university. No longer an untouchable."

"That's a good story," I said.

"This is India. Anything can happen."

The Hindu holy man seemed to be plodding around us now, perfunctorily.

"Varanasi is the city of Shiva," Singh continued, glancing at the holy man. "He is the god of death and destruction. But this is not to be considered strange. Everything has an expiry date. Shiva is not the ending. Shiva is the god of transformation. It is no bad thing. Come," he said, looking again at the holy man, "we have overstayed our welcome."

We walked back down the steps. The holy man held his hand out for money and I gave him 100 rupees. That's only about two dollars. And when we were back in the narrow alleyways, we broke off again, following Bhanu.

"Bhanu," I asked, "how dirty is the Ganges? What about all those body parts?"

"They are cleaning it now, slowly. The fish have come back."

"But the body parts," Amie said, "there must be heaps of them."

"Most of the ghats are for bathing. Some are for laundry, but not now. The river is too much silt."

"You just said it's not dirty."

"No, it's not dirty. This is the end of the monsoon season. The Ganges is very high now. It is …"

"We should go bathing," Jess said. "Tomorrow. What do you think?"

Bhanu looked uncomfortable. "It is going very fast now."

"So it's clean?"

"Yes, but …"

"No worries then."

"Tomorrow, you have a free day. I will not be with you."

"Then tomorrow we'll go swimming in the Ganges. Who's in?"

"You must stay by the shore," Bhanu said, looking even more uncomfortable. "Do not go out in the current."

"Can everybody swim?"

"Please," said Bhanu. "Can we go back to hotel now? It is a little bit side of late."

We were trudging through the dim back alleys again. I think I was fiddling with my camera when I looked up and almost got bowled over by four men carrying a body on their shoulders. The lump of the corpse was mostly under a gold brocade cloth, and they were literally jogging with it, trying to get it to the ghat on time for their allotted spot. I just had time to register that it was a dead body and that they had almost knocked me down, or that I had almost tripped them up and made them drop it, and they were gone. I saw the face, though. The mouth was lolling open. That I remember. That's burned into my memory like a scar.

India is like that. It's like a slap in the face to everything you thought you knew.

Our brains are difference engines. They have evolved to detect changes in the environment and then generate reactions. They've gotten pretty good at predicting these changes. They anticipate them and the whole range of human emotions are tied directly into this purpose. In fact, that's precisely what emotions are.

Darwin spoke of this, but he only catalogued a few basic emotions. Psychologists today talk of literally hundreds of emotions. One theory classifies them by the three aspects of valence, intensity, and focus. Valence is polar — either an emotion is positive or negative. You are hurrying to catch the ten o'clock bus, for instance. You arrive just as the bus pulls up and you jump on with satisfaction. Or, you arrive just in time to see the bus pulling away without you and you experience frustration and anger. It's pretty simple.

The aspect of intensity is also straightforward. It's just the depth to which we feel an emotion. Missing a bus is no big deal. Having someone close to you die definitely is. It's the difference between feeling frustration and utter devastation.

But it's the third aspect which really separates emotions out into their different manifestations. This one's called focus and it refers to what has caused the emotion. The focus can be an event (like a bus arriving on time) or it can be an object (loathing or loving mussels, maybe). Or there can be something called a moral focus as well. That's when you approve or disapprove of an idea.

In the morning, I went with the Australian girls. They were wildly adventurous, these young women. They'd worked themselves into a quivering excitement about bathing in the Ganges. I, on the other hand, wasn't too thrilled about the idea, but I promised to go along with them anyway, at the very least to take photos.

We'd dipped back into the maze of alleys, not really sure of what we were doing, and within a few hundred metres we were — as could be predicted — hopelessly lost. At a featureless intersection, a little girl appeared, no more than ten years old. She was making money by applying *bindi* to people's foreheads. Bindi is the dot, usually red, worn between the eyebrows. It's the sixth chakra, the seat of what is called "concealed wisdom." She was selling cheap paste-on little dots. Her eyes widened at the foreigners coming at her.

"Where you go?" she asked.

"Assi Ghat. We want to bathe."

"Assi Ghat is too, too far."

"Well ..."

"There is another, closer. Come, I take you."

She whirled around and we followed. After only a couple of confusing turns, we went down a long alleyway and emerged out onto the river. There was a lonely little ghat there, almost empty. Only two old men washed in the river there, one of them bald, his shiny brown head just peeking above the water.

The Aussies and I looked at one another. This was it. Amie laughed and headed straight for the water. The girls had all worn their oldest, most ragged clothes, things they were planning on throwing away anyway. "You are to bump your head under three times," the little girl called, bubbling joyfully now at the sight of white people going in the water.

I hadn't planned on it. Or maybe I had. I'd worn swim trunks under my pants just in case, so it was only a matter of taking off my shirt and shoes. Here I was at one of the most holy places on the subcontinent. The Ganges was right there in front of me.

I tried to reason with myself. The cremation ghats, I knew, were downstream and no body parts could possibly come up this way. The water, too, was high and roiling quickly along. It had to be at least sort of clean. I looked down at the water. My soul was at stake here. Or at least the dark edges of my sins.

I stepped down toward the water. It was a milky greenish-brown. The old men looked up at me and one of them bobbed his head and flashed the most wonderful smile. I think that's what did it.

I put a foot into the water, and it was deliciously cool. I went down another step and hit sandy bottom. There was no slime. I was up to my knees in it now.

The little girl was on the ghat. "Head down," she said. Dom had a camera aimed at me. She was laughing and encouraging at the same time. Amie was already in. I waded out a bit further, hunched down, shut my eyes, and dunked right under. I can't say that I felt my sins floating away. I can't say I felt anything other than a welcome dip on a fiercely hot day.

Everyone was grinning at me as I came up. The girl was beaming even more broadly. "Two more," she insisted.

And down I went, twice more. Everyone did it. We all eventually emerged dripping and grinning, back up onto the ghat, pulling towels over our wet things, squeezing out the water from our hair. The little girl sat down in front of Jess and took out a squeeze tube of henna. In only a few moments she'd covered most of Jess's inner forearm with thin fine lines. Her face was scrunched up in concentration and when she finished she stood back. It was a stylized peacock, wrapping up around Jess's hand and arm. We bent around the design, astounded at the girl's abilities.

"You go to school?" I asked.

She gave me a derisive look as if school was only for chumps.

"Where you go now?" she said, standing up.

"Back to the main street, I guess. Back to our hotel."

"Come then, I take you. Now look first," she insisted, as if she'd taken us out on a field trip, as if she were the schoolmarm looking after us. "Do you have everything? You forget any cameras? Any bags?"

We checked the steps around us dutifully.

"Okay, we go." And off she trotted.

Later on, we all agreed that this was one of the highlights of the whole trip. A special moment. I knew my friends back home would balk. I knew they'd cite reports of bacteria counts and floating bodies. But they weren't there. They couldn't know what it was like.

Amie went with off with the little girl to find a yoga studio. The rest of us pressed back into the chaos that is India. Women flowed by in dazzling saris, bright indigo blues and swirling saffrons and yellow the colour of sunflowers. Some of the men wore long white cotton shirts down to their knees with white pantaloons underneath. An ascetic stood on one curb. Here, they're called *sadhus,* holy men. His hair was in dreadlocks halfway down his back. He was entirely caked in mud. Even his face had a thick layer over it so that his eyes stared out luminously. He looked like some kind of swamp monster, though I was getting used to these sorts of apparitions. His eyes landed on us and I wondered if he could tell. He made no gesture, no head bob or smile to show that that he'd seen us, and although I knew it was ridiculous, I'd like to think that he approved. Our wet clothes stuck to us, our hair was clearly sopping, and there's only one place we could have come from. We'd bathed in the holy Ganges and we were all, I think, feeling quite proud of ourselves.

Bhanu was relieved to see us, though he didn't say much of anything. After we'd changed, Bhanu gathered the full group. There were eight of us now, since several more had joined us from Nepal, and we all went out for something to eat. I had vegetable thali and it was delicious. "Tell me, Bhanu," I said, tearing at a piece of garlic naan. "Would you have gone in?"

"Oh, I have. I'm not a strict Hindu, though. Not so much."

"Where are you from?"

"Jaipur." He looked up at us and smiled shyly.

"We're going there later, right?"

"Yes, we go there."

"How are you goin' on these tours anyway?" Amie asked. "Do you like it?"

"This is my second."

"And before that?"

He stopped and looked off into the distance. "I work in the National Park at Ranthambore."

"You were doing tours there?"

"Not so much people. I work with animals."

"What kind of animals?"

Two of the new people perked up from the end of the table. They were Andy and his girlfriend, Nat. "Andy," she said. "Tell them what you do."

"I'm an elephant keeper. I'm the elephant keeper at the Melbourne Zoo."

"No kidding," I said. "Bhanu, what animals did you work with?"

"Tigers," he said. "I work with tigers."

That caught us unawares. Andy shook his head and whistled. "How many are left, out there, in the wild?"

"Seventeen hundred and fifty one. No more." Bhanu looked at his watch. "But we must go just now."

"Where are we going now?"

"Ceremony at the Ganges. You will see."

"What ceremony?"

"An *aarti*. A ceremony for the Ganges. It is start tonight." He turned fully on me. "You can see some music there. I told you this is holy month. Now you will see."

For a third time, then, we went back to the ghats. Tuk tuks appeared as always and beelined us down into the chaos. This time there was more human traffic. Thousands of people were jostling and funnelling down into the alleyways. I looked for our girl but couldn't see her. I never saw the swamp monster again either. Just a monkey, perched up on a cement pillar, looking down at us with disdain.

We followed the crowds out onto a massive ghat. The Ganges was in front of us, inky black in the night. On the far side of the river, two or three kilometres away, were the twinkling lights of villages. We'd come up onto the ghat just as they were starting. At the edge of the ghat, just at the edge of the river, stood five Brahmin priests. They were chanting.

"What's this?" I whispered over to Bhanu.

"It is Sanskrit," he said, "not Hindi. It is from the Vedas."

Each priest stood on a separate marble shelf. Each in his left hand held a bell by a wooden handle. They rang these rhythmically and in tempo with one another. To the right side were drummers, hammering on double-ended drums and one man conking away on something like a cowbell. On the other side, though I could barely hear it, was a reed organ pumping like an accordion. It was all a little discordant.

"This is Agni Pooja, a fire worship," Bhanu said, and, as if on cue, some other men brought out what looked like teapots leaping with fire. Each priest took one and they went through an elaborate gesturing, all in sync, holding up the fire pots, swaying the smoke up into the air like ribbons from a rhythmic gymnastics event.

In the shadows beside us, I could see a conically shaped temple rising up over us. Its bricks were fire red, though it was almost lost in the darkness. We were on the Dashashwamedh Ghat. It's mentioned in texts from the second century C.E. but it's even older than that. And something like this ceremony has been practised here without interruption for two thousand years.

The bells rang on and the fire pots danced in the hands of the priests, the smoke swirling in beautiful dancing wisps and curls. When at last they finished, they cast flower petals down into the Ganges. They floated like confetti out over the blackness of the river.

◀᠅ **LISTEN 13.1**

We shuffled off and followed Bhanu down a ramp at the side of the ghat. A woman there was selling *diyas*, tiny floating prayers, the size of the palm of your hand. They are woven from *maljhan* leaves and fastened together with twigs. In the little saucer-like container are flowers, marigolds and rose petals, and in the middle a candle flickering hesitantly. We took our diyas to the water's edge and released them, and they trailed out into the current, like a row of little stars, twinkling and bobbing, like hope itself.

Keshava Rao Nayak came strutting down the street as if he owned it. That's no small feat in Varanasi. The traffic parted for him like the Red Sea for Moses. Keshava, though he was sixty years old, had a mane of black hair that could only be described as luxurious. It flowed out behind him, bouncing as he walked. It was part of the effect. He strode up to me and eyed me up and down.

"You are the student?" he said at last. He was a lot shorter than I but he eyed me like a mountain climber in front of a very easy peak.

"Yes. I ..."

"Come. I am Keshava."

"The International Music Ashram?" I said.

"This is me, yes. Come."

I'd contacted the International Music Ashram before I arrived. The name was a bit of a misnomer. It was actually just Keshava's house. This, it turned out, was just a few metres off the Dashashwamedh Ghat where we'd been the night before. There he and his son conducted music lessons.

I'd signed up for sitar lessons. Visions of George Harrison and the Beatles had danced though my mind before I'd come to India. It was one of my reasons for coming.

"Watch your head," he said when we reached the entrance. We climbed up a steep flight of steps and he led me into a cement room the size of a bedroom with only a single light bulb dangling from the ceiling. Shelves on either side were stacked with drums.

Keshava nestled himself down crosslegged on the bare floor, inviting me to do the same. Keshava was actually a tabla player. It was his son who would be teaching me sitar. His wife came in carrying a tray of chai tea.

"Shyam come here soon," he said, slurping at his tea. "I wait with you." On the wall was a painting and in it a woman was holding a sitar.

"Please," I said. "What's that?"

"This," he said, "is Saraswati. She is god of music. *Wati* it mean 'female' but *saras* mean 'flow.'" I kind of liked that. Music is like the flow of the river.

"My family," Keshava went on, "we are musicians for three hundred years, living here. Nowhere else." He jutted out his chest proudly and started naming everyone back to his great-great-grandfather; what instruments they played, who they had played for. Indian classical music does have this lineage, I knew. The discipline and knowledge passes from a master to a disciple. It is rigorous and there are no short cuts.

"I am sixty years old," Keshava said, finishing. "I have many students."

"Many like me? From other countries?"

"Some, yes. One German man, he stay for three months. He improve greatly."

"Tabla?"

"Yes, tabla."

"Always," he said, "teaching come from heart." He placed a hand on his chest. "Not from brain. If teacher not relax, student not relax." I think he was telling me to relax. I was squirming a bit on the hard floor.

He pulled a pair of tablas toward himself. "I play for you?"

"Yes. Yes, please."

He twisted the larger of the drums around, arranging it on the circle of cloth that it sat on. He adjusted the angle, then paused, focusing. He raised his head, sticking out his chin, and began to play.

It was one of the most extraordinary performances I've ever heard. Classically trained musicians are venerated in India, just like the great classical musicians in the West. And here was a master, sitting in a little concrete room under a bare light bulb. His fingers flipped between positions and strikes, like a concert pianist. He leaned in and doubled the tempo. It was extraordinary. The opulence of tones he got out of those drums, the sheer range of sounds and the speed at which he rang through them, was dazzling.

 **LISTEN 13.2**

"Wow," I said, when he'd finished. A face had appeared at the open door and Keshava looked up. "Ah cha," he said. "Here is Shyam." He rose, nodding to his son. His head bobbed once and I thought there was a signal. *Here is a foreigner,* he was saying. *He knows nothing ... but he is earnest. Tell him about our music, about our theory and history and it will be enough.*

Shyam looked at me. He had a warm, kind face, an intelligent face. He was wearing only a sleeveless T-shirt and khaki shorts. He had a thick moustache like his father's, though there was none of the swagger, none of the bravado.

Leaning against the wall was his sitar. He nestled himself cross-legged as his father had done and pulled the sitar over his lap. It was a beautiful instrument, elaborately painted with tuning heads running the length of the neck. The sound box was made from the shell of a pumpkin, delicately shellacked and round.

"What will you know?" he asked.

"Tell me about the ragas." Ragas were pieces in Indian classical music. "Each one represents a particular mood, is that right?"

"Raga," he said, "is Sanskrit word. It mean 'colour.' You understand? Each raga have their own mood, as you ask. If there is no any mood, so that is not raga."

He played a run on the sitar. There are twenty strings on the thing. Four of them are drones, vibrating sympathetically when the others are played. Ten or so form a sort of harp-like arpeggio. He tumbled his finger down these and the scale tinkled through the room.

He leaned forward and began what I can only describe as a lecture. "Time is most important factor in North Indian raga, because the all day, the twenty-four hour, we divide in eight part. Four part we call morning, four part we call evening. And in the each part we have the mood of raga. Listen. This is Raga Todi."

He played a scale. Well, not quite a scale. In Indian classical music, each raga is identified with certain notes, a certain sequence of notes, so that even the ascending notes are not quite the same as the descending. It's a pattern of notes. A mood and an emotion.

"Like this we start the story. We start like waking up. Then we go more fast, fast. We play many kind of material, many kind of rhythm, and the possibility of what we can do with the raga."

Sitar lessons in Varanasi.

"So, it's improvised?"

"Improvised, yes. But the notes must only be this ones. This one Raga Todi, raga of morning."

He played a bit more, tilting his head into it, hunching over the strings, closing his eyes. It was serene and lovely — just like morning.

 **LISTEN 13.3**

There is something universal in how music translates emotions and moods. There are at least two studies I know of where Indian ragas were played for Western audiences. People who'd never heard a sitar before were remarkably adept at identifying the emotions portrayed — joy and sadness, anger and peace. Another study took thirty second slices of music from three different cultures, Indian, Japanese shakra, and Western classical music, and played them to people from all three cultures. Everyone was completely accurate at identifying the emotions in their own culture's music but they were also almost as accomplished at getting the moods right in the others.

So why is this? Why should sound so accurately convey human emotions?

"Raga," Shyam said, "have minimum five notes. Maximum seven. This one Raga Kedar, raga of nighttime. Listen now. This note called *wadi*. It is central note of raga." He played a note — it wasn't the tonic of the scale. Indian ragas don't work quite like our Western scales. "Wadi mean 'speak,'" he said. "At beginning, we come back to wadi again and again, slowly, slowly. Play this note, play that note, but always come back to wadi. We fix it in the listener ear.

"Three other kind of note we have. Each different for different raga. *Samadi* is harmony notes, the notes go best with the wadi. Look, I try and explain you." He played a bit more, touching on the central note, then extending out to others, brushing across them, rising up through several then coming back to the wadi. "Third," he said, is *unamati*. Other note, not too importance. We come to them later."

Music and emotion are both based on anticipation. Much has already been written on this. The simple physics is that there are notes that go with other notes. We can predict which ones will come next. They come like buses arriving at our stop just when we need them. We pleasure at the expected fifth. Our brains pull toward the major third. And we long for the resolve back to the tonic.

Something like this goes on in ragas too. But there's more to emotion and music than the simple anticipation of pitch. Music has a rhythm too, so that a slow beat, like our heartbeat, is the physical manifestation of calm, of gentleness, and possibly a little sadness. Joy is expressed in faster tempos. That much is obvious. But there's even more.

"We have fourth kind of note," Shyam went on. "It called *vivati* — rare note. It not usually played. Only to extend the beauty." He played for a few minutes, unbroken by talk, but he nodded at me when he was going to his vivati. He leaned into it, squeezing it out above the rest, and I could hear it. It was just that kind of note that sent shivers down the spine. He smiled when he saw my reaction. "Just so," he said. "Just so."

A sitar is different from a guitar, or any stringed instrument that I know of, in that the metal frets are high, high above the fretboard. By pressing down on them you can get as many as five distinct notes on any given place on the fretboard. "It for more emotion," Shyam said.

He bent at a string, waggling it in a way that would have made B.B. King jealous.

Shyam sat with me for more than two hours, playing ragas, explaining the complexities of Indian music. It was a seminar of the highest standards. After a time, Keshavi appeared at the door, pushing his head in once and then hovering in the entrance, standing over us. He was telling his son, I think, that the time for lessons was over.

The Taj Mahal floats like a summer cloud. Off in the distance, it shimmers, almost too perfect to be real. We'd come into Agra on an overnight train from Varanasi. The city was quieter but only minimally. At the gates of the heavily secured area around the Taj Mahal, the beggars came at us again. One boy had a grotesquely bent spine. He walked on all fours, crablike, his face down by the pavement but tipped up to us imploringly. It was heartbreaking and disturbing. So much desperation within a few hundred metres of the opulence that is the Taj Mahal. But again, India is like that. Always there is the slap.

No cars are allowed in through the security gates, and you must hop aboard a little electric shuttle bus to bring you closer. They're desperately afraid of terrorism here, of the possibility that someone could place a bomb in the most beautiful building in the world.

The Taj Mahal was built by the Mughal emperor Shah Jahan in the early 1600s. It took twenty-two years to build; twenty thousand workers and a thousand elephants to haul the white marble from far off Rajasthan. The jade and crystal came from China. The turquoise came from Tibet and the sapphires from Sri Lanka.

But here's the thing. It's a tomb. A tomb to love.

Jahan and his wife, Mumtaz Mahal, were head over heels in love with each other. When she died in childbirth, Jahan was devastated. He buried her in the garden and set about building the world's greatest monument to love. When it was finally complete, her body was transferred and it lies to this day in the very centre of the Taj Mahal.

When it was done, Jahan made damn sure that there would never be an equal to this building. First, he paid out compensation to the families of the master artisans, so much wealth that seven generations of descendants from each of the masters would never again have to worry about money. And then he cut the thumbs off of every master artisan so that, without that opposable digit, they could never carve marble or set jewels again.

We arrived in the middle of the afternoon in the dripping heat. Under a hot indigo sky, the domes and towers of the Taj Mahal gleamed. On the pathways leading up to it scattered groups of people wove their way to and fro. A long line of women in orange and bright pink saris wound up the left side like a necklace of jewels. I stood for a moment just taking it all in. In all my travels, truly, I have never seen a more beautiful scene.

Andy and his girlfriend disappeared for a while. "There are no elephants here," someone joked. "I wonder where Andy's gone."

But when they came back, Andy was a little flushed. Something had happened. "Look," said Nat, holding out her left hand. The girls gathered around the glittering diamond ring to ooh and ahh. "He just proposed to me," she said. "Right here, at the Taj Mahal."

Travelling back to the hotel, Bhanu rode in the tuk tuk with me and Amie and Dom. Amie turned to him again. "Another one, Bhanu. When are you going to get married?"

"He's married to his tigers," said Dom.

"How many have you seen with your own eyes?" I asked.

"Just forty-eight."

"Aren't they dangerous?"

"If a tiger kills three people, we must label it a man-eater and it will be taken to a special place."

"But not killed?"

"No, isolated. A fenced area."

"Hey, wait a minute," I said. "It has to kill three people before it's a man-eater? What about the first two?"

"Could be accident."

"Accident?"

"Startle the animal. It does not mean to kill."

"And the second?"

"Same, same. It get three chances then it know human taste and it is man-eater."

I'd never heard Bhanu talk so much. He babbled away about tigers all the way home. "I show you photos," he said. "I show you photos."

Back at the hotel, we could barely get in. A crowd had gathered, spilling right out into the parking lot. The lobby was draped with flowers, like beaded curtains. "What's happening here?" I asked Bhanu.

"It is wedding."

"Ahh, that's perfect." I glanced over at the Australian girls.

"A Hindu wedding can go on for three days," Bhanu said. "This is beginning."

Someone grabbed at us. I think it was the uncle of the groom. "Please," he said with a characteristic head wobble. "You are invited. You must come."

It was the ring ceremony. We were whisked in. The man brushed people aside, making way for us. The bride and groom sat on a golden settee at the back of a room up on a sort of pedestal. He had just put the ring on her finger and they both looked a little overwhelmed. This was an arranged marriage. Most here still are. "It is not two people getting married," the uncle explained to me. "It is two families getting married."

The music was just beginning. It wasn't live. They had a DJ playing dance mix versions of Bollywood songs. *Filmi gīt,* they're called, songs written just for the movies, and their big, over-the-top dance numbers. In no time the dance floor was filled. I was pulled into the mayhem. So were the girls. In fact, we were treated like rock stars. People surrounded us, taking our photos then asking shyly to be in the photos with us.

People handed us their small children and we danced awkwardly, holding them. The infants wore dark mascara around their tiny eyes to ward off evil. And there was liquor too. A lot of it.

The uncle grabbed my arm, trying to show me the steps to the dances: an upthrust hip and a palm stabbing at the air. I gave it my best shot and there was laughter and more flashbulbs. Another uncle came in at me. He signalled for me to stand on one leg. Then he hooked the calf of his own leg behind my upraised leg and we just whirled, our right legs locked together, jumping like pogo sticks in circles around each other. It was a blur, a joyful bedlam.

It's important to say here that there's more music in India than I could possibly write about. Their Indian classical music, the discipline of the sitar and tabla, are about the same as classical music in the West. That is, they're respected but not really a central part of life. Bollywood is different. It's ubiquitous. Even it is an ancient art form, though, the tripartite entertainment that is story, music, and dance. That hasn't changed since the *Ramayana*.

There's folk music, too, and each region has its own sounds and instruments. I'd seen two stringed fiddles called Ravan Hatta. And at a temple, I heard a band of four or five men playing shenai, a reed instrument almost like a soprano saxophone.

But it's Bollywood that is absolutely everywhere. I think we finally escaped the wedding around midnight. Three or four hundred guests lingered there and it seemed like I had to shake hands with everyone on my way out. Many implored us for more photos and many thanked us gravely, placing hands over their hearts or touching their foreheads. A river of smiles. A sea of magnanimity.

Singh, our alternate guide, took over in Jaipur again. Funny, because both Singh and Bhanu were from Jaipur. which is the capital of Rajasthan, the pink city they call it, and yes, all the buildings are painted a shade that falls somewhere between amber and salmon. They took us up to a fort — the Amber Fort, in fact — on a hill high above the city.

Rajasthan is a different state with different customs, a different language, and a different history. An immense wall hooked over the hills around the fort, for the fort was really the grand palace of the Maharaja. The wall looked for all the world like the Great Wall of China, and it seemed to go on for many, many kilometres. "This," said Singh, looking out over a terrace, "is the third longest wall in the world."

"What's the second?"

"Nobody cares about second."

"You don't know?"

"Yes, I know. It's at Kumbhalgarh near Udaipur, also in Rajasthan … but nobody cares." He paused. "Listen, everyone knows that Neil Armstrong was the first man on the moon but nobody knows who is the second."

"I think it was Buzz Aldrin."

A snake charmer in Jaipur.

"I never heard of him," Singh said with a snort. Then he looked at me and laughed. "Come," he said. "There is too much to see."

Jaipur is filled with palaces. The City Palace is an architectural masterpiece, lined with arches and capped with cupolas. The Water Palace rises up out of a sparkling man-made lake, and, looking over the centre of town, sits the exquisitely named Palace of the Winds.

At the central gate of the Amber Fort, elephants decked out in garlands and brocades ferried in the gullible tourists. Andy was watching them carefully. Touts launched out at us, selling cheap jewellery and mock *safa* hats. A couple of the girls bought them and popped them on, until they were told that these sorts of turbans were only worn by men.

Down by a stone wall, a reedy flute was sounding. Bhanu looked over at me.

"You are interested in snake charmer music?"

"Snake charmers. Absolutely, yes."

We followed the sound and came upon a man squatting down, knees up to his chest. He played a double-fluted instrument with a whining, reedy sound. In front of him, in a woven basket, a cobra was rising up, the telltale neck flaps opened wide, forked tongue darting in and out.

"Oh my god."

"It is okay," said Bhanu. "The venom is taken out."

In fact, the cobra was a small one, maybe three feet long. The man played on, a simple little tune. It could've been a folk melody from almost anywhere. The cobra bobbed and swivelled, seemingly in time to the music. It's not the music, though. It's an illusion.

Some people think snakes are deaf. That's not true either. They can hear well enough, they just don't give a damn about music. What they're cueing in on is the movements of the snake charmer. He sways back and forth as he plays. It has nothing to do with the music. Movement is what keys the difference engine in a snake's brain.

And it's not just some sort of circus trick. This is an ancient art in India. It didn't occur to me until Bhanu reminded me, but snakes are the animal most closely associated with Shiva. It's a religious thing. Snake charmers would have been on hand at holy festivals for thousands of years. The snake in the Hindu religion represents wisdom and eternity.

It used to be that they bashed out the snake's teeth to keep it from poisoning anyone. For a while snake charming was completely banned in India. Now they have come to a compromise. The venom is removed (how, I don't know) and the snakes can only be kept for twenty-two days. Then they must be released back into the grasslands and another snake must be found. And so the snakes, like the cows, are protected. Twenty-two days becomes the new eternity.

◀≀ **LISTEN 13.4**

On one of our very last nights together, Bhanu graciously invited us to his house in Jaipur. The Aussies and I packed into a tuk tuk and travelled for a very long way. It grew quieter. We could hear crickets and see stars in the sky. The tuk tuk puttered up to a wide, dark space and out of the shadows came Bhanu. About him were three dogs, obviously very much his, and very much concerned about these intruders. Bhanu spoke a few quiet words to them and they came snuffling up to us one by one, allowing themselves to be patted. We were on a large lawn and behind it was probably the finest private house I saw in India. Inside, I could see that the floors were marble. Bhanu had us sit out under the stars, though, and he brought out his photographs of the Bengal tigers to look at under the lamplight. Clearly this was the one true love of his life, and the photos were spectacular. He had tigers leaping, lurking in the undergrowth and running full tilt, ripping with muscles and grace.

When it grew cooler, we went into the house. It was a beautiful place, unlike anything I'd seen yet in India. Bhanu sat on the couch, talking to the Australian girls. I was up looking at some photos on the wall. To my great surprise, there was one of Bill Clinton shaking hands with a man. The next one over, even more surprisingly, was of Jacqueline Kennedy, her arm around the very same man. And it was signed by her, right across the picture. "Bhanu," I said, startled. "Who is this man?"

"That is my grandfather."

"Your grandfather knows Jackie Kennedy?"

"Yes. He was, well, something like the prime minister of Rajasthan."

"You've been holding out on us."

"Here." Bhanu got up and went out of the room for a moment. He came back with another photograph. It was much older and showed a grand old gentlemen in a turban with whiskers that went almost to the end of his shoulders.

"This is my great-grandfather. The Thakur of Bagru. He was the right-hand man of the last Maharaja."

"You're descended from royalty?"

"Yes, it's a little bit side of true." Bhanu's head bobbled. My difference engine clicked.

The world is indeed a strange and perplexing place. I'd experienced surprise and shock in India. I'd experienced fear and shame and despair. But I'd also experienced wonder and laughter and epiphany. I'd seen burning bodies but I'd also seen candles floating like stars down the Ganges. I'd heard master musicians and danced at an Indian wedding. I'd seen beggars and sacred cows and all the crushing exuberance of life among a billion others. And in the quiet of Bhanu's sanctuary, I'd become okay with it. The slap had lost its sting.

14

Russia and the East
There Will Your Heart Be

I KNOW A LITTLE PLACE IN MOSCOW CALLED THE SPUTNIK HOTEL. IT's worth staying there just for the name alone. Outside, there's a statue of Yuri Gagarin, the first man to go into space. He stands rigid, in high Communist style, arms perched as if he's just about to launch himself off his pedestal: to infinity and beyond.

Inside the Sputnik, in the faded lobby, I had my first experience with a pickpocket. I was sitting on a couch going over my map when I heard a voice behind me. "I'm terribly sorry, but I think that man is trying to rob you."

I looked down to see a hand creeping toward the pocket of my jacket. I looked up at the pickpocket and he stared at me, daring me to do something about it. Then he stood up and walked away, almost nonchalantly, as if nothing were amiss.

"I am sorry," came the voice again from behind me. "I thought I should warn you." I turned to see a slight young man sitting on the other side of me and I swivelled around to him. His accent was Australian, though not a thick one.

"Not very good, was he?" I said. "That wasn't even close."

"They're really everywhere, though they're not usually so brazen.

"You been here long?"

"I've been here for three days."

"I just arrived."

"My name's Michael," he said, extending a hand. It was loose and flappy. He was a little awkward, my new friend, and he reminded me of someone, though I couldn't quite place it.

"Are you waiting for the city tour?" I said.

"Hmm, yes, we were told to meet here."

A few others were beginning to congregate. There was Elli from New Zealand and Steve and Gabby from the United States. We chatted amiably until our guide strode in, a statuesque Russian beauty named Tatiana. She looked like a James Bond double agent and when she spoke it was with a deep and smoky Russian accent. *Perfect,* I thought.

Tatiana led us out and down a few blocks to the Leninskiy Prospekt metro station. We went down a long wooden escalator and into the world's most fantastic subway system. I'm not kidding. One station has stained glass windows like a church. Komsomolskaya Station is like a palace. It has vaulted ceilings and chandeliers. Real chandeliers dripping with cut glass baubles the size of your fist.

Tatiana clicked ahead of us in her high heels, her pencil-thin eyebrows bobbing whenever she stopped to explain something. We came back up to the street level in front of a massive cathedral of white marble topped with shining copper domes. They shimmered under the grey skies like a Russian Taj Mahal. "This," Tatiana explained, " is Khram Khrista Spasitelya. Is largest Orthodox Cathedral in world."

The domes were of that elongated shape I'd seen in pictures. "Onion domes" they call them. I took out my notebook to jot that down. Michael tipped into me. "What is it you're writing?"

"The onion domes," I said. "I was just thinking it might make a good metaphor for the stuff I'm writing. You know, peeling away the layers."

Tatiana eyed the two of us but did not falter in her speech. "Cathedral here was built in 1812. It is thanks for defeat of Napoleon."

"You can thank the long Russian winter for that," Steve, the American, whispered over to us. Michael harrumphed and looked uncomfortable.

"In 1931, cathedral was destroyed to make room for Palace of the People."

"But," Steve began again. He was a straight-up, no nonsense thirty-something from Denver. "If it was completely destroyed, then what the hell are we looking at here?"

"All marble was taken for metro. This you have seen."

"Down there? That was from the cathedral?"

"Here was only hole remaining," Tatiana continued, ignoring him. "Palace of the People was never built. Soon came Great Patriotic War. It was very hard for Russia. We have saying: 'Every family lose somebody in this war. Every family. That," she looked directly at Steve, "we will never forget. And that, you cannot imagine."

"Bah," he said under his breath.

"After glorious victory," Tatiana continued, looking back at the cathedral. "We make hole into swimming pool."

"You've got to be kidding."

"The great Moscow Pool was largest swimming pool in world." Tatiana whirled off towards the entrance.

"Of course it was," Steve said. "Glorious swimming pool."

Michael hummed uncomfortably behind Steve, feeling that he was starting to make a scene, but Tatiana was already clicking off towards the cathedral. Michael lurched after her and, again, there was something about him that reminded me of someone. What was it? Something about the way he walked, a little stiff, a little formal.

We entered through a wrought iron door and inside there were dark icons on the walls. It was a massive building, the central dome rising ten storeys above us. Tatiana strode out into the middle. There were no pews, no seats at all, just a huge empty space.

Somewhere up past the altar, a service was going on and I could hear singing. "We never forget out beautiful cathedral," Tatiana continued. "In 1990, we have change. We have permission from the government to rebuild cathedral." She eyed us coolly. "We build it exactly the same, exactly as we remember. This you see now."

I could only focus on the singing. It was like heaven's own choir. I couldn't see the people singing but their voices rose up in a swell of minor chords, reverberating through the whole cathedral. It was rich and full and extraordinarily beautiful.

Now, I don't know much about the Russian Orthodox Church but I do know that there are no musical instruments. There are no church organs or bells. No guitars or violins or trumpets. Only the human voice, as primordial as the constellations.

I was transfixed. I don't know how many voices were singing, ten, twenty, maybe. I got out my notebook. I was going to write something about how it was the same as that long-ago flute in the paleolithic cave; all the same things were at play, but just then, Tatiana leaned in to me.

She whispered, huskily, "Write in your notebook …"

"Pardon me?"

"This singing. This is true soul of Russia." For the first time, she was off her prepared speech. For a moment, her eyes softened, drifting away, and we both just listened. Her eyebrows arched into something resembling wonder, then the moment passed and she snapped back to herself again. She nodded once at me, rather formally, then turned back to address our group.

"When cathedral was rebuilt, we have not funds from government. The people of Moscow give money. Over one million people donated rubles. One million. This is will of Russian people."

Tatiana picked up her pace and we popped out between two buildings and into a massive plaza. Along one side of it were the red brick walls of the Kremlin. Down at the other end were the fairy-tale spires of St. Basil's Cathedral. The onion domes on St. Basil's were like striped ice cream cones, peppermint and vanilla and cherry.

"Here," announced Tatiana, "we have Red Square."

The skies were lowering grey above us and only a few people bustled across the massive square, making it look even bigger, a vast empty expanse of cobblestones and distant spires.

"Red Square," Tatiana began, "is not named for Communism. This is misconception. Red, for Russian people, means beauty and life. We have long winters. We have no colour for long winter months and so, for us, red is …"

"Poignant?" I said.

"Yes, it is so," she said, turning her piercing glare on me. "We go now to Mausoleum."

"Lenin," whispered Michael.

Up near the walls of the Kremlin was a small black granite building, monolithic and cold. A queue of people was lined up there, straggling out like a breadline. Tatiana waved us in behind them. "I wait for you on the other side."

"You're not coming?" Michael asked.

She didn't answer but strode off across the cobblestones. "I guess she's seen Lenin before," Steve said. "I don't imagine he's changed much."

The line moved quickly. Just at the entrance, one of the soldiers wobbled his gun at Michael, who froze. "Oh dear," he said.

The soldier barked something at him but he didn't move. Someone in front of us hissed back that he had to take his hands out of his pockets, to show respect. He yanked his hands out and the soldier lifted his gun. Then he tottered on into the mausoleum. It was right at that point that I knew what Michael reminded me of. It was C-3PO, the robot from *Star Wars*. The protocol droid. That was it exactly.

We were ushered into a dark room. On a stone slab there was Vladimir Lenin, preserved since his death in 1924. Apparently, it's a closely guarded secret how he was embalmed. He looked like he was just sleeping there. Even his thin moustache was perfectly trimmed, though his colour was waxy and slightly yellow. We hurried by, Michael still muttering his "oh dears" until we came out again into the square on the other side. Tatiana stood watch there like a prison guard.

"Come," she announced again as we bumbled to keep up. "Now we go in Kremlin."

For some reason, the front gate of the Kremlin is up a ramp. I remember as I walked up it that here I was, a Cold War kid from Canada, walking right through the front door of the Kremlin. It would have been unthinkable, even twenty years ago. But here I was, striding amongst ghosts.

We passed in under the Troitskaya Tower. It was topped with a ruby red five-pointed star, still there, though I would have thought it the quintessential symbol of Communism. We walked along the side of the Palace of Congress and came out into an open area called Cathedral Square.

At the foot of the bell tower was a massive cathedral bell, just sitting there on the pavement. "Here," she said, "is world's largest cathedral bell."

"Of course it is," said Steve.

The bell was huge, I had to admit.

"Never to ring," Tatiana went on. "Fifteen-ton piece of it is here. You can see."

"Ah," A great chunk of it had broken off like a tectonic plate.

"We have fire here in this church. The bell grows hot ..."

"Red hot."

"Just so. It grows red hot and when fire hose hit it ..."

"It cracked. Wow." I tried to imagine what that must have sounded like. The one and only peel of the great bell, a wrenching explosion of eight thick inches of bronze.

"We go now to Armoury." Tatiana clicked off and we trailed after her. To our right an area was blocked off. "What's down there?" I asked.

"Is official residence of president."

"Right there?"

"Yes."

Steve stepped forward. "Can we go in?"

"Not allowed." She stopped. "Is official residence."

"All the leaders lived there?"

"Yes."

"Even Stalin?"

Tatiana turned her withering stare on him. "Yes, even he. Also many czars and to be included also, Napoleon Bonaparte."

"Wow."

We passed by, though Steve's head swivelled longingly. Down another short lane was a large square building called the Armoury. It had once been the storage house for the royal arsenal but is now, in essence, the museum of the Kremlin. Inside it was a bit of a whirlwind. Tatiana took us through rooms filled with things like the royal carriage of Catherine the Great and the ivory throne of Ivan the Terrible.

In hall number two, there was a row of glass cases and Michael literally skipped over to one of them. "There they are," he whispered reverently. "Oh, I've been waiting for this."

I joined him. In the glass case in front of us were ten of the only remaining Fabergé eggs in the world. Michael hovered in front of them like a little boy in a toy shop. And toys they were.

"The Fabergé eggs," Tatiana announced behind us. I leaned in around Michael to see them. Even Steve was goggling over his shoulder. And Gabby, his wife, had pushed around the edge of him. These little treasures were worth tens of millions of dollars each. Fabergé was a Swiss jeweller hired by the czar to make an Easter egg surprise for his children. And the first one was such a success that for every Easter afterwards, until the execution of the royal family in 1918, there was a Fabergé egg wrought entirely from jewels and precious metals.

Each egg has a "surprise." My favourite was the Trans-Siberian Railroad Egg. It had a little toy train inside. In the display case, they'd set the train out, five miniature cars, each one no larger than your thumb and each one fashioned out of silver and gold and platinum. The whole thing could be wound up with a golden key, like an old clock, and the tiny train would actually run along a track on the outside of the egg. The locomotive at the front had a diamond for a headlight and the last car had two little rubies for taillights.

Michael pointed to another one, a golden egg set in a bowl, with spires and onion domes rising from it.

"That one is the Moscow Kremlin Egg."

"How do you know that?"

"I have been waiting to see these." All the writing was in the Russian Cyrillic script, though I could make out the date: 1906. That made me think that this egg in particular would have been handled by the last of the czar's children, the mysterious (and some say the sole survivor of the Revolution) Anastasia.

"What's this one have inside?"

"Hmmm," Michael said. "It's a music box."

"No kidding?" Steve said.

"Yes. It plays the czar's favourite Easter hymn."

"The world's most boring hymn?" said Steve.

"Shhh," said Michael. "It's serious."

Tatiana swept us onward after that through further rooms with fur-lined crowns and things like the Orloff Diamond, the third largest diamond in the world.

Steve harrumphed at that one. "Third largest," he scoffed. "Big frickin' deal."

Tatiana left us on our own after the tour of the Kremlin. She marched off into the grey streets without a backward glance. Michael and I wandered across Red Square and out to what looks like another palace but is in fact the G.U.M. department store. That stands for Glavnyi Universalnyi Magazin, which means, in typical Communist eloquence, the Main Universal Store.

We didn't stay long. Michael wanted a souvenir to remember Moscow and he picked through the aisles like a treasure hunter. I found a little something too and we headed back, down into the marble halls of the subway stations and back to the Sputnik Hotel. Outside, Yuri Gagarin greeted us, still holding his hands by his side like a swimmer about to take off from the starting blocks. Good luck to you, Yuri. May you one day finally leave that pedestal and find your infinity.

Later that night, I asked Michael what he'd bought and he looked a bit uncomfortable but rolled out a large package wrapped in brown paper. "I simply had to buy this," he said, pulling out a clump of cheap plastic the size of a drinking cup. It was a crude approximation of the Moscow Kremlin Egg, and I laughed when I saw it.

"It plays music, too," he said. He was already thumbing at a key on its side. "Listen ..."

I wondered how they were going to translate the choral singing, the czar's favourite hymn, but that's not what came out of Michael's egg. In the lobby of the Sputnik Hotel, a tinkling emerged. It was a sweet little tune, though it was hesitant and mechanical. This wasn't at all the music of the czars, I thought. This was a simple Russian folk song, hued with melancholy, and even as the spindles and cogs of Michael's egg turned and chimed, I could imagine the sound of a balalaika off on the frozen steppes, a fire lapping at the hearth in a peasant's hut, the snow swirling outside.

◀€   **LISTEN 14.2**

Neither of us said anything. We just listened until it wound down, slowing a bit, lurching once and then stopping. Michael looked up at me when it finished, a silly grin on his face, and he turned to wind it up again. The little melody started chunking out again and Michael pointed down at my bag. "What did you buy?"

"Two hundred and thirty one rubles for this." I pulled out a little wooden doll

"A matryoshka doll. Ooh, let me see. Let me see."

I passed it over and he eyed the hand-painted little doll. She was the shape of a miniature bowling pin. She was delicately painted with a red shawl draped over a swirl of blonde hair. Her face had big doe eyes and red circle cheeks. Michael turned it over and over, eyeing the painted embroidery of her dress. Then he twisted it and pulled it apart and inside was a smaller doll, painted in exactly the same way: red shawl, green embroidered peasant dress, blonde hair. He laughed and pulled that one apart too and inside was another. And inside the third one was the smallest of all — a baby matryoshka doll, no bigger than a grape.

"If I might say," began Michael, "maybe this is the metaphor you are looking for." Michael's egg was still clunking away in the background and I thought that, yeah, that was an idea. The phenomenon of music is multilayered. It's got a pretty little surface but that's just a simple matter of the physics of sound waves. That's only the shell.

There's something inside the painted doll that is music.

Our group travelled on together after that. We pulled a few marathon bus journeys and an overnight train that brought us down through the northern forests of Poland and into Warsaw. The old city there is called Stare Miasto. It was almost entirely destroyed at the end of the Second World War, and almost half the population was killed, but, just as we'd seen in Moscow, there are long memories here. It took fourteen years but they rebuilt the whole centre of Warsaw, exactly as it once was.

I went out for a walk by myself when we first got there and I was coming down a wide boulevard when I came across an old man sitting on a bench playing an accordion. He held it on his lap, pumping away at the alabaster keys. His white beard was neatly trimmed and on his head sat a jaunty cap.

◀᠄   LISTEN 14.3

The accordion squeezed out a Slavic melody, a little thing in a minor scale, though something of it hung in the air in a sophisticated, almost jazzy way. I imagine that he sat there all day playing various pieces. Musicians are often thought to have stellar memories. Many of them can play hundreds if not thousands of songs by memory. What this really means is that they've become very good at "chunking" the music. Musicians "hear" the underlying structures — the chord patterns, for example — and then it's easy to build the rest over top of that. There are several layers to this sort of memory, but it's a bit like playing chess. If you know the basic moves each piece can make, you begin to see certain patterns emerging over and over.

That's the mechanical part. What's important about music is something else. It's the feeling you put into it. It's the slight lag behind the tempo, the nuances of the phrasing, all the human qualities that tell you there's a real person playing.

The old man finished his piece and looked up at me. I'd been standing there awhile.

"You are first time to Poland?" he said.

"Yes."

"Is Krakowskie Przedmieście," he said, sweeping an arm out to indicate the broad boulevard. I already knew it was the central street leading into the old city. "Here," he continued, "is Copernicus." He pointed down the street and I knew what he was talking about. Just outside of the gates of the Science Hall of the University of Warsaw was a marble statue of Nicolaus Copernicus.

"Yes," I said, "Copernicus." I balled up a fist to represent the Sun and circled my other hand around it, orbiting it.

He chuckled. "Ya, good," he said. "And here," he turned, pointing a long finger at a church just down the other way, "is Chopin."

Now, I knew that Chopin was Polish. He lived most of his life in France and most people assume he's French. He certainly sounds French.

"Chopin," the man said again, sensing my confusion. He tapped out a little bit of a Chopin prelude on his keyboard. "Chopin, ya?" he said, and he took his hand and thumped it against his chest. He was looking for a word in English. "Go in church. You see. You see."

241

So I did. I thanked the man and dropped a few coins in his accordion case. He went back to pumping out his folk tunes and I went directly down the street to the Holy Cross Church. A patina of green hung on the old copper roof and at each side there were square bell towers. I went up the steps leading to a marble-bannistered balcony then entered the darkness of the church itself. There was no one really around. It took a while for my eyes to adjust and still longer to find it, but there it was, encased in one of the pillars. Chopin's heart.

The composer left instructions from his deathbed that his heart should be buried in Poland. The rest of him is buried in a cemetery in Paris but his heart was removed and, or so the story goes, preserved in a cask of brandy for the long trip back to Warsaw. And there it lies, encased in a pillar of the church that was only a building or two away from the place where he grew up. Carved onto the pillar is a little epitaph. It reads, in Polish, "For where your treasure is, there will your heart be also."

And, yes, I thought, that's just what I'd been looking for. With Copernicus swinging the Earth around the Sun, with Russian dolls that come apart and peeling onion domes, there is a centre to all this. And the centre is the human heart. Everything comes from the musician's intention to reproduce his or her own deepest feelings. To produce something beautiful and meaningful, something emotionally charged. Something that will touch others and let us know that we're all in this together.

Further down into Poland is the pretty little city of Krakow. We all headed for the huge medieval town square. At one end are the double towers of St. Mary's Cathedral, and we could see that a crowd was already gathering under the north tower. Up at the top of this tower, every day, a golden trumpet appears in the highest window. The trumpet sounds out a simple little tune that everyone in Poland knows by heart. It's called "Hejnał Mariacki" and this whole ritual is broadcast over the Polish national radio station. It's become a sort of musical signature for the country itself.

What's interesting, though, is that tune never properly ends. The trumpet player always stops just before the last note, pretty much in mid-melody. He just stops. There's a reason for this, of course. It marks a particular moment in the city's history, a moment in the year 1241 when an invading army was approaching the city walls.

From the high tower, the bugler, placed there deliberately as an early warning system, saw the dust of the horses approaching and sounded the alarm. He played the "Hejnał Mariacki" but before he could get to the end, an arrow took him through the throat. Nevertheless, the alarm had been sounded. The city gates were slammed shut, the battlements were manned, and the marauding army was turned away.

◀⁓ LISTEN 14.4

So, the trumpet player today — and presumably every day for 672 years — stops in the melody just when that original bugler died, to commemorate his selfless act. We often associate music with events in this way. The stories get locked in our collective memories. They serve to distinguish us as a group, as a people, and I guess that's like the next shell out.

There are even instances, like this one, where a little phrase can come to represent a whole nation. And it brings up an interesting question: Is there music that is particularly Russian, say, or Italian, or, for that matter, Rajasthani? Can you hear a few bars and, like a language, just know that it comes from a particular part of the world?

Well, one of the most intriguing studies I came across looked at just this idea. In 2003, researchers Patel and Daniele looked at more than three hundred musical themes from sixteen different composers, some specifically English (Edward Elgar, for example — think "Pomp and Circumstance") and some specifically French (Debussy — think "Clair de Lune"). And, in a very carefully controlled study they did find something that could be considered particularly French or English about the music. What it turned out to be was a sort of mirroring of the language, in particular the way the stress falls on syllables in French or English. It's complicated, but basically, the music either followed the patterns of languages in which the stress patterns are quite variable (English) or languages in which the stress on syllables is quite uniform (French). The study was replicated in 2008 with over eight thousand pieces of music from American, Austrian, English, German, Swedish, French, Italian, and Spanish composers, and they came to exactly the same conclusion.

So, to at least some degree, it is true. We can hear music — even aside from the particular instruments of a place — and be able to recognize where it comes from. It's a carryover effect of the language spoken in those places. Language and music did develop from the same evolutionary root, there's no doubt about that. Both mark us as a people. Language describes our worlds. And music? Well, music is the glue that binds us together.

The second pickpocket came at me on the overnight train to Bucharest. In the middle of the night, I lay on the little foldout couchette, listening to the clattering of the train. I was restless and not sleeping, and through my semi-conscious state I started to pick out another sound. A sort of gentle rattling.

Now, these night trains are often the haunt of thieves and night crawlers and all manner of the strange and unusual. Through my sleep-less blur, I began to realize a man was trying to break into our cabin. I turned around quickly and the first thing I saw was that the compartment door was just sliding open. That was unsettling, since I knew for a fact that I had chained it from the inside and locked it both at the top and the bottom. But there it was. The door was open a good hand's width wide.

I didn't see anyone at first, but as I continued to stare at the gap, a face appeared and a small flashlight beamed in at me. It shone in through the crack and above it I could see the thief. I could see his face. It's burned into my episodic memory. In fact, I'm pretty sure I could still pick him out of a police lineup if I had to.

Anyway, he took off down the corridor when he saw that he'd been busted, and I just lay there with my heart pounding, wondering what I should do. I reached down to check that my bag was still there. It was. Michael and Steve and Gabby were all in the cabin with me, but they were all fast asleep.

I thought of yelling. I thought of waking the others. But I don't know, I was still half asleep and it occurred to me that this man, this thief, prob-ably had a knife or something. I don't mean to say he'd use it on anyone, but he probably had something sharp to slash open bags or slit through straps, so I didn't attempt to go after him. He didn't get anything anyway.

I closed the door again, locked it, and spent the rest of the fitful night listening. I kept imagining that I heard that rattling again, again and again, when, like an Edgar Allen Poe story, it was really just my own heart thumping. In the full light of morning, I told everyone about it. Steve, of course, said that he would have chased the guy down and beaten him up. "Frickin' gypsies."

"Gypsies?" Michael yelped.

"Why would you think he was a gypsy?" I broke in.

"They're all thieves," said Steve, pounding a fist into a cupped palm.

"You know, Steve, I have gypsy blood in me."

"You do? Should I be watching my stuff more closely?"

"Maybe you should."

My great grandmother, Audrey Adams, was born in a gypsy caravan in southern England in the late 1880s. I don't know much about it. I only knew her briefly when I was really little. We called her Broken Grandma because she was in a wheelchair. My only memory of her is of a frail old lady well into her nineties. Still, from her I guess I can claim that I have at least a few drops of gypsy blood pumping through my steely British veins.

We think now that gypsies — or more properly the Roma people — originally came out of northern India. They hightailed it out of there sometime around the ninth century C.E., though we're not sure why. The name "gypsy" comes from the mistaken belief that they'd come from Egypt. They didn't. Over the centuries they migrated across Asia Minor and out into Eastern Europe, especially Romania, which still has the largest Roma population in the world.

For a while they were a slave class in Eastern Europe. They're still heavily repressed and in all those years many of them have refused to settle down. They're a people apart, nomadic almost, and yeah, some of them are pickpockets. I've seen gypsy children working the crowds in Paris and in Rome, just like something out of *Oliver Twist*.

They're also fine musicians. Many of them have become known throughout Eastern Europe as a professional class of musicians. They're the ones you hire to play at your wedding. You watch the silverware, I guess, but if you want the best band, you hire the gypsies.

A couple of hours later, we were hauling down through the hills of northern Romania. The train stopped at the station in Brasov, which is the capital of the province of Transylvania. Michael had his face pressed to the glass because we'd told him it was Transylvania. Not far off is the real Dracula's castle, and I think Michael just wanted to see what vampire country looked like. By noon, though, our train pulled into the tattered old city of Bucharest.

That evening, our last night together as a group, we all went to a restaurant on the outskirts of town. It looked a bit like a barn. There were at least a couple of chickens up in the rafters while we were eating. I don't know what they were doing up there, but they flapped around, pecking at the crossbeams, all the time we were there.

After we ate, we ordered some pints of Romanian beer and the entertainment came on. Of course, it was a gypsy band. In Romania, specifically, these gypsy musicians are Lăutari, and they are some of the finest musicians on the planet.

The band was fronted by a clarinet player, and oddly enough, beside him a man playing the pan pipes. There was a fiddle and a drummer and a cello and a hammered instrument like a marimba. An odd assortment of instruments, but when they kicked into their performance they sounded like a Dixieland jazz band hopped up on steroids. They played incredibly fast, burning through the melodies, racing along at breakneck speed.

◀╏ LISTEN 14.5

After a few songs, a line of folk dancers came out in front of them with much knee-slapping and high-kicking. Oktoberfest meets the Mongol hordes, I thought. As the night progressed, the band played even faster and the dancers triumphantly managed to keep up with them, even providing some rhythms themselves, slapping away with their hands at all parts of their bodies.

Rhythm patterns are complex throughout the Balkans, not only Romania, but in Bulgaria and Albania and the sad war-torn states of Bosnia, Serbia, and Croatia. Most of Western pop music is in 4/4 time. It's easy and straightforward to dance to. But throw in a 5/4 pattern and watch the dance floor clear. No one in Western Europe quite knows what to do with two legs and five beats. For Roma musicians this is child's play.

Through many of the Balkan states, you will hear a beat called *Kopanica* that rings in at 11/8 time. In Bulgaria, a meter called *Sandansko Oro* is set at mind-blowing 22/8 time. It was explained to me that it's actually one bar of 9/8 and then one of 13/8 — as if that makes it easier.

But it's not as impossible as it sounds, because they don't count the meter like we do. They think of it as more like Morse code with patterns of short beats and long beats. So they might have short, short, short, long and then short, short, long, short, short. Think of it like a pattern in spoken speech. Shakespeare, for example, was famous for his iambic pentameter. Your high school English teacher would have bored you to death with this observation. The pattern is five pairs of short and long. Da Dah, Da Dah … Da Dah, Da Dah, Da Dah. "But Soft, what light through yonder window breaks." Do you hear that?

Just speed up the tempo by a factor of ten and you've got one possible gypsy pattern. The Lăutari band I was hearing were roaring along in 8/8 time, a relatively straight time signature for them, but lightning fast.

The dancers were all in white. The men had red sashes tied around their waists and the women wore embroidered red aprons. They flung each other across the floor, occasionally raising their hands above their heads to clap along to the rhythm. The men kicked their legs up sideways, slapping at their heels with their palms. The women whirled behind them and the band played ever faster and faster.

We ploughed through a number of pints of beer until, finally, the presentation part of the dancing had apparently finished. The dancers came out into the crowd, grabbing people — Steve, for one — by the elbow to get them up dancing. Gabby went with him and the unfortunates who had been grabbed formed a large circle with the dancers, all interlocking arm in arm. The band roared back into life and the circle began to spin. You didn't need to know any steps. Everyone just held arms and circled together in a sideways and wildly out of control conga line. Michael slunk down in his chair at the inappropriateness of it all.

I got up to have a go as well. Why not? My gypsy blood was pumping. I tried to dip in with Steve and Gabby but missed them going around. No matter, someone parted and I jumped in, linking arms and spinning with the rest. Flying around to the music, I narrowed my eyes and tried to imagine that I was in an old gypsy caravan. I kind of hoped my Broken Grandma could see me now.

You've got to wonder if there's something in the DNA of people that makes them good musicians. Like these Lăutari. They were fantastic. Or, people often point out how eight different generations of the Bach family produced nothing but extraordinary musicians. Well, the truth is that there's not a stitch of evidence that it's in our genes. Or at least, there's no one gene that accounts for musical ability. I suppose there are things like fine motor control, good memory for rhythms or melodies, and maybe perfect pitch. On the whole, though, it's not in our genes.

It comes from living in a family, and a wider community, who value music. It comes from long, hard hours of practise and it comes from the collective memory of our larger group. It's no coincidence, then, that the major events of our lives are ennobled with music. Music defines us. It comes from the deepest parts of who we are.

We said our goodbyes that night. Steve and Gabby were leaving for Istanbul. Michael was flying home. I was heading west. It was actually kind of sad. It's funny how quickly you can get attached to other people. For all their quirks and funny ways, I will really miss them. And to this day, whenever I hear a little chiming music box, well … it makes me think of Michael's plastic egg.

My last stop was a special one. I was headed for Italy to see the Carnival of Venice, a two-week spree of masques and balls and parades and music dating back almost nine hundred years.

Venice is called the *Repubblica della Serenissima,* the Serene Republic. I've always liked that. I arrived by train but then took a water taxi up the Grand Canal to the Rialto Bridge. I'd found a little hotel there just a few steps away from Marco Polo's house. It was on a small canal, one of the thousands that course through the city. A gondola floated by. At the back was a gondolier in a striped shirt and straw hat, poling it through the water. On the cushions in the middle sat a figure dressed all in black and wearing a mask.

These ornate masks date back to a time when there were strict divides between the social classes. For the time of the carnival, at least, it no longer mattered. You were in disguise. Better than disguise, you could be whoever you wanted to be.

The Carnival this year was themed *Sensation Sestieri 6 x 6.* That meant that each of the six districts, the sestieri of Venice, was supposed to represent one of the senses. For the sixth sense they had imagination. Really, it was more interesting on paper than it was in reality but it did make me think about a few things. In the Santa Croce district, by the train station, the sense of smell was represented. Now, everyone has had the experience of smelling something — fresh baked bread, a certain perfume, a whiff of tequila — and having it cause an avalanche of vivid memories. We don't know why exactly smell should do this. One theory has it that the olfactory nerve is just very close to the hippocampus, where our memories get sorted.

The auditory cortex also happens to be pretty close to the hippocampus and it's probably the only other thing besides scent that evokes such strong memories. Nothing else seems to come close. I should clarify, though, that it's not the hippocampus which stores the memories. It just sorts them. Memories are widely diffused through the brain.

Music is something like this too. It's widely diffused. It seems to have tapped into all sorts of neural networks — movement and memory and emotion. For that reason, it's become something central to our sense of personal identity. Something that not only defines us as a group, but something that defines us as individuals.

In a little square in the San Polo sestiere I came across a little piece of magic. I was coming around a corner, just wandering, half lost, when the lane opened up into a small square. In the middle was an old fountain, dry as a bone, and just in front of it was a man dressed for the Renaissance. He could've stepped right out of a painting by Raphael or Fra Angelico. He was bent over a lute, a wonderful ancient-looking instrument, and he was plucking out some pretty intricate counterpoint. Counterpoint is where two different melodic lines twine together. It arrived at about the end of the Renaissance and is pretty much the hallmark of the Baroque period in music. And one composer above all others was its master.

"Bach?" I asked the man when he finished.

"Yes." Other tourists were walking by. He looked pleased that someone had stopped to talk to him.

"Are you from Venice?"

"No, I am from Hungary. I come only for the festival."

"And the piece you played …"

A lute player at the Carnival of Venice.

"It is the Bourée in E minor for Lute. Bach wrote it on keyboard but it was meant for the lute."

🔊 **LISTEN 14.6**

"Can you play another?"

"Yes, of course."

He began again, the familiar melody of "Jesu, Joy of Man's Desiring," one of Johann Sebastian Bach's most enduringly beautiful pieces. This one is a cantata, a choral work for several voices. It's been transcribed over the years for solo piano, for organ, and for lute or guitar. It's been used in movie soundtracks and is popular at weddings. It's been covered by everyone from the Beach Boys to the Mormon Tabernacle Choir. And here it was at the Carnival of Venice.

But that's hardly anything compared to how far Bach's music has risen. I guess you could say it's the next shell out. Right out of the solar system. In a leap of real imagination, the engineers at NASA, way back in

1977, launched the Voyager I space probe and included a recording on it, a literal gold record with three pieces by Johann Sebastian Bach. By the time the big rockets had dropped away, Voyager was no more than a metal shell the size of your washing machine. By 1979, Voyager had passed by Jupiter. By 1998 it had passed the orbit of Pluto and entered interstellar space, becoming the most distant object ever launched by man.

Voyager is just about 18 billion kilometres from the sun as I write this. And about 40,000 years from now it will come to the next nearest star in our galaxy. On the golden disk there are instructions, in simple stick figures, of how to build a machine to play the music. And if anyone out there ever does find it and if they listen to it, we shall be adding another layer, the shell of a Russian doll, to the long history of music.

What will they think of Bach, I wonder? What will those little green people think when they hear his prelude and fugue in C major? It makes you wonder, doesn't it?

PART FOUR
Musical Intelligence

15

VIENNA
The Sound of Genius

Schönbrunn Palace sits like a wedding cake on the outskirts of Vienna. Pediments and casement windows line the lemon yellow walls like icing. Marble statues jut up from the roof as if they'd been squeezed out of a baker's tube. Inside are the apartments and offices and state banquet halls of the once mighty Austro-Hungarian Empire. For eight hundred years the Hapsburg family ruled half of Europe from this great confectionary. And for a few brief decades in the late eighteenth century, the place played host to a trio of musical geniuses the like of which the world will not soon see again.

I arrived, fumbling up the stairs from the U-bahn. At first, it was almost impossible to take the whole palace in. There are several wings containing fourteen hundred rooms. It spills out across four or five city blocks. I walked into the grounds and a carriage clopped past me, the blindered horse trotting across the cobblestone courtyard with a load of tourists. So I veered left instead and walked along a wing called the Orangerie. This had been a sort of greenhouse two centuries before. They kept lemon and orange trees through the winter there. It was also where the royalty had their most lavish parties, summer picnics even in the most dire and grey of Viennese winters.

Around the back were vast gardens and fountains and I climbed a staircase there, up onto a balcony that overlooked the rolling parklands with, off in the distance, a view of the Gloriette, a grand ornamental gate up on a distant rise. Hedges and rose gardens and golf-course-like greens spread before me.

Somewhere down the paths here, I imagined a young boy arriving with his father in 1762. Wolfgang Amadeus Mozart was six years old and he clutched in his tiny hands a piece he'd written himself. His father, Leopold, a brutal taskmaster by some accounts, hustled the young boy in with his sister. The gleeful Leopold Mozart had managed to arrange a performance for the two of them in front of the empress herself.

I ducked in through a passageway that brought me back out to the front of the palace, and there I bought an admission ticket and an audio guide. A visit to the palace today is a highly regulated affair. You're channelled down the hallways in strict progression. Photography is forbidden and you are kept from even touching the walls by thick velvet ropes. I held the audio guide up to my ear and pushed the button for station number one. A voice spoke to me in a clipped Austrian accent and off I went into the maze of rooms. Marie Antoinette, the electronic voice insisted, grew up in the apartments down this hallway. Napoleon slept in this bed over here. The Archduke Ferdinand, whose assassination would trigger the First World War and the end of the Hapsburgs, played with his toy blocks on the parquet floor here, just beneath the mirror.

Somewhere in the guts of all this glory, I stopped in one long room, a widened corridor really, now called the Hall of Mirrors, though it was, in fact, just a sitting room for Empress Maria Theresa the First. The empress was a sort of Queen Victoria of her time, staid and regal, mother to kings and royalty across the continent. And it was here that the six-year-old Mozart was ushered in to sit in front of a clavinet. The empress's entire entourage would have been there, her secretaries and handmaids, and they all looked to the empress for signs of boredom.

The empress nodded and the little boy set his plump fingers over the keys. He looked once at his father and then he began to play. The empress cocked her head at the first notes and then as the rush of beauty came at her, dazzling, almost impossibly perfect from the hands of this tiny boy, her expression relaxed and she allowed herself a smile. At the end, she clapped, quite wholeheartedly, and the little boy genius pushed himself down off the bench. The whole room was filled with applause and the boy, not knowing any better, maybe a little overcome by the adoration, jumped up into the empress's lap and planted a big fat kiss on her cheek.

That would have cost an older man his head, but for the little wunderkind it earned him more laughter and applause. And a first footnote in the history books.

So much has been written of Mozart that it's hard now to know what is true and what is apocryphal. The story of the empress is well-documented and I was standing in the room where it actually happened. The little boy was not only miraculously, almost supernaturally talented, he was also very charming.

I eventually wound my way out of the palace, but I lingered there in the cobblestone courtyard even as the doors to main palace were locked. It was exactly six thirty. Evening was closing down over the spires of Vienna but I had to wait. In the Orangerie there was to be a concert that night. A chamber orchestra was going to play Mozart in one of the places where he himself had performed.

The crowd of tourists began to dissipate and a different audience began to arrive, in tuxedos and evening gowns. I was most certainly underdressed but I was ushered in along with them, into the great glassed hall. The interior was dazzling. The walls were white but there were elaborate fixtures everywhere, carvings in the shapes of spears and shields and draping cloths — all of it gilded in gold. All the panelling bore mouldings, also gilded in gold, so that, under the blaze of the cut glass chandeliers, they traced lines of liquid fire across the walls.

Mozart had played in this very room soon after he'd moved to Vienna from Salzburg. There'd been a competition on February 7, 1786, between him and the court composer, Antonio Salieri. By all accounts, Salieri won. That might surprise you. What had happened was that Salieri's composition was played by court musicians, the best in the land, while Mozart's piece was played by amateur musicians, a couple of them from his own extended family. He didn't stand a chance.

I tried to imagine Mozart standing there, perhaps over by one of the windows. He was still young, but he was now surrounded by the best of Vienna. The emperor himself had given Mozart the idea for his little piece, another reason why it may not have been so good.

We all took our seats and the fluttering of paper and shuffling of chairs gradually died down. There was silence and then applause as the orchestra took the stage. This was a chamber orchestra, about half the size of a full symphony orchestra; a little less brass, not quite so many violins, almost nothing for percussion. And then the conductor, Sebastian Aigner, came out to a great roar from the crowd. Aigner had trained with the great Vienna Philharmonic. He bowed modestly then turned to his players, raising his baton. Thirty-one musicians raised their instruments. A trumpet flashed under the chandeliers. The warm cinnamon-coloured wood of an old cello sat under a waiting bow.

They began with an excerpt from *The Marriage of Figaro*, perhaps Mozart's most famous opera. The violins opened with a swirl of notes. Then the woodwinds came in with the theme, and four bars in, with a mighty whoomp, the entire orchestra took up the same theme. And I knew it. I'd heard it dozens of times before in movie scores and television commercials and black tie galas.

Mozart himself conducted the first performances of *Figaro*. It was one of his first big successes and the newspapers of the day largely praised it. There's also a record that, on that opening night, someone (we're not sure who) paid professional hecklers to boo from up in the first balcony. They booed so loudly that at times they drowned out the singers. This was not unusual in those days. Things were tough. The audience, especially for a comic opera, could be a rowdy bunch. How unlike that it was tonight. The audience around me sat politely. Even a squeaky chair somewhere in front of me brought a few heads swivelling around with disdainful glances.

It was lush and lovely. To the left of the stage were the strings. To the back was the brass section, the trumpets punctuating the chords, sizzling above them. They quieted and then the gentle woodwinds took over with a hollow melancholy refrain. The cello and a single contrabass — a walnut-coloured veteran — pumped behind them like a deep, soulful heartbeat. There was a wide spectrum of timbres, colouring the music like the palette of a painter.

 **LISTEN 15.1**

It took thirty-one players to produce this one piece of music. Their synchronization was perfect, and even the feeling or mood that emerged was a whole. A single thing. And this was because of the conductor.

Isn't it strange? The musician most responsible for bringing out the soul of it all wasn't even playing an instrument at all. Maestro Aigner stood at the front, waving a thin stick in the air.

I watched him carefully. I could see how he was controlling the tempo. How when he raised a cupped palm upwards, the dynamics of the orchestra would swell up in volume, how he pointed at and cued the various sections, how he stabbed with his baton to get the specific articulation of notes that he wanted. And at the end, with a circular motion of both hands, he rounded off the last long note, and between his forefinger and thumb pinched off the last trailing timbres, closing them to silence.

A genteel smattering of applause followed the excerpt. Maestro Aigner turned and bowed slightly, formally, then returned to his music stand to flip the pages to the next piece. I looked down at my program. It was Haydn's Symphony Number 92, popularly called the Oxford Symphony. Joseph Haydn wrote 112 symphonies in all. In fact, he's been called the father of the symphony, a towering figure in Vienna long before Mozart arrived. The orchestra played the second movement, an adagio, a slow, beautifully structured piece in three sections. It began in a major key then went to a minor section and ended again with the major. This is important. Classical music actually refers to a specific period of music — pretty much covering the period from Haydn's birth to his death. It's music that has a highly structured form both in length and in melodic arrangement. Pieces stick to their key signature. They resolve on the tonic. They don't often flirt with peculiar time signatures.

Haydn was the master of this period but the young Mozart was already knocking at the door of the Romantic period that was to follow. He and Mozart knew each other quite well. Haydn was almost thirty-five years Mozart's senior but they played together in string quartets with Haydn on the violin and Mozart on the viola. Imagine that.

I sat through the symphony, enjoying it, but thinking that, yes, there was a predictability about it. I felt like I always knew what the next note or chord would be. I want to be really clear here that this comes only from hindsight, from the benefit of two hundred years of perspective.

In Haydn's day, this would have been the height of creativity. Haydn, to a very large degree, all but invented the forms and structures of classical music. And nobody could have predicted what was to come. Nobody could have predicted the blazing comet that was Mozart.

When the symphony finished, there was a short intermission and I went outside to wander around the gardens. Night had fallen and a full moon rose over Vienna. Inside, framed in the great arched windows, I could see the bustle of evening gowns and tuxedos scrambling for a glass of wine, consulting their programs like dictionaries. The stage was now empty. They'd turned down the spotlights so that the walls there were lit with a gentle tangerine hue, almost like the inside of a seashell.

Out in the gardens, in front of the window, people passed back and forth, silhouetted, the tips of their cigarettes dancing like fireflies. I walked out into the darkness, trying to see the stars, but I didn't make it far. I heard them announce that we should take our seats again and I scurried back to find my place.

When I sat down again, there was an excitement rippling through the audience. The next piece was the one we'd really all come to hear. They were going to play some excerpts from one of Mozart's very last compositions, *The Magic Flute*.

Maestro Aigner came out again, and this time two singers came out onto the stage along with him. Judith Halász was the soprano. She wore a dress which, in contrast to the black attire of the orchestra behind her, was a firebrick red. It had spaghetti straps and it sparkled when she moved. To her right was the baritone, Vesselin Stoykov. Aigner raised his baton and an E flat major chord swelled out into the room. It hovered in the air and pulsed once at the end. I was watching the conductor's hands again, watching how he literally pinched the air to cut off the sound. Then the next chord, a C minor, with that same faint pulse of rhythm at the end. Then a higher inversion of the E flat. It was as if Mozart had taken Haydn's complete movement and written it into three chords. Alex Ross, the music critic for the *New Yorker* magazine, once wrote of this opening that "it's as if Mozart has written the emotional stages of an entire life in three bars: hope, pain, wisdom."

How did he do it? It's only three chords. What is it about these three chords that can wrest so much emotional gold out of us? Somehow, in the total effect — all the different timbres of the orchestra, all the notes and harmonics and even that little rhythmic pulse at the end — somehow it stirs the most profound feelings in us. It's the conductor at the front who controls it, who unleashes it, but what we would like to think is that we are hearing exactly what Mozart wanted us to hear and exactly what he intended us to feel — in fact, what he himself would have felt on first composing it.

And that, right there, is the genius of music.

The overture ended, and Judith Halász now stepped to the front of the stage. Her dark hair cascaded down the back of her neck. Stoykov, the baritone, came forward beside her, dressed in the most formal of tuxedos. They were to sing the famous duet of the second act, the "Papageno," which comes towards the end of the opera. Halász lifted the palms of her hands in front of her, as if to hold up the very air, as if to command it, to spill it out like a god. And the orchestra began.

There's a section about halfway through the duet where Stoykov, playing the part of Papageno, brings out a set of magic bells. In the background, this is played by a percussionist on a glockenspiel. But it looks as if the singer is playing them. The bells tinkle, sparkling above the orchestra in a melody as beautiful as any you are likely to hear. The notes danced and splashed and Stoykov sang his lines between them. The audience, and I include myself here, were absolutely entranced.

◀︎ᵉ **LISTEN 15.2**

Mozart himself conducted *The Magic Flute* on the opening night in September 1791. He died just nine weeks later at thirty-five, a tragedy that is almost too unbearable to imagine.

St. Stephen's Cathedral rests in a cobblestone square at the centre of Vienna. An ornate gothic tower rises up on its south side. The top of the tower was lopped off by a bomb during the Second World War but they've rebuilt it, and you can see the newer stones, whiter and cleaner, starting about halfway up.

Across the square, an arched passageway leads you under a building and out into a quieter side street. Mozart lived here at Domgasse number five between 1784 and 1787. These were his glory years in Vienna. He was at the height of his fame and prosperity, moving in the highest circles of society, well known even to the emperor himself. It didn't last long, though. Mozart's years after he moved out of this apartment were sad and ignoble and wracked by illness and poverty.

These apartments are now a museum. The whole building has been taken over by the exhibits, though Mozart and his wife rented only the rooms on the first floor. These would have been the most exclusive rooms in the place. If you look at the outside of the building, the windows get smaller as you go up. There were no elevators, so the rooms further up the stairs were less desirable, less a mark of status.

In these rooms, he wrote *Figaro*, the Prague Symphony, several piano concertos, a couple of horn concertos, a few violin sonatas, and five string quartets. Clearly he was prodigious and most of what he wrote here we would unabashedly called genius. But what does that really mean?

Most experts now realize that there are many different kinds of intelligence. The authority on the subject is Howard Gardner out of Harvard. Gardner recognizes seven intelligences, including mathematical intelligence, spatial intelligence, verbal intelligence, and, yes, musical intelligence.

Musical intelligence, though, is less well defined than the others, probably because we assume we know exactly what it is. But do we? Certainly musical intelligence must include things like having a good sense of melodic patterns — being able to identify and remember tunes. It probably includes an intuitive understanding of chord sequences — what chord will most naturally follow the tonic, which minor will go with it, and that sort of thing. All these things are the stuff of musical theory. It's just that people with musical intelligence "get it" rather easily. They intuit it rather than learn it.

But loads of people have these sorts of talents. It's not unusual. More refined, perhaps, is the gift of perfect pitch. It's thought that only about one in ten thousand people still have that. I say "still" because it looks as if most infants are born with perfect pitch. It's one of those things that gets pruned out of the growing brain if it's not needed. So even that may not be particularly special. The trick of knowing that it's an A flat when a spoon is dropped on the floor is impressive, but it also doesn't really account for genius.

I walked up the creaky steps from street level and into the actual rooms of Mozart's apartment. *He was really here*, I kept thinking. The legendary Wolfgang Mozart. He walked these floorboards. He looked out that window. Of course, the place has changed. None of the furniture is Mozart's and even the walls have been reconfigured to allow for the flow of people through the museum, but this was the place. This was where he wrote some of the world's greatest music.

Up on the walls, there are glass cases containing bits and pieces of his life. There's an original program from *The Marriage of Figaro* and, over in the next case, a copy of some of his handwritten scores. I bent into the glass, trying to see around the barred reflections of the fluorescent lights. His notes were spidery, though quite legible, and I could pick out the melodies easily enough.

Mozart wrote in his letters that many of his pieces came to him on long carriage rides — to premieres in Prague or Berlin, for instance. The music seemed to come quite fully formed and he simply wrote it down, almost without changes. Or that's what he said.

A lot of research into genius has moved away from the idea of some sort of innate talent. Studies into childhood prodigies are now focusing on the emotional disposition of the child. There seems to be what's called a "rage to master." These precocious children are very intent and very focused on the task of learning. There's also considerable evidence that a good mentor must be present. In this case, it was Mozart's father — no small musician himself — who had the young boy practising hours a day by the time he was four. Leopold Mozart may have been a strict taskmaster but that was the only way Wolfgang could have become so quickly proficient. And there's a tender side that's often lost in the retelling. Leopold apparently took great care to write down the simple melodies that his young son was writing. He seemed to know that even from the earliest days this boy was showing a remarkable determination to compose.

There's nothing magical here. It seems to be a case of a reasonably talented young boy who simply worked harder than anyone else. The Swedish psychologist Anders Ericsson arrived at the idea that ten thousand hours of practise will make you an expert in any given pursuit. He looked at professional musicians, master chess players, and professional athletes to come up with this number. And, lest you think it's easy, you should know that ten thousand hours is a pretty unforgiving amount of time to invest. You would have to practise three hours a day, seven days a week for almost ten years — steadily, without a break or holiday — to reach your ten thousand hours. It's a lot.

Mozart probably reached that number by his early teens. The things he wrote as a child are cute. I've heard his first symphony and it's amusing but by no means startling. On the other hand, pieces he wrote when he was fifteen are now staples in the orchestral canon. Pieces as good as anything anyone has ever composed.

Malcolm Gladwell later popularized the idea of ten thousand hours in his book *Outliers,* but Gladwell — and fair enough — also considered social context. This included things like the time of year you were born, access to the best technology, or, in the case of musicians, access to the best musical instruments and outstanding teachers. Perhaps most important is the level of the respect or status given to musicians in that particular society at that particular time.

All this holds true for Mozart. Quite in contrast to the idea we might have of the solitary genius working in isolation, we know now that Mozart was out almost every night, going to concerts, meeting other musicians, listening to others' works critically and thoughtfully. He was surrounded by music. He was practical and very focused on his work. He wrote and re-wrote much of what he was hearing, grabbing onto phrases as they came to him, noting them down before they could be forgotten.

Prolific composers such as Mozart have innumerable melodies coursing through their heads. Part of Mozart's genius lay in selecting which melodies he would work on, in knowing which ones were good and which ones should be discarded as ordinary and predictable. My favourite quotation on genius is apt here. It comes from the philosopher Arthur Schopenhauer: "Talent hits a target no one else can hit; genius hits a target no one else can see."

Figaro was a popular hit, for sure, but later, by the 1790s, Mozart was writing things that nobody else had ever attempted. In his last summer on Earth, in dire poverty with two children running around his feet, in a one-room apartment, gravely, gravely ill, he wrote his three final symphonies. He wrote them — three full symphonies — in less than six weeks. It's astounding, and all the more so that in them he was at his best, writing the finest structures and melodies of his career. The strict classical forms of Haydn, the resolutions to the tonic chord, the allowable key changes and meters, even the allowable chords — never a diminished or augmented seventh — are there, but there's more. He avoided the expected cadence, surprising the listener, delighting the connoisseur with the unexpected. There's a richness and experimentation that had not been heard before. And a sublime beauty. In them, Mozart was knocking on the door of a new age.

It was indisputably Mozart. What I mean is that no one else was doing it. No one else could have done it. In a letter to a friend, Mozart wrote, "Why my productions take from my hand that particular form and style that makes them 'Mozartish' and different from the works of other composers, is probably owing to the same cause which renders my nose so large or so aquiline or, in short makes it Mozart's, and different from those of other people. For I really do not study or aim at any originality."

Still, he must have had a sense. He must've known that he was doing things that no one else could do, things that were indelibly stamped with the deepest part of his being. Even two hundred years later, when we hear a conductor lead an orchestra through one of his pieces, what we want to say is that we are hearing Mozart. We are literally hearing the essence of that man. That's perhaps the strangest mystery in all of music. One that is at the heart of everything.

Up on the second floor of the Mozart House, there were more displays and in one small case up on the wall by the door, there was a locket — no more than the size of the face of a wristwatch. I moved in closer. On it was painted a street scene of Vienna, a man with his back to the viewer. It was delicately rendered and quite beautiful. I looked down at the label and read that this was actually a locket owned by Mozart. This little locket travelled around, at least for a season or two, in the pocket of Mozart. It's something he would have held in his own hand.

It was the only time, really, in that museum, that I felt something touch me. Besides his music, all the rest of him has vanished. We don't even really know where he's buried. He was so destitute at the time of his death that they carted him off and dumped him in a pauper's grave with five or six other bodies.

Mozart's death mask.

Wolfgang Amadeus Mozart died at one o'clock in the morning on December 5, 1791. In a glass case up on the third floor of the museum sits the plaster cast of his death mask. It's eerie as hell. The eyes are closed but the plaster of Paris, or whatever it is they used, was actually dried over Mozart's dead face. He doesn't really look how you might think. Too many movies and portraits have left us with idealized portraits of him. But there he is. That's him. A man who died at a shockingly young age. A genius, yes, but a man all the same. A noble soul and a soul I'd like to think can miraculously still be heard every time an orchestra plays his exquisite music.

Einstein's brain was removed not eight hours after his death. They'd planned it carefully, hovering around him as he died so that they could get a first crack at it. The pathologists conducted the removal in a laboratory at the University of Pennsylvania and what they found when they opened him up was a brain that was actually a little bit smaller than normal. Undaunted, they pushed on, photographing it from all angles and finally cutting the brain up into 240 little one-cubic-centimetre blocks. These little blocks are now scattered all over the world. They've been poked and prodded more than the brain of anyone else who's ever lived. It's a bit sad, really.

It was only much later that a closer examination of the photographs revealed something extraordinary. In 1999, almost thirty-five years after Einstein's death, Dr. Sandra Witelson noticed that Einstein's brain was missing something called the lateral sulcus. It's not a chunk of the brain, actually, it's a fissure, a sort of canyon in the grey matter that runs up outside the parietal lobe.

What that means is that he didn't have a natural separation between two particular parts of his brain. It was connected in a way that most people's are not. And these were the parts to do with mathematical and spatial reasoning — exactly what he excelled at. The real question is: was he born with that abnormality, that Darwinian slip of genetics, or did his brain grow that way? Did his brain actually rewire itself and physically change over a lifetime of work? Would sheer focus and concentration — ten thousand hours or more — do that?

We think now that the answer is yes. In a landmark study in 2011, it was discovered that the brains of taxi drivers, of all things, were significantly rewired because of their work. Their brains were literally changed.

In particular, this happened to the taxi drivers in London, England. Now, London is a massive city and its streets are nothing like the grid patterns we find in North America. It's a geographical spaghetti bowl and a taxi driver in London studies for many years to acquire what's called "the Knowledge." The cabbies are quite proud of this and a good driver will actually know pretty much every little side street and weaving lane in London — thousands and thousands of them.

And for these drivers, there is measurable growth in the posterior hippocampus, the part of the brain that forms things like mental maps and calculates the shortest route between any given point A and point B. It's amazing.

Mozart's brain is lost to us. But we do know that the brains of professional musicians are quite unlike any others. Oliver Sacks, perhaps the world's most famous neurophysiologist, has written that it's very difficult to identify the brain of a visual artist or a writer or even a mathematician, but that he can almost instantly identify the brain of a professional musician.

The corpus callosum, for one thing, is enlarged in musicians. Non-musicians process pitch and melody in their right hemisphere and language largely in their left. Active musicians seem to be more global in how they perceive and produce these things and that takes the corpus callosum, literally a chunk of connective tissue the size of your hand that rides below the two hemispheres. Musicians with perfect pitch also have an enlargement of the planum temporale in their left hemisphere. We're not exactly sure why. There are loads of other structures, like the caudate nucleus, which coordinates and plans body movements. All of these areas are more prominent in active musicians. Indeed, there are as many as thirty different regions of the brain, thirty different neural networks that are called into play when we are performing music.

It's important to say, though, that to the best of our knowledge right now, musicians are not born with these brain differences, probably not even geniuses like Mozart. It's possible, I suppose, that they may have more of an inclination, some sort of genetic tipping point, that may accelerate this process, but in general they have rewired their brains through their hours of practise and study. In fact, they've rewired their brains just by thinking about music. As many studies have shown, musicians don't need to actually be practising on their instrument. The same motor neurons are put into play when they simply imagine themselves playing.

So, what about the rest of us? What about us mere mortals? Well, that's an interesting point. Whether or not we are professional performers, almost everyone is an expert at listening to music. Think about it. Surely, you've listened to more than ten thousand hours of music in your life. We may not be able to sing like Celine Dion or play the cello like Yo-Yo Ma, but we have been listening to professional musicians for years and years. And this has an effect on our brains.

There's a valuable little piece of brain real estate up near the front called the medial prefrontal cortex. The basic activity of this brain region seems to be project management. These executive functions match up our actions in accordance with our internal goals. They integrate new sensory information with what we already know about ourselves.

It turns out that this area also lights up when we're listening to music. And that's interesting, because this centre of executive functions is about the closest thing we have to a physical structure containing the sense of ourselves. It's been called an autobiographical neural network, not quite the seat of the soul perhaps, but definitely the place where we think, reflectively, about ourselves.

And, probably, where we think about others, where we recognize others as autonomous beings. It's where we surmise that other people also have feelings and motives and consciousness, exactly like our own.

If you take U-bahn line four almost as far north as it will go you will eventually arrive at Heiligenstadt. It's a part of Vienna now but in Beethoven's day it was an unimportant little hamlet on the outskirts of town. Beethoven lived here four or five different times. That's no surprise. The man lived in at least thirty different places. Seems he couldn't sit still.

Heiligenstadt is special, though. Immediately after I stepped off the train, I could feel the sense of tranquillity about the place. There are lots of parks and big shady trees. I walked up a quiet road, turned a corner and came into a sort of cul-de-sac. There's a house here — number 2, Pfarrplatz — where Beethoven lived from April to October, 1802. He wrote a few things here, the most important of which is something called the Heiligenstadt Testament. And it's not a piece of music at all.

For lack of a better word, it's a suicide note. He was only thirty-two when he wrote it. This was a young man who was as fine a concert pianist as any in Europe. He'd come to Vienna to study under Haydn. He'd won competition after competition and by all accounts he was simply dazzling on the keyboard. But here in Heiligenstadt, he could no longer escape the problem that had been dogging him for years. He was losing his hearing. He was quickly becoming completely and irrevocably deaf.

Imagine that for a second. One of the greatest musicians of all time, deaf. It's like Picasso going blind. It's like Shakespeare going mute. What greater cruelty could fate have in store?

Beethoven hid his deafness as long as he could, but eventually it was too real to ignore and he slowly closed himself off from the world. He moved up to Heiligenstadt on his doctor's advice — to give his ears a rest — but this clearly didn't work and one October day he sat down to write his last will and testament.

It's a heartbreaking read, this testament. "What a humiliation," he writes, "when one stood beside me and heard a flute in the distance and *I heard nothing.* It was impossible for me to say to men speak louder, shout, for I am deaf. Ah, how could I possibly admit such an infirmity in the one sense which should have been more perfect in me than in all the others."

"Farewell," he writes at the end, "and do not wholly forget me when I am dead."

But here's the thing. He never sent the letter and he certainly never committed suicide. The letter was intended for his brothers, but they never saw it, nor did they ever know of its existence.

For the rest of his life, Beethoven hid it away amongst his other papers. Why he even kept it is a bit of a mystery, unless of course you consider that he wanted to be reminded of this low point in his life. That, and perhaps the turning point that followed.

I always think that something profound happened to Beethoven in those weeks up at Heiligenstadt. At some point in that fateful autumn he must have decided that, damn it all to hell, he wasn't going to let something like deafness stop him from being the greatest composer who ever lived. It is precisely this steel-willed resolve which most surely marks

Beethoven's greatness. You can hear it in his music, in the storm and power of the symphonies that were to come.

He had come to communicate with people through notepads and by having them shout in his ear. He sawed the legs off his piano so that it rested directly on the floor and he lay beside it, thumping out notes, feeling only their reverberations through the thick oaken floorboards. He could no longer hear the outside world, but the music was still there tumbling around in his mind. And what music it was.

I wrote much earlier in this book that music is not in the ears at all. It is, as a point of fact, entirely in the brain. There's no truer proof of this maxim than the story of Ludwig van Beethoven.

I went to hear a concert of Beethoven piano sonatas. It was at the Église Saint-Julien-le-Pauvre, the oldest church in Paris. It's small and medieval. Outside, the building is unadorned, just pale pink-grey bricks and a few spartan windows. There are no statues, no gargoyles, no flying buttresses or towering spires.

When I went inside, it was dark. Thick columns held up a barrel-vaulted ceiling and, at the front, a few rows of wooden chairs had been set up. In front of the ancient altar, a Steinway grand piano sat incongruously, as if it had been left there mistakenly. Its polished black lid was propped opened like a coffin. I sat where I'd be able to see the pianist's hands, and the ivory keys shone like teeth in the dark medieval apse.

A small crowd, maybe fifty people, had come to hear the pianist Jean-Christophe Millot play. Millot studied at the National Conservatory of Paris. In fact, he won first prize there. He's won international competitions from Milan to Portugal, though this concert was to be different.

I had the perfect seat, but just before things started an elderly French woman came in pushing her husband in a wheelchair. I had to shift my chair over, a little behind a pillar, unfortunately, so that there was room for the wheelchair. The man in it huddled under a woollen blanket, barely turning to acknowledge me, but his wife — I assume it was his wife — thanked me in French and sat down in a chair on the other side of me.

Millot walked up the side aisle from the back of the church. He wore a tuxedo but it was strange seeing him have to walk through the whole church to squeeze by a few people to even get to the piano. He sat down, shuffled in the piano bench, and then seemed to look at the keys for a few moments, meditatively, as if he were willing the music to come out of them. Then he sort of nodded to himself and laid his long fingers over the keys.

And the music of Beethoven lifted up into the airy darkness of the church, shimmering off the ancient stones, sublime and sparkling waves of melody.

Millot would play two sonatas that night. It's funny, the program was completely in French, though I recognized the first sonata — it was the *Pathetique*. The second, though, was a mystery. The program had it written as "Claire de Lune." I thought Debussy wrote *Claire de Lune*. Something was amiss here.

Millot spilled through the first one in short order. The French woman beside me tugged at my sleeve after it ended. "*Il joue trop vite*," she insisted. He is playing too fast. It was a little fast, I thought, but I didn't really have the French for a discussion. Maybe the pianist was showing off his technique on the fast bits. Maybe he'd played it so many times before that he was just sort of running through it. It did, though, seem a little flat emotionally because of it.

He made up for that in spades on the next piece. When he began the so-called *Claire de Lune* sonata, I had to laugh at myself. Within the first three notes, I understood my confusion. *Claire de Lune*, in French, is moonlight. This was the famous *Moonlight* Sonata. Three notes in and I looked around. The rest of the audience were enraptured. The old man in the wheelchair beside me closed his eyes. He rocked ever so slightly as the melancholy triplets bled into the deep and sonorous opening chords. There's nothing else quite like it.

◀€ **LISTEN 15.3**

The *Moonlight* Sonata was composed in 1801, just a few months before the Heiligenstadt Testament. That's astounding. Beethoven was writing this piece just when he was coming to terms with his deafness. It's something that burbled up from the very depths of his soul. Classical sonatas are not structured like this one. This one opens with a heartwrenching adagio. Beethoven himself marked the score with the words *tutto questo pezzo delicatessimamente*. It must be played delicately, very delicately.

The Romantic movement elevated feeling over rules, passion over structure, and here was its bellwether. From the tortured mind of a young Beethoven, railing against his oncoming deafness, came this excruciating piece of beauty.

And so, beyond the beauty, the Romantic movement cast up another idea. From it grew the idea of the solitary genius, the individual rising above the rest, rising above his or her own fate to touch the sublime.

On my last day in Vienna, I walked around the Ringstrasse. It's a broad avenue that replaced the ancient medieval walls that once encircled the oldest parts of Vienna. Now it's a collection of colossal stone buildings and opulent palaces. It's all meant to impress, a visual metaphor for the power of the Hapsburgs. The State Opera House is here and the parliament buildings and the old war ministry. They're all grand staircases and columns, cupolas and arches. But if you keep following the Ringstrasse up around to the north, in the direction of the Danube, you will come to some smaller side streets.

One of these is the Mölker Bastei, and at number eight there's another one of Beethoven's residences. It's old. You enter into a courtyard that looks as if it were meant for carriages and then up a set of steps to the fourth floor.

Even on the landing there, there wasn't much to see. Three doors stood closed but one had a small historical plaque on it and I gently pushed it opened. There was a desk just inside the entrance. A university student sat behind it and he looked up from his book, seeming almost surprised to see a visitor.

I paid my two euros and pushed opened an inner door, coming into a large room with thick plank floorboards and whitewashed walls. In the centre was a very old piano. Whether or not it actually belonged to Beethoven I'm not sure, but it was certainly of the kind he used to play. Nothing else was in the room except for one of those old upright radiators under the window. I was all alone so I walked around to the keys. Of course there was a sign in German saying please not to touch it. And over the yellowing keys, there was a strip of plastic.

Beethoven's piano.

I couldn't help it, I was completely alone, so I inched over to the keyboard and snuck the tips of my fingers up under the plastic covering. There was just enough space there to poke my fingers through so they lay over the keys. I formed a C minor chord. This was a special key for Beethoven. It had, he thought, a stormy, heroic quality, kind of like himself. He used it in at least fifteen of his most important works, from the *Pathetique* Sonata to the Third Symphony and even the opening of the famous Fifth.

And I pressed down, ever so gently. Of course it was louder than I thought and the chord rang out through the room. Almost instantly, the door pushed opened and the university student gave me his best shaming glare. I backed away apologetically, but I had to do it. Just to imagine that my own fingers had touched the same chord as Beethoven's. My version of Mecca, I guess, a pilgrimage to greatness.

In the next room was a kind of desk with drawers. The top ones were opened and in them sat papers from Beethoven. Handwritten musical scores. They were just scraps, really, and I'm sure the most important papers are in larger museums. All of the scraps, though, were pieces he'd written right in this apartment. On the top of the desk, a shelf was open and one particular sheet of music was prominently displayed. A little label below it told me that it was from Beethoven's Fifth Symphony. The Fifth. The mighty Fifth with the opening four notes that might be among the most famous notes in all of music. Ba Ba Ba Baaah. In Morse code, short-short-short-long is read as the letter V, so that in the Second World War this opening was used to mean victory. Beethoven himself commented on the four notes, saying "Thus Fate knocks at the door."

I bent down to look at it more closely. I wanted to see if I could read a bit of it. To see what part of the symphony it might be from. I couldn't tell at all, it was such a scribble. In fact, I realized that there was nothing complete about this. It was more like a notepad of ideas, a run of quarter notes here, a marking there in German, and a few numbers, which I think were probably bar numbers. It was more like a sketch pad where maybe he was trying out bar twenty-four of just the second French horn part.

But this is how genius works. "Works" is the key word. It was the scrap of an idea, something that had come to mind and something that he had quickly jotted down before it could be forgotten. But it was a part, a small part, of the thing that would become one of the greatest pieces of music we know.

One of Beethoven's techniques — and the Fifth is a great example of this — is to set up some small motif. Then, through the rest of the piece, he brings it up again and again, only slightly changed, taken over as a rhythm rather than a melody, switched to a clarinet line instead of a swell of strings. But our minds seem to recognize it, echoing through everything.

And we know he worked slowly, almost painstakingly. Mozart polished off three full symphonies in a single summer. Beethoven worked for years. He worked on and off on his final symphony, the *Ode to Joy*, for more than seven years. And all the time, his fame and his genius grew and grew.

The Ninth Symphony premiered in Vienna on May 25, 1824, and Beethoven decided, though he was completely deaf, to conduct the concert himself. It was, in fact, the first time he had appeared on a stage in over twelve years.

There are many accounts of this night. Despite Beethoven being on stage, it was really directed by the theatre's resident Kapellmeister, Michael Umlauf. Beethoven actually sat over by the edge of the orchestra, beating out the tempos. Nevertheless, he turned the pages of the score and watched the movement of the bows for clues as to where they were. Sometimes he stood up and gesticulated wildly, almost dancing with the music. He really couldn't hear a single note the orchestra was playing but he heard the whole glorious thing in his own head.

At the end of it all, his back was to the audience. It was a packed house that night and the audience absolutely erupted into applause. In fact, there were five standing ovations. One of the singers, a woman named Caroline Unger, was standing near the old man. She realized that, with his back turned to the audience and not hearing a thing, Beethoven was not aware that the crowd was on its feet. She took a couple steps, reached for the old man's arm and gently turned him around. And the audience, knowing the master could no longer hear, began to throw their handkerchiefs and hats in the air. They raised their arms and waved and jumped, and not a single sound was heard by Beethoven — though it's said that there were tears in his old eyes.

16

Ireland and Scotland
The Celtic Soul

I hired a bike on the tiny island of Inishmore off the west coast of Ireland. You can wheel around the whole island in about an hour and it's like a couple of hundred years have dropped away from the calendar. Horses and carts clip-clop up the little lanes between piled rock fences. Old stone farmhouses look out over sheep pastures to Galway Bay.

I stopped at one particularly pretty view and propped my rented bike up against a stone fence, but before I could get my camera out, a man appeared in big rubber boots. He waved down at me and came clumping across his fields. Mr. Connelly was his name, and he ended up taking me around the farm that had been in his family for centuries. Up near the top of a hill, he showed me his Fairy Tree. It was windblown and gnarled and on its scraggly branches were dozens and dozens of little tatters of cloth, rippling in the breeze like raindrops in a puddle.

"It's been here forever," explained Mr. Connelly, touching one of the strips of cloth. "I remember it as a boy. You're to put a ribbon up here if you have troubles on your mind. Then the fairy tree will sort you out."

He stopped and looked hard at me. "Now don't you go thinking we're all believing in leprechauns riding unicorns," he said. "If you ask me if I believe in fairies, the short answer is 'no.' On the other hand," he paused thoughtfully, "out in County Claire, on the mainland, your man there went about building a new motorway. There was a fairy tree directly in the way and there was so much ballyhoo over it that they had to reroute the whole thing. Cost a pretty penny. So no, I don't hold with no fairies, but it doesn't hurt to respect them either."

We walked back down to the road. "Are you here to find your ancestry?" he said, clumping along.

"My ancestors were from the Outer Hebrides — Scotland," I said. "I'm going up there after this."

Mr. Connelly nodded.

I felt like I needed to add more. "Though I've heard," I went on, "that way back they came from Ireland."

"Many folks do."

We walked back in silence and when we'd come back down to my bike, he turned to me one last time. "You'll be off to see the Dun now, I suppose?"

I was. *Dun* is the old Irish word for "'fortress." The one I was heading for was as old as any on the planet. As old as the tales of Homer. As old as the trumpets of King Tut. The difference was, for the first time I was in a place where the history was, maybe, at least partly my own.

I rode down a path that skirted the beach. The tide was out and it was blanketed in kelp. I saw a seal out on the rocks, sunning itself in the pale Irish sun. Then I turned toward a long hill and pedalled up the slope for a kilometre or so. This is where most people who come to the island end up. Dun Aonghasa, two rows of semicircular stone walls that date from the Bronze Age. The semicircles don't have a back wall. The land there just drops off into nothingness, sea cliffs that crash down a hundred metres to the ocean below. There's no fence or guardrail and I crawled, literally on my hands and knees, over to the edge to look down. Far, far below me, the Atlantic was frothing and crashing up against the rocks. I scuttled back and lay back on the grass for a moment, breathing heavily.

We don't know a whole lot about the people who lived here or where they came from, but outside the fort there are more rock walls, which were probably enclosures for animals — no different a life really than our Mr. Connelly's. There have been people in Ireland for thousands and thousands of years, living by the sea, burning the peat for warmth, raising cattle and sheep and holding the fairies to account for their troubles. The Picts melded into the Celts and the Celts cross-pollinated with the Norse.

These Celtic peoples, in fact, once covered most of Europe. They were known as *Keltoi* by the Greeks and *Galli* — the Gaels — by the Romans. Both words meant "barbarians." Today the old Gaelic languages are heard in only the most remote pockets of the British Isles, like here on Inishmore. The men working on the ferry spoke the old Irish and it was good to hear. It's on signs all over the Republic of Ireland but there are few people who really still use it. Celtic music, on the other hand, is as alive as it ever was.

That night I was back in Galway, which itself is a pretty little town on the coast, the heart of one of the finest music scenes on the planet. I found my way down to a little pub called Tig Cóilí, a name which literally means "the house of music." Its front is fireplug red, like an expanded version of one of those old British telephone boxes. Inside, it was already crowded. A man shouldered by me with a pint of beer in each hand. I took the opportunity to ask him if there was going to be music tonight.

He stopped and looked at me, a little surprised. "There's always music."

"Who's playing?"

"Why, whoever shows up."

And at around nine o'clock, at a booth near the front, two men and a woman sat down and plucked their instruments out of their cases. This was no hired band. These were locals who had just come down to play a song or two with their neighbourhood friends. Both the men played mandolins, although one was almost as big as a guitar. The women brought out a violin, though I guess around here you'd call it a fiddle.

They began with a reel. The fiddle and the smaller mandolin played exactly the same melody, a strident, dancing flurry of notes, while the larger of the mandolins chunked out the chords. The crowd noise still buzzed behind the musicians. They weren't really playing for anyone but themselves. It was all just a part of the *craic*, another old Irish word that means all the gossip and the talk, all the fun and social interaction that happens in places like pubs.

I watched as a younger woman came in and sat down with them. "Can I play a song with you, then?" she asked, fishing something out of her coat pocket. It was a penny whistle, thinner than a recorder and made out of brass, but much the same thing really. I don't know where she came from and I took it that the others didn't know her, that she wasn't a regular. It didn't seem to matter. She had an instrument and she wanted to play. They all put their heads together for a minute or two, nodding, deciding on a song, and when they broke apart, the penny whistle launched into a sprightly little jig. The fiddle doubled her exactly, both women's fingers flying over the frets and stops, missing not a note, playing as if they were one. The men on the mandolins glanced at each other, broke into grins, and then off they went too, playing jubilantly, effortlessly, as if they'd all known one another for years.

🔊 **LISTEN 16.1**

This is what music is all about. There were heads nodding around the room, and many of the patrons had stopped their chatter to listen. There was something special going on and I remembered what someone told me once about Celtic music. It has just two speeds, they said.

There are jigs in the key of pure joy. They leap and dance and rocket with delight. And then there are the slow songs, laments of such sweet longing that even the angels turn from their prayers to listen.

Just south of Galway are the Cliffs of Moher. There the raw Atlantic slams up against the rocks, sending flues of sea spray up into the winds. It's a cold, eerily beautiful place. On top of the cliffs is a round tower, O'Brien's Tower, the seat of the clan chief who once ruled these lands.

A path twists along the cliff edge and I walked along it, mindful of my footing. The wind gusts have sent people over the edge and I'd just come up to a plaque mounted on a rock. It was in memory of the people who have lost their lives here — some of them on purpose. I bent down to read it and just then I caught a faint tinkling of notes drifting in and out on the sea winds. A little further along I found the source. Sheltered behind a low stone wall was a woman playing a Celtic harp.

She sat on big red cushion over a blanket-draped stool and she tucked into the harp, plucking out a sorrowful little tune. It was almost

Celtic harp at the Cliffs of Moher.

too perfect. The winds were flipping her long rust-coloured hair in front of her face but she didn't seem to mind. And she wore a long peasant dress, as if she were performing at some medieval feast.

Her hands danced across the strings. They kept darting up to flip little levers at the top of the strings too. It was intricate and almost hypnotic, like a weaver at a loom. When she finished, she tipped her head at me and dropped her long fingers from the strings.

"That was great," I said. "Is that your own piece or ..."

"No, that's a traditional one."

"It was really beautiful."

"O'Carolan."

"I'm sorry?"

"O'Carolan. The most famous harpist in Ireland. He wrote many pieces."

"Is he from Dublin?"

She looked at me strangely. "He died four hundred years ago. You've not heard of him?"

"No, I ..."

"O'Carolan was the master. He was blind, they say."

"Like Homer."

"Well, yes, I suppose a bit like Homer."

"And those little levers at the top of your harp, what do they do?"

"Ah," she said, flipping one for me to hear. "They raise the note."

"A semi-tone."

"That's right. Are you a musician yourself, then?"

"Yeah, I play a little."

"Shall I play another?"

"Yes. Yes, of course."

Her name was Lewena and she played up here at the cliffs for the tourists who wandered by. A little cardboard box by her feet had a handful of coins in it. I stood listening for a long time. The harp, you see, is the national symbol of Ireland. It's everywhere, on the back of their coins, on their coat of arms. And a silhouetted harp is the logo for that most famous of Irish exports, the black draughts of Guinness beer.

Still, this was the first harp I'd seen in my travels around Ireland. They're never played in the pubs and I asked Lewena about that when she finished again.

"Well, it's too heavy, isn't it?" She pointed over at her dolly, leaning against the rock wall some ways off. Her coat was draped over it and she had a bag there, everything she needed for the day. "It was the instrument of the court." She paused, drawing in a long breath. "It was not for the small folk."

"The small folk?"

"In the royal courts, it was used to accompany poetry. Like Homer, as you say."

"For telling stories?"

"Something like that, I imagine."

◀᠎᠎᠎ LISTEN 16.2

I left Lewena, dropping a few bills into her cardboard box. She tipped her head at me one last time before I walked back down to the buses, thinking again about stories and language and poetry.

Language, clearly, is about conveying meaning, about trying to get an idea across. Music is not. It's a sort of communication, all right, but it's not about the passing on of information. They both come from the appropriation of basic mechanisms in our auditory cortex. I know that sounds dry but it's true. Language and music grew from the same place, like twins who have gone off in their own directions. Language arose to pass along meaning and music arose to pass along ... what? Emotional connection? A sense of belonging? Maybe a sense of ourselves.

I was thinking all this when I climbed on the bus for Dublin. There is a direct one, an express bus, but I chose instead to take the one that travelled the back lanes. I wanted to see a bit more of the countryside.

The road signs pointed off at each roundabout, this one heading to Limerick, that one to Tipperary. Are there any place names more lyrical than that of Ireland? For that matter, are there any people more aware of the power and beauty of language? Few countries can rival the poetry of Ireland. This little green island has produced Jonathan Swift, Oscar Wilde, George Bernard Shaw, Samuel Beckett, W.B. Yeats, Seamus Heaney, and that most musical of all writers, James Joyce. And, really, that's just barely scratching the surface.

So, when I finally got to Dublin, I went on a little pilgrimage to see one of the most famous books in the world. In the great library at Trinity College, they keep an illuminated manuscript called *The Book of Kells*. It contains the four gospels and it was handwritten, probably in the middle of the ninth century C.E., on vellum. Vellum is prepared sheepskin and it's held the ink over the centuries. In fact, the book is a treasure house of illustration. It's said that all the designs of Celtic art can be traced back to these pages. Even the colours are magical, derived from materials like shellfish and beetles' wings and crushed pearls.

The book was probably made by monks on the holy isle of Iona, just off the coast of Scotland. Iona was attacked and looted in the year 1009, but when the Viking raiders found the book, they were more interested in the jewel-encrusted cover than its pages. They ripped off the cover and left behind the vellum. The surviving monks recovered it and fled to the abbey at Kells just north of Dublin. In 1661, the manuscript was taken to Dublin and it's been here in this library ever since.

No wonder the Irish are in love with books and words.

I went upstairs after seeing the book to the Long Room, the oldest and grandest room in the Trinity Library. Many of the great Irish writers worked here at the benches and tables, hunched over their quills and ink under the shelves of ancient manuscripts. Jonathan Swift likely wrote sections of *Gulliver's Travels* right in this room. Oscar Wilde thought up a few good quips here. There's a whole centre in the English wing named after him as a matter of course. But off in the corner, there was something I hadn't expected. Just near the stairs down to the gift shop and the exit is a glass case containing an ancient harp, one of the oldest ever found.

The Trinity College Harp is a beautiful thing, dating from the late 1400s and made out of oak and willow with brass strings. Given its workmanship, it was almost certainly a part of some royal court. In fact, it's exactly the harp that is duplicated on the Irish coat of arms and the silhouette that graces each and every cask of dark Guinness beer.

I thought I recognized it.

It's amazing it even survived, because by the 1700s, when the English had taken over Ireland, harps were banned. In fact, they were often burned by the English and the harpists were often executed. It was too easy for them to rouse the people with the old songs and so, by 1720 or so, the harp had all but disappeared. The music of Ireland moved from the royal courts to the "small folk." The simple instruments took over, penny whistles and bodhráns (what they call the poor man's tambourine), and the music went where the people went, and that was down to the pubs.

There's a riddle about Dublin. How can you cross from one side of the city to the other without passing a pub? Simple. You just stop at every one. So, with the evening coming on, I headed down to St. Stephen's Green and a pub there called O'Donoghue's. The place is a rabbit's warren of rooms. The old plank floors are uneven and warped and the walls are festooned with photos of the past.

I found a small room off to the side and ordered a Guinness from the bar there. The woman behind the taps poured me a glass three quarters full then left it to still on the bar for a few moments. "Will there be music tonight?" I asked. I should have known better.

"Do you want some Irish coffee too?" she snipped.

"What?"

She laughed. "Another tourist came in here last week. He asked for an Irish coffee — you know, whiskey in your coffee." She stopped to mop the bottom of my glass. Then she held it up to the tap again and filled it to the brim with a great frothy head. She passed it over to me. "Then the tourist asked, 'Which part of Ireland grows the coffee beans?'"

There was laughter from the people all around the bar.

"They're grown just up behind the Irish coconuts," said a man to the left of me.

I took my pint of Guinness. It wasn't warm as most people say but then it wasn't cold either. The man to my left asked me what I thought of it. He'd been waiting for me to take my first sip. I'm sure I had a Guinness moustache from the foam.

"You can buy Guinness all over the world now," he went on, "but we have a saying here. Guinness doesn't travel. It doesn't taste quite the same anywhere else."

"It is good."

"Tell me that it isn't the milk of angels?"

"It's good. It's really good."

"Listen," said the bartender, looking at me over the taps. "You're in luck tonight. See your man over there? The older one? He'll be playing tonight."

I turned around. The man was elderly and almost bald. He wore little round glasses. He could've been someone's grandfather. He sure didn't look like a musician. But of course, half an hour later, there he was with his penny whistle sitting amongst a group of locals at the front.

The man seemed to be the focal point of the little group, calling out the order of the songs. He sang, belting out the old songs like an opera star, but mostly he played the penny whistle, his fingers trilling and tapping and fluttering like a butterfly that never quite sets down on the branch.

Tonight the group was all elderly men, in their sixties or older. One played a guitar slung across his large belly. Another was dapper in a fedora and vest and played a small mandolin. The third was a man who could've passed for Santa Claus in the off season. He had his snow-white hair slicked back and he wore suspenders. He had a big white beard too and he spun out the Celtic tunes on a larger mandolin, rocking his head in time. A woman appeared later. She'd brought a bodhrán. It's the drum of Celtic music, played with a tipper — a drumstick that's held in the middle so that both ends alternate in a sort of walking thump. Occasionally, for accent, the tipper is used to hit the wooden rim, producing a good loud crack.

They rollicked in time to one another, laughing and taking sips of their beers between songs. They fitted as closely as stones and bounced as happily as clouds. I always say that the best musicians play with the beat, urging it on, anticipating it before it really comes. Music is not just a matter of mathematics. It's more than the harnessing of sound waves. The penny whistle bent into the high notes, squeezing out the emotion rather than the precise pitch. And they all bobbed their head in time with one another. They scrunched up their faces. Their lips tightened and their foreheads creased. They were putting their whole selves into this music and I could feel that. I could feel that as plain as day.

I went up to get another pint of Guinness.

"Well. What do you think?" asked the bartender.

"They're good."

"They're grand," she said. "I've been working here for six years. Your man there has never missed a Saturday night. Never."

I went back to listen some more and noticed that, as in a lot of the pubs, the walls were covered in old photos of musicians. There were photos of some of the great writers as well. There was one of William Butler Yeats staring out across the years, a handsome young man in this portrait, with a wild mop of hair. He'd once written "How can you know the dancer from the dance?" It's one of his more famous lines.

And it's completely true. How can you know the singer from the song, for that matter? It's the same thing. When I heard these musicians playing, I was hearing the very deepest parts of who they were. I was, if I may say so, hearing something of their souls.

I heard the pipes just down the rain-blackened road from Edinburgh Castle. I'd been walking up the Royal Mile, a cobblestone stretch that rises up from an inlet called — and I love this — the Firth of Forth. At the very top of the Royal Mile is Edinburgh Castle. It rests on a pinnacle of volcanic rock like a crown. This, some would say, is the heart of Scotland.

I wouldn't. That's not even close.

The rain was pattering down steadily. Dark clouds were washing in from across the firth. I'd heard the piper clearly enough, though — those bagpipes cut through almost anything. He was about halfway up the Royal Mile, in front of an old stone wall, pacing back and forth like one of the Queen's own guards, blowing the pipes for all he was worth.

I stopped, of course. The man was in full regalia: a kilt with the tartan of the Royal Stewart and over his shoulder a long scarf that matched it. On his head a high felt hat rode up like those of the guards at Buckingham Palace. His boots had white covers and across his mid-section was a sporran — a sort of belt purse with tassels. This was full military dress and he was marching through the puddles, guarding nothing but the stones of the wall.

I looked up at the rain, but I thought *As long as he can stand it, so can I,* so I stood and listened to him run through a number of tunes without stopping. Finally, he let the pipe drop from his mouth and with a last wheeze from the actual bag, the bellows, he stopped to eye me.

"You don't mind the rain?" I said.

"Achh, I'm immune to it," he said. "Where are you from then?"

"Canada."

"You don't mind the snow?"

"Touché. Tell me, what was that last piece you played?" I asked.

"That was 'Mrs. John McColl.'"

"And the one before that?"

"That's called 'Mrs. McPherson from Inverran.'"

He looked at me and we both broke into grins. "I know what you're going to ask," he said.

"Yeah, what's with all the Mrs.?"

"That I don't know. It's just what they're called." He looked up at the sky. "You know, maybe it is getting a wee bit wet."

"Has it been raining for long?"

"Weeks, I'd say." He heaved the bagpipes down.

Bagpipes are large, that's for sure. Besides the bag, which is as big as a sheep's stomach and probably originally derived from one, there are three pipes like smokestacks sticking out of the top. These are the drones, the unbroken notes that run underneath the melody. Two of the drones are the same. They sound out a note that's an octave below the tonic note of the chanter — the flute part of the bagpipes. The third drone, and the longest one, is two octaves below.

And yes, I know that bagpipes are the butt of jokes everywhere. For me, though, they're something majestic. Maybe it's my roots showing but I love the sound of these things. To me, they're stirring and, sometimes off in the distance, they strike me as melancholy and haunting.

And I think it has to do with the drone. Whenever the chanter comes down to hit a fifth above the drone, it rings and reverberates, and it's like the world comes into focus. When the chanter hits the major third above the drone, I get shivers down my spine. It's like all those Pythagorean ratios made manifest. It's the basis of harmony and melody, right there in front of your ears.

I left the piper to take apart his bagpipes. Another block or two up towards the castle, I came across a bronze statue of the philosopher David Hume. He's dressed as a Roman senator, which I found a bit bizarre, but it's his left toe that really sticks out on this statue. Literally and metaphorically. It's at chest level on the sidewalk so that tens of thousands of people have taken to rubbing the toe for luck as they pass by. David Hume's big toe shines almost golden from all the polishing, even in the dark drizzling rain.

Hume was an empiricist philosopher, which means that all we know, all we are, comes from what we've experienced. It's not so much about reason or logic or figuring it out. It's about what our senses have brought in to us. We have built ourselves, and the universe we live in, out of visuals and fragments of sound, out of scents and touches and tastes.

I'm not entirely sure about that, but I was just then thirsting for another pint of Guinness. Or at least the Scottish equivalent. And I wanted to see if the music would be as much a part of the pub scene as it was in Ireland. There were plenty of pubs, that was for sure. Under all the gables and sandstone turrets of the Royal Mile, I chose one called The Mitre.

The Mitre dates from 1873. The wood on the handrails has been polished down almost as much as Hume's big toe. Green felt wallpaper embossed with thin gold lines covered the walls and a hammered copper roof arched overhead. The Mitre got its name from the fact that, before it was a pub, it was the house of the local bishop. His ghost is said to haunt the cask ales, unhappy perhaps at the turn his living room has taken.

And sure enough, the Celtic Soul dances here too. Three men were already sitting by the front window when I got there, one on guitar, one on fiddle, and another who, well, sat on a wooden box and simply drummed on it with his hands.

When they stopped to take a break, I asked him what kind of wood it was.

"Plywood," he said, a bit confused. "I just found it."

"Are you guys from here?"

"We live here now, but we're from up around Dundee," said the guitar player. "We're called MacPolvo."

"I'm heading past there on my way up to the Hebrides Celtic festival," I said. "Have you ever played there?"

"You come to find your roots then?"

Why does everyone ask me that? "As a matter of fact, my ancestors did come from the Hebrides," I said. "A long time ago."

"Hebcelt is on the Isle of Lewis, right?" said the drummer.

"Yeah, I'm going there tomorrow."

"Ach, bring your waders," he said. "It'll get wet."

"Here," said the guitar player, nodding at the others. "We have a song from the Isle of Lewis. Maybe you'll hear it up there."

They launched into a sad song — a lament — a song of leaving home. The songwriter, Murdo MacFarlane, was forced to leave, like a lot of Scots, when his ancestral lands were bought out from under him. They call that time The Clearings and most of the poor Scots got on the ships with only the rags on their backs. A few tried to hide out in the caves but the English overlords used dogs to hunt them down. It was a dark time. The time in which my own ancestors had come to Canada.

The guitar player sang in Scottish Gaelic. He sang it sweetly and with feeling. The angels, I thought, would stop to listen to this one.

"Ach, enough of that," he said when the final note trailed off. "Here's something a little more cheery. This one's from the Napoleonic Wars. It's about the rubbish they tell you to get you sign up."

They launched into it. The drummer pounded on his plywood box. I later learned that it is a real instrument. It's called a *cajón* and probably comes from flamenco tradition. Really it had a thumping good bass. And, like the bodhrán, the drummer could get a lot of different sounds out of it. He was actually really good, driving the rest of the band along, pumping like a heartbeat, striding and swaggering like a soldier just back from the wars.

◀ᛁ LISTEN 16.3

Rhythm is another of those neural networks we've locked into. Our whole body floats with it, the automaticity of it, the feel of moving, of all our muscles working in coordination. The crowd was with MacPolvo that night. The beer was sloshing and the elbows were swinging.

When they'd finished that song, the guitar player, who seemed to like to say a little something about every piece, said, "This one's about the year the barley crop failed. There was no whiskey that year. Now, there's a hell of a lament."

The drummer laughed and they crashed off into another wild jig. The drummer pounded at his plywood box, the guitar player sang bawdily, and the shy fiddler behind them sat on a heat register by the window ledge and sawed off some really great fills.

The next morning, I took a train up through the highlands to Inverness. It took a good part of the day but I was nowhere near finished. I went as far as the train lines would carry me and then I had to take a bus up another couple of hours to the tiny village of Ullapool. It's here that you catch the ferries to take you across the Minch, the long stretch of sea between Scotland and the Western Isles.

The Western Isles are properly called the Outer Hebrides, as raw and stark an archipelago as you will find on this planet, home to pirates and fishermen, to Vikings and monks and ghosts. This was the ancestral land of my mother's side of the family. This was where they'd come from.

The next morning I got on the ferry. There were musicians climbing on board as well. It was hard to ignore the guitar cases and drums. They'd all come to play the HebCelt. A flutter of seagulls followed the ferry along, dancing on invisible strings, squawking and swooping above us. One by one they flew off, leaving us to make the crossing alone. The seas darkened. A wind kicked up and the ship began to heave and lurch.

On the ferry over I sat by a woman who must've been at least eighty. She was crinkled and bent and in front of her on the table she had assembled her breakfast. I watched as she touched her bowl of oatmeal then tapped a finger on the spoon beside it. Then she touched the rim of her tea cup. It was steaming. She looked up at me just then, having noticed I was watching. She smiled and simply said, "Remember. Remember everything."

The ferry eventually pulled into a bay on the Isle of Lewis. I walked down the gangplank and out into Stornoway, the biggest town in all the Western Isles. Every year, they put on the Hebridean Celtic Festival in the castle grounds here. It draws something like twelve thousand people, tripling the size of the town and bringing Celtic musicians in from all over the world.

The day was shaping up to be sunny and bright, which was rare for these parts. There was still a cold stiff breeze, though. We were pretty far north, halfway out to Iceland really, and I only had time to get through the town and out across a bridge to Stornoway Castle, where the festival was to be held. I stopped there and off in the distance again I heard the pipes.

This time it was a whole marching band, coming up the high street. Ten pipers with a drum major at the front. He marched proudly with a massive bronze sceptre. Behind the pipers came a dozen or so drummers, rat-a-tat-tatting. They marched up and over the bridge and out onto the castle green.

There's nothing like the sound of a whole troupe of pipers. It's warm and rich. It's the voice of the Highlands. The pipers formed a circle and played "The Sailor's Hornpipe." They played another and then another and the crowds began to gather around them, murmuring at first, then clapping and finally cheering wildly with all their hearts. And that was how the festival began.

◀᛭ **LISTEN 16.4**

Pipers at Stornoway Castle.

HebCelt is three full days of music beneath two big-top tents. The biggest performers would play in the blue candy-striped tent, huge names like The Proclaimers and The Waterboys, a Scottish band that started in the eighties. They were famous for a tune called "The Whole of the Moon." They have a new album based on the poetry of W.B. Yeats. How can you tell the dancer from the dance?

And there were others, like Julie Fowlis, a local girl who'd done well for herself. She had a song in a Disney movie and was making the most of it now. Under the smaller of the circus tents were the up-and-comers. There was even a duo from Canada, Qristina and Quinn, a brother and sister from Victoria. The boy was only sixteen but he could play the guitar as well as anyone. For three days, cold but mercifully dry, I wandered back and forth between the tents.

The thing is, though, this was a show. Twelve thousand people came for the headliners, and a thousand hands lifted small squares of light — cellphones — to film it all, what used to be, I guess, the waving of Bic lighters. It was all very, very different from the musicians I'd seen holding court in the pubs. It almost seemed like they were different kinds of music, completely different kinds of things.

It's a funny world we live in now, presenting musicians as celebrities. You have to remember that for tens of thousands of years music was performed by the community. Many voices chanted together. Drums were banged in unison. Dancers danced in time with the rhythms. We get fooled because that's not how it's done today. The Western world, especially, has shifted so that we have a very lucky few who are professional musicians while the vast majority of us are passive listeners. We have singer-songwriters, some who we elevate to the status of celebrity, some who we heap with fame and riches, and we just sit and listen to them. But that's not how music has been for most of our history.

Thomas Edison changed all that even further. On July 18, 1877, he made music permanent. He fixed it for the first time on a wax cylinder, making a single performance universal and intractable. For a hundred years now, it's been polished to a sheen. It does not allow for mistakes or a whole lot of improvisation or abandon. And it's everywhere. The average fourteen-year-old today will hear more music in a month than my Celtic ancestors would have heard in their entire lifetimes.

The funny thing is it really doesn't change things all that much. All of us in the audience, while we may not have the skills of those up onstage or those on our digital recordings, well, we're still expert listeners. And I don't mean that facetiously.

Let me explain because this is important. We know that musicians play off each other in subtle, almost subconscious, ways. We know that neurohormones like oxytocin are washing through the brains of people who are singing together. Music produces an enigmatic and profound connection with other people. It's linked inextricably with movement and emotion and language and it works in some pretty subtle ways.

Consider this: Glenn Gould, one of the greatest pianists who ever lived, is said to have rarely actually practised. That sounds almost unbelievable until you know that what he did instead — and just as carefully and painstakingly — was mentally rehearse the music in his mind. He's on record as saying that he would play entire pieces over and over in his mind, literally hundreds and hundreds of times, until he felt that he had it right — and all this before he would actually touch a piano keyboard. We know now through many studies of brain imaging that the exact same motor neural pathways are fully engaged in a person who only imagines music rather than one who actually plays it.

Music seems to work at a level that goes beyond the physical sound waves. Beethoven is another example. He was completely deaf by the time he composed his Ninth Symphony. He simply heard it all in his mind.

What I want to say here is that music exists in the mind in a very special way. And in the big picture, this still holds true for us in the modern world. As I've said, we've now elevated musicians to a special social status. The rest of us have forgotten our musical roots. And yet we are really good at listening to music. You see, even a passive listener, like me in the crowd, listening to The Proclaimers walking five hundred miles, well, our minds still lock into the music in much the same way as the performers do. When we listen to music, our brains mirror the brains of the musicians. I realize that sounds a bit flaky, a little new age, but it is in fact largely true.

What they're feeling, we're feeling. In essence, it's the best way we have of being truly aware of each other. Not just the physical presence of another person but something deeper. A connection with who we really are, deep down. Music is the one way we've found to truly touch another person's soul.

On the last night of the festival, I did something quite different. A smaller performance was going to run way up on the other side of the island. I actually rented a car just to get there. The car was about the size of a toaster oven and I trundled across the rocky barrens. It was beautiful out there in the middle of the island.

A mist came chasing down the hills and out over the moors. The sun was catching it just right so that a rainbow rode out in front of it, billowing as if it were blown along by the clouds, reds and purples and greens tumbling down the hillside across the glen.

I went past crofts (ancient farmhouses) then along a coastline of crashing waves and rocky shores, up to a little town called Borve. Now, to call Borve a town is to call a canoe the *Titanic*. They did have a nice little community hall, though, and just behind it is a set of standing stones as old as Stonehenge. They form a little circle there, though they haven't yet been excavated. Older by far than Mr. Connelly's Fairy Tree.

The band came on at 8:30. They were the Angus Nicolson Trio from the Isle of Skye, from a town called Slate. Angus himself was quiet. He played the penny whistle and at times the bagpipes. There was a guitar player and also a drummer with long, stringy hair. His name was Andrew MacPherson and it was he who did most of the talking.

Towards the end of the evening, Andrew and Angus both brought out penny whistles — though they were almost as big as clarinets — hollow tubes as long as your forearm. The guitar player started in on some chords. "This," Andrew announced, "is a song from the Isle of Barra."

◀≷ LISTEN 16.5

That caught my attention. I was heading for Barra the next day. Little Barra, the last of the Hebridean Islands, and my own ancestral home. My ancestors had left there two hundred years ago and, as far as I knew, no one in my family had seen it since. The musicians started playing this sweet little song and it was shatteringly beautiful. Chills raced all up and down my spine.

After the show, I asked Andrew what it was called.

"That one?" he said. "Why that one's called 'Mrs. McLelland from Tyna Yardee.'"

And I could barely hold back my laughter.

I finally came to the end of the world. I took a little prop plane that landed on a cockleshell beach on the north shore of the Isle of Barra. It was a very small plane. They can only land here when the tide is out, jumping down over the sand dunes to a long, flat stretch where the wheels of the plane splash up walls of water from the tidal pools.

There's nothing between Barra and Canada, nothing but five thousand kilometres of angry grey ocean. I caught a lift in a little white van around the single lane track to the south end of the island. In the harbour there, right out in the water on a little rocky island, is a castle. Kisimul Castle, it's called, one of the oldest castles in Scotland.

This castle has sat fat in my imagination for all my life. I'd seen a picture of it years before in a *National Geographic* magazine, and I knew that it was the seat of the MacNeils of Barra. My mother was a MacNeil.

She'd grown up on a farm on Cape Breton Island several generations in, speaking Scottish Gaelic.

Kisimul Castle, you've got to admit, is a very fine name. It's sort of dark and moody, just as an old castle name ought to be. Rising above it on the shore is a little village appropriately named Castlebay. The houses are built of the same dark stone that peeks through the highland grass, the same stone, too, that shapes the walls of the castle. The village was quiet. An old man rode by on a rusty bicycle and a solemn line of sheep meandered down the main street. Behind it a sharp hill rose up, almost a small mountain, just to remind you that this is still a part of the highlands.

There's a small fishing boat that will take you out to the castle. A man in an orange vest will spin you out there for a couple pounds. It takes all of five minutes. When he dropped me off, he said he'd come back to get me in an hour or so. "What do you mean? I have the place to myself?"

"Looks as if you do."

I walked up the sea-wet steps and in through an iron gate under the old battlements. The place was rebuilt in the 1930s and there's a stone longhouse inside, still the official home of the clan chief. It's locked but you can go through some of the other chambers and towers. One was the ancient dining hall. It was pretty much empty, though I lingered there awhile in front of the great gaping fireplace. In ancient days this would have been the place where music was played. I tried to imagine it. I tried to imagine myself among these people.

But it was just so silent and empty. I went back out and up a set of stairs to the oldest part of the castle. The tower there is three storeys high and I went right to the top floor, creaking across the old wooden planks of the floorboards. There were narrow windows open to the sea. One way was the Atlantic and the other way was the village looking down on us. I coughed once, clearing my throat, and the sound echoed across the stones.

And I knew what I had to do.

I'd learned a song, you see. It was an old song, a hundred, two hundred years old, I don't know. It was all in Gaelic but I'd learned it as best as I could. My grandmother used to sing this song out there in her Cape Breton farmhouse. Accompanied by the crackling of the fire in the pot-bellied stove, the clanging of iron pots and a sweet smell of oatmeal porridge, she'd sing it to the little girl who was to become my mother.

And here I was ready to sing it again. "Oh chì, chì mi na mórbhe-anna," it begins. "Oh I can still see the great mountains."

It was a lament, a song of remembering like so many I'd heard before.

◀ᠻ **LISTEN 16.6**

"I see in my dreams," it goes on in translation, "the lands of my youth. I will hear them speak in the language I cherish. I'll be received there with love when I reach it, and I'd not trade that for tons of gold."

So here I was. And I'd not trade it, they were right. I'd not trade it for all the gold in the world.

I sang the song for myself. I sang it for my ancestors. I sang it for all I was worth. And maybe, I thought, the angels did stop to listen. Maybe. Because it really was the sound of my soul.

I'm writing these very words only a little bit later on that same day. I'm looking out at the castle in the bay. The setting sun has just caught it and the ocean is sparkling around it. Out past the entrance to the har-bour, the Atlantic is surging and bringing in the tide.

Somewhere out there, drums are thumping on an African beach and the ragas of sunrise are ringing out across the ghats of Varanasi. Somewhere out there, a rumba sounds down the cobblestone streets of Havana and a whale sings to the underwater cliffs of Tahiti.

Bach is sailing through the stars and I, here on a forgotten island, sit above a castle, thinking that I am ready. I'm ready, now, to go home.

BIBLIOGRAPHY

Anderson, Jon Lee. *Guevara: A Revolutionary Life*. New York: Grove Press, 2010.

Briggs, Philip. *Ghana: The Bradt Travel Guide*, 2010.

Brooks, David. *The Social Animal: The Hidden Sources of Love, Character and Achievement*. New York: Random House, 2011.

Campbell, Kay Hardy. *Recent Recordings of Traditional Music from the Arabian Gulf and Saudi Arabia*. Boston: Middle East Studies Association Bulletin, July 1996.

Cross, Ian and Iain Morley. "The Evolution of Music: Theories, Definitions and the Nature of the Evidence" in S. Malloch and C. Trevarthen (eds.), *Communicative Musicality* (61–82). Oxford University Press, 2009.

Darwin, Charles. *Descent of Man*. Harmondsworth: Penguin, 2004.

Darwin, Charles. *On the Origin of Species by Means of Natural Selection.* Mineola, NY: Dover Publications, 2006.

Doidge, Norman. *The Brain That Changes Itself.* New York: Viking, 2007.

Dutton, Denis. *The Art Instinct: Beauty, Pleasure and Human Evolution.* New York: Bloomsbury Press, 2009.

Enzensberger, W., U. Oberländer, and K. Stecker. "Metronome Therapy in Patients with Parkinson's Disease." *Der Nervenarzt,* 68(12):972–7, December 1997.

Foster, Brian. "Einstein and His Love of Music." *Physics World.* January 2005.

Garland, Ellen, *et al.* "Dynamic Horizontal Cultural Transmission of Humpback Whale Song at the Ocean Basin Scale." *Current Biology,* Volume 21, Issue 8, 687–91, April 14, 2011.

Hajime, Fukui. "The Effects of Music and Visual Stress on Testosterone and Cortisol in Men and Women." *Neuroendocrinology Letters.* No's 3/4. Jun–Aug. Vol. 24, 2003.

Hart, Mickey. *Songcatchers: In Search of the World's Music.* National Geographic, 2003.

Huron, David. *Sweet Anticipation: Music and the Psychology of Expectation.* Boston: MIT Press, 2006.

Janata, Petr. "The Neural Architecture of Music-Evoked Autobiographical Memories." *Cerebral Cortex Journal.* 19 (11) *http://cercor.oxfordjour-nals.org/content/19/11/2579.short,* 2009.

Jourdain, Robert. *Music, the Brain and Ecstasy: How Music Captures Our Imagination.* New York: William Morrow and Co., 1997.

Lansing, Stephen J. *Perfect Order: Recognizing Complexity in Bali.*

Princeton University Press, 2006.

Levitin, Daniel J. *This Is Your Brain On Music: The Science of a Human Obsession*. New York: Plume, 2007.

Levitin, Daniel J. *The World in Six Songs: How the Musical Brain Created Human Nature*. Harmondsworth: Penguin, 2009.

May, Elizabeth. *Musics of Many Cultures: An Introduction*. Berkeley: University of California Press, 1980.

Molnar-Szakacs, Istvan and Katie Overy. "Music and Mirror Neurons: From Motion to 'E'motion." *The Journal of Social Cognitive and Affective Neuroscience,* December 2006.

Nettl, Bruno. *The Study of Ethnomusicology: Twenty-Nine Issues and Concepts*. Champaign: University of Illinois Press, 1983.

Nidel, Richard. *World Music: The Basics*. New York: Routledge, 2005.

Palmer, Robert. *Deep Blues: A Musical and Cultural History of the Mississippi Delta*. New York: Viking, 1982.

Panksepp, Jaak. *Affective Neuroscience: The Foundations of Human and Animal Emotions*. Oxford University Press, 1998.

Patel, Aniruddh and Joseph Daniele. "An Empirical Comparison of Rhythm in Language and Music." *Cognition 87*. B35–B45, 2003.

Patel, Aniruddh. *Music, Language and the Brain*. Oxford University Press, 2008.

Peretz, Isabelle and Robert Zatorre (eds). *The Cognitive Neuroscience of Music*. Oxford University Press, 2003.

Pinker, Steven. *How the Mind Works*. New York: W.W. Norton and Co., 1997.

Reeves Sanday, Peggy. *Divine Hunger: Cannibalism as a Cultural System.* Cambridge University Press, 1986.

Rentink, Sonja. *Kpanlogo: Conflict, Identity Crisis and Enjoyment in a Ga Drum Dance.* University of Amsterdam, 2003.

Reznikoff, Igor. "On the Sound Dimension of Prehistoric Painted Caves and Rocks. Musical Signification. Essays on the Semiotic Theory and Analysis of Music." *Approaches to Semiotics 121.* New York. 541–57, 1995.

Rumi, Mevlâna Jalâluddîn. Translated by Helminski, C. and K. *Introduction to Rumi: Daylight.* New York: Threshold Books, 1999.

Sacks, Oliver. *Musicophilia: Tales of Music and the Brain.* New York: Random House, 2008.

Sadie, Stanley, ed. *The New Grove Dictionary of Music and Musicians.* London: Macmillan, 1980.

Salimpoor, Valorie and Mitchel Benovoy, Kevin Larcher, Alain Dagher, and Robert Zattore. "Anatomically Distinct Dopamine Release During Anticipation and Experience of Peak Emotion to Music." *Nature Neuroscience.* Nature America, Inc., 2011.

Schlaug, Gottfried. "The Brain of Musicians" in *The Cognitive Neuroscience of Music.* Oxford University Press, 2003.

Storr, Anthony. *Music and the Mind.* New York: The Free Press, 1992.

Thompson, William Forde. *Music, Thought, and Feeling.* Oxford University Press, 2009.

Unyk, Anna, Sandra E. Trehub, Laurel J. Trainor, and Glenn E. Schellenberg. "Lullabies and Simplicity: A Cross-Cultural Perspective." *Psychology of Music,* 20; 15, 1992.

INDEX

ALSO BY GLENN DIXON

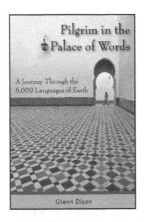

Pilgrim in the Palace of Words
A Journey Through the 6,000 Languages of Earth
978-1554884339
$24.99

Pilgrim in the Palace of Words is about language, about the words that splash and chatter across our tongues. Some six thousand languages are still spoken on the planet, and Glenn Dixon, an expert is socio-linguistics and a tireless adventurer, travels to the Earth's four corners to explore the way these languages create and mould societies.

As one philosopher said, languages are Houses of Being. After doing graduate work in linguistics, Dixon wanted to visit these houses or "palaces" himself, to stroll along their sidewalks, knock on their doors, and peek in their windows. He wanted to see what they were hiding in their basements ... even if it meant a little bit of trouble. In some cases, a whole lot of trouble! Join him on his adventure as, with wit and humour, he works toward a real understanding of how and why we communicate the way we do in the Global Village.

Visit us at
Dundurn.com | Definingcanada.ca | @dundurnpress | Facebook.com/dundurnpress